✓ **W9-AYN-408**

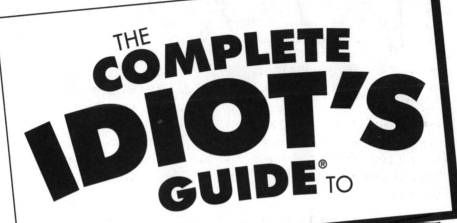

The Crusades

by Paul L. Williams, Ph.D.

ALPHA

Publisher
Marie Butler-Knight

Product Manager
Phil Kitchel

Managing Editor
Jennifer Chisholm

Acquisitions Editor
Gary Goldstein

Development Editor
Doris Cross

Production Editor
Katherin Bidwell

Copy Editor
Cari Luna

Illustrator
Brian Moyer

Cover Designers
Mike Freeland
Kevin Spear

Book Designers
Scott Cook and Amy Adams of DesignLab

Indexer
Tonya Heard

Layout/Proofreading
Angela Calvert
John Etchison
Sherry Taggart

Contents at a Glance

Contents

Appendixes

Foreword

When we think of the Crusades, some vivid images spring to mind: the armored knight sporting a cross on his surcoat, splendid mosques and palaces of Eastern opulence, dusty pilgrims trudging their way to Jerusalem. Perhaps we remember some evocative names such as Bohemond, Saladin, and Tancred, or half-forgotten places such as Antioch and Tyre.

We may not think of the horrors of war, the dangers of ignorance and fanaticism, and the prejudices that continue to divide Christians from Moslems to this day. But they are some of the most important things we can learn about from studying this dark yet fascinating era.

It all began more than 900 years ago in a world very different from our own. The Middle Ages were a time of uncertainty and peril, when famine, disease, or invaders could strike anyone at any moment. With life so tenuous for so many, the idea of a glorious afterlife was vastly appealing; and the church that assured its followers that they would see paradise had an influence that was in some ways stronger than that of most religions today.

So when the head of the Catholic Church called for a Holy Crusade, people listened. Hoping for salvation, or seeking personal glory, or for the sake of political expediency, they took up arms and journeyed to the Holy Land in the First Crusade.

Historians have numbered eight significant Crusades that took place over the course of 200 years. During that time, the Holy City of Jerusalem was captured by Christians, established as a kingdom ruled by the Western invaders, and ultimately retaken by Moslems. Crusading orders were created, such as the Knights Templar, who took the monastic vows of poverty, chastity, and obedience, and took up the sword as well. Ill-prepared pilgrims and warriors alike starved or died of heat prostration on the road to Jerusalem. Thousands of innocent Moslems and Jews—and even some Christians— were massacred in the name of Christ. And throughout the crusading centuries, East met West in ways that would change both worlds forever.

What started this phenomenal movement? Who were the crusaders, and why did they fight? What did the peoples of the Eastern lands think of this massive influx of Western warriors? And how can any war be considered "holy"?

The answers to these questions and more lie in the book you hold in your hands.

With humor and enthusiasm, Paul Williams describes the world of the Middle Ages and the events that began in 1095 in vivid detail. Here you'll meet crusaders such as Godfrey of Bouillon, the deeply religious leader of a Frankish army, who wrestled a bear—and won. You'll learn why the Europeans called the Moslems "Saracens" and what modern banking owes to monastic knights. You'll even discover how one crusader's case of dysentery was instrumental in the conquest of Jerusalem. So get ready for a tour of the tumultuous Crusades. And when you're through, you'll understand the basics of one of the most fascinating periods in history.

—Melissa Snell

Melissa Snell is the Medieval History Guide for About.com and has studied the Middle Ages for more than 20 years. She lives in the beautiful central Texas countryside with too many dogs.

Introduction

The Crusades changed everything. It changed the way we think. It taught us the scientific method and the breakdown of plant and animal life into genus and species. It brought about Scholasticism and the art of making distinctions for clear and precise thinking. It introduced us to works of forgotten philosophers. It brought about a rebirth of knowledge. Without the Crusades, St. Thomas Aquinas would never have thought of combining religion and philosophy into one great intellectual system.

It changed the way we believe. It taught us about other religions and other lifestyles. It freed us from the confines of parochialism and gave us an awareness of different cultures and different peoples. With this knowledge came an awareness of geography that didn't exist before—an awareness of distant lands and distant peoples. The Italian merchants who thrived on the Crusades learned to make good maps of the Mediterranean; the monkish chroniclers transmitted to Europe a conception of the vastness and variety of Asia. The zest for exploration, travel, and trade was stirred. Without the Crusades, there would not have been a Marco Polo, let alone a Christopher Columbus.

It changed the way we eat. It introduced us to spices such as pepper, ginger, cloves, and cinnamon. Cooking after the Crusades was no longer bland and tasteless. It brought to our plates maize, rice, sesame, shallot, scallion, and carob. It presented to us melons, lemons, peaches, apricots, cherries, and dates. Without the Crusades, there would be no chocolate cake, no ice cream, no cookies, and no candy. For many of us, the greatest discovery of the crusaders was sugar.

It changed the way we live. It gave us glass for our houses made from silica, soda, and lime—and Venetian glass made from refined sugar. Our houses became opened to sunlight, and with sunlight came sanitation. Our cathedrals acquired magnificent stained glass windows that originated with the enameled glass of the Moslems. Mirrors now replaced polished bronze or steel. In this way, the Crusades taught us to look at ourselves for the first time in history.

It changed the way we dress. It gave us silk, muslin, velvet, and damask to replace drab clothes of coarse and heavy wool. It informed us of colors that could come from dyes: red, pink, blue, green, purple, yellow. The world became more beautiful and intriguing. In fact, the first fashion fad was caused by the very First Crusade.

It changed the way we smell. It taught us to take baths on a regular basis and to use toilets. It introduced us to scents, powders, and perfumes. Before the Crusades, we were smelly beasts, who stank (according to the Moslems) of rancid cheese. But after the Crusades, everybody and everything smelled better.

It changed the way we love. It taught us the joys of lovemaking, of sensuality, that were unknown to the Western world. After the Crusades, everyone was sexier.

It changed the way we look. It caused men to return to the old Roman custom of shaving the beard and women to rediscover the art of applying makeup. Suddenly, even plain people looked comely.

It gave us other things as well, including inventions from the crossbow to the compass. Eventually, in the backwash of this great event, we came upon such things as gunpowder and printing.

There is nothing about the Western World that the Crusades didn't change. It freed serfs from bondage to the medieval manor. It gave rise to nationalism and national interests. It brought about the collapse of feudalism and the rise of capitalism. It helped create a middle class. It consolidated all Christians under the supreme authority of the Roman Catholic Church. And, as it gave rise to papal power, it also planted the seeds of the Reformation. The first voices of protest against the Latin Church were raised in opposition to the Crusades.

The Crusades is an epic story. It is a tale of knights in shining armor, of high romance, of chivalry and pageantry, of incredible courage and heroic deeds. But it is also a tale of barbarism and brutality on a grand scale, of horrors beyond measure. It is not a story for the timid or the faint of heart. These pages drip with blood and guts and a fair measure of illicit sex. In fact, several chapters very likely may cause you to shudder, scream, or rip out your hair. If so, this is all well and good. History such as this confirms one thing: that man, despite his outward appearance of sense and sensibility, remains an irrational animal, capable not only of works of transcendent goodness, but also acts of unspeakable evil.

Surely, the task of any writer of history is to present, and not to preach. I have tried to abide by this rule. But the Crusades unfold as a play scripted by a medieval moralist. The story is of the great conflict between Islam and Christianity over the Tomb of the Holy Sepulcher. It begins with lofty speeches and high hopes and it ends with bitter accusations and crushed dreams. The drama is peopled with intriguing and complex characters, from heretical sinners (Frederick II) to saintly kings (Baldwin IV). It offers scenes that stir our imagination—a great Christian king defying an entire Arab army to engage him in combat, and shock our sensibilities—bloodthirsty crusaders killing and cooking captured Turks before the walls of Antioch. The story moves to an intensifying climax—the great clash between Richard the Lion Heart and Saladin, and a perfectly conceived denouement—the sacking of Constantinople, the Byzantine city the crusaders were sworn to save.

The Crusades, of course, never really ended. They persist to this day in the conflict between the Jews and Palestinians over the same issues; even the atrocities—the killing of innocent men, women, and children—haven't changed. Barbara Tuchman, the great historian, once spoke of the past as a "distant mirror." It is an apt image. By looking into the past, we inevitably come upon reflections of our times and ourselves, and more often than not, we may be disturbed and startled by what we see.

How to Use This Book

This book will guide you from the First Crusade to the last. It's divided into seven parts:

Part 1, "The Medieval World," transports you from the Dark Ages to Pope Urban II's vision of a crusading army saving the Eastern Emperor from the Turks, and (not incidentally) luxuriating in the beauty and riches of Constantinople at the dawn of the Renaissance.

Part 2, "The First Crusade," follows the Holy Army from the Crusade of the Poor, led by Little Peter, to the crusaders' conquest of Jerusalem.

Part 3, "The Formation of the Latin East," takes you to a Middle East with an established crusader presence, increased entente with the Moslems, and increased trade and wealth. You also meet the Knights Templar and the Hospitallers, get a feel for the Arab world of the time, and for the concept of *jihad*, as demonstrated when Zengi, the Moslem leader, goes on a rampage against the Christians.

Part 4, "The Second Crusade: A Dream of Kings," grabs you by the scruff of the neck and takes you from the siege of Damascus to the Horns of Hattin.

Part 5, "The Third Crusade: The Rage of a Lion," presents the great conflict between Richard the Lion Heart and Saladin, the ruler of all Moslems.

Part 6, "The Fourth Crusade," conveys you from the Grand Council in Venice to a hellish excursion that ends with the fall of Constantinople.

Part 7, "The Collapse of the Crusades," carries you through the Fifth, Sixth, and Seventh Crusades, where you'll meet a Christian emperor with an Arab harem, a saintly king in search of relics, Mongols, and Mamelukes; and witness the final medieval conflagration between Islam and Christianity.

Extras

Throughout these pages, you'll encounter sidebars, little boxes that will help you follow the course of the various Crusades:

Warrior Words

Read what's here for definitions of terms used in the text, and their linguistic or historical background.

Christian Chronicles

Here you'll find excerpts from the many records and chronicles of the time, and insights and fascinating historical details about the events and personalities in the text.

Crosscurrent

This is where you can read a bit about some of the many problems, oddities, twists, and turns of the Crusades.

Crusade Aid

Here, you'll find helpful tips to direct you on your pilgrimage with the crusading armies.

Appendix A, "Glossary," collects the terms used throughout the book in one place, and adds some more. Also, check out **Appendix B, "Further Reading,"** for comprehensive works on the Crusades; general overviews; detailed scholarly accounts; books about specific aspects of the Crusades, such as the individuals, weaponry, and art; and a list of a few of my personal favorites.

And when you get confused, or if you're just interested in details, don't forget that there's a chronology of the Crusades and two maps following this section.

Note that when the term "church" appears without adjectives but is capitalized (as in "the Church"), it refers to the Latin Church, or what we now call the Roman Catholic Church.

Acknowledgments

I am midway on my pilgrimage to the City of God. The way has been fraught with many dangers, toils, and snares. I have managed to slay a fair share of dragons, to save one or two damsels in distress, and to battle a host of wicked windmills. I have only managed to stay the course due to the love and support of my wonderful wife, Pat, my darling daughter, Katie, and my spiritual guide and sister, Judith Schmitt. This book would not be possible without the assistance of my steadfast secretary and friend, Mary Riggall, my angelic literary agents Sheree Bykofsky and Janet Rosen, and Gary Goldstein and Katherin Bidwell of Alpha Books. You can't have a Crusade without a cross, and my cross is D.V. Cross, the development editor of this text, who has a wonderful ability to give form to matter.

Trademarks

All terms mentioned in this book that are known to be or are suspected of being trademarks or service marks have been appropriately capitalized. Alpha Books and Pearson Education, Inc., cannot attest to the accuracy of this information. Use of a term in this book should not be regarded as affecting the validity of any trademark or service mark.

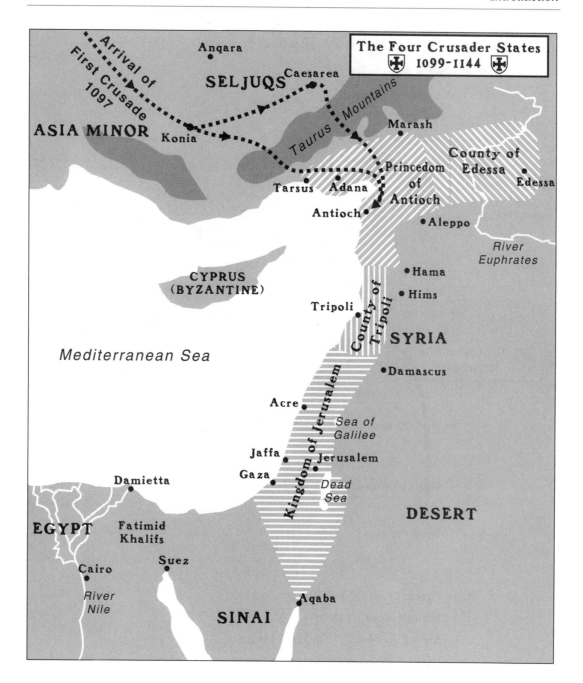

Angara

SELJUQS Caesarea

ASIA MINOR Konia

Taurus Mountains

Marash

County of
Edessa

Edessa

Tarsus Adana

Princedom
of
Antioch

Antioch

Aleppo

River
Euphrates

Arrival of
First Crusade
1097

The Four Crusader States
✠ 1099-1144 ✠

CYPRUS
(BYZANTINE)

Tripoli

County of Tripoli

Hama

Hims

SYRIA

Mediterranean Sea

Damascus

Acre

Sea of
Galilee

Jaffa

Jerusalem

Kingdom of Jerusalem

Gaza

Dead
Sea

DESERT

Damietta

EGYPT

Fatimid
Khalifs

SINAI

Cairo

Suez

Aqaba

River
Nile

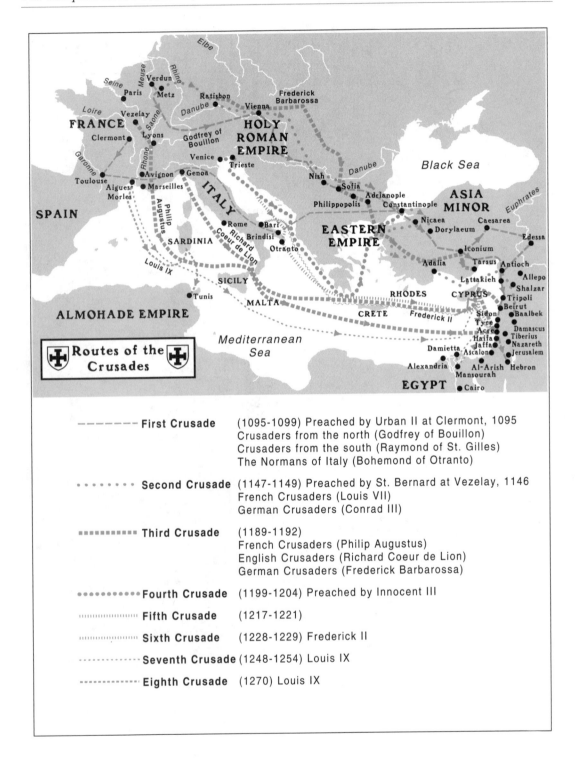

Chronology of the Crusades

1096	Proclamation of the First Crusade at the Council of Clermont
	Persecution of Jews in Europe
	Arrival of the Christian armies at Constantinople
1097	Battle of Dorylaeum
	Siege of Antioch
1098	Baldwin becomes Prince of Edessa
	Battle of Antioch
1099	Fall of Jerusalem
	Godfrey of Bouillon becomes first ruler of Jerusalem
	Latin Kingdom of the East formed
1110	Establishment of the University of Paris
1120	Foundation of the Knights Templar and the Hospitallers
1122	Birth of Eleanor of Aquitaine
1123	Crusader Decree of First Lateran Council
1144	The Fall of Edessa to the Moslems
1146	St. Bernard of Clairvaux preaches the Second Crusade
1148	Withdrawal of crusaders from the Siege of Damascus
1154	Occupation of Damascus by Nur ed-Din
1160	Composition of the *Cid*
1163	Construction of Notre Dame de Paris begins
1170	Death of St. Thomas à Becket
1174	Death of Nur ed-Din
	Saladin takes over Damascus
1182	Birth of St. Francis of Assisi
1183	Aleppo submits to Saladin
1186	Battle of Hattin
	Jerusalem conquered by Saladin
	Pope Gregory VIII proclaims Third Crusade
1188	Imposition of "Saladin Tithe"
1188	Start of Third Crusade
1189	Drowning of Emperor Frederick Barbarossa in Cilicia
1190	Richard I of England takes Cyprus
1191	Conquest of Acre by Richard I and Philip II
	Battle of Arsuf
	Treaty of Jaffa
1198	Pope Innocent III proclaims Fourth Crusade

1202	Sack of Zara
1204	Fall of Constantinople
	Establishment of Latin Kingdom of Constantinople
1209	Establishment of Cambridge University
1211	Start of Construction of Reims Cathedral
1212	Children's Crusades begin
	St. Clare founds "Poor Clares"
1213	Pope Innocent III proclaims Fifth Crusade
1215	Signing of Magna Carta
1218	Siege of Damietta
1221	Defeat of crusaders at Mansurah
1225	Birth of St. Thomas Aquinas
1229	Sixth Crusade under Holy Roman Emperor Frederick II
1237	Mongols invade Russia
1239	Proclamation of Crusade against Holy Roman Emperor Frederick II
1244	Fall of Jerusalem to the Khwarisimians
	Battle of La Forbie
1245	First Council of Lyons deposes Holy Roman Emperor Frederick II
1248	Seventh Crusade under King Louis IX of France
	Capture of Damietta
1249	Defeat of the Seventh Crusaders at Mansurah
1250	King Louis IX arrives in Palestine
1251	Shepherds' Crusade starts
1258	Mongols conquer Bagdad
1260	Baibars becomes Sultan of Egypt
1265	Birth of Dante
1266	Birth of Giotto
1268	Mamelukes conquer Antioch
1270	Death of St. Louis in Tunisia
1271	Marco Polo sets off for China
1274	Second Council of Lyons
1291	Fall of Acre

Part 1
The Medieval World

So you picked up this book and you think you're ready to go on a great Crusade to save the Holy Land from the infidels. You probably fancy yourself a knight in shining armor or a lady of high romance. Well, listen up, readers! You're not fit to enter the ranks of the crusaders. I don't care if you're the Chairman of the Board of IBM or a chump from Cambridge. Most of you don't know your mail from your mace, or the Dark Ages from the Renaissance. I am commissioned to prepare you for the Holy War. And you can't go on this military venture without some basic training in medieval history. You're not going to like it. I'm going to push your noses in the dung and the dirt of the times. You're going to scream and shout. You're going to be offended. But I'm not here to protect your sense and sensibility. I'm here to get you in shape for the Saracens. If you have a weak stomach, put this book back on the shelf and back out now. If you have the guts, turn the page, and enter boot camp.

Welcome to the Middle Ages

> **In This Chapter**
>
> ➤ European life before the Crusades
>
> ➤ Starving peasants opt for serfdom
>
> ➤ The feudal system takes hold
>
> ➤ The Christian faith provides hope
>
> ➤ Ignorance and illiteracy bolster religious zeal

The Crusades changed everything about the Western world, from the way we dress to the things we eat, from our methods of banking to our bedroom behavior. No subject is more compelling or more interesting. But we have to start with an understanding of the circumstances that gave rise to this earth-shaking event. Why were hundreds of thousands suddenly willing in 1095 to embark on a three-thousand-mile trek to save the tomb of Jesus Christ from Arab hands? Why didn't earlier Crusades take place when the Moors overran Spain and Armenia? Why weren't the Christians incensed enough to unite against the Moslems in 1010, when Al-Hakim, the mad caliph of Cairo, destroyed the Church of the Holy Sepulcher in Jerusalem? Why did great multitudes go on the march in 1095, when the Turks had committed no extraordinary act of aggression against Christendom? Why the wild and suicidal assaults on trained armies by peasants, women, and children when their way of life was not at risk? Why the Crusades?

...on, we must visit Europe at the time of the first Christian mil-
...d of warning: You definitely won't like what you find when you
...d foreboding world.

...ness of Daily Life

...d is filled with strange sights and sounds. The people are smelly and dirty.
...air is long, matted, and filled with lice. Their teeth are broken and decayed.
...breath is as fetid as a sudden outburst of sewer gas. Their faces are scarred by
...x and covered with grime. Their clothes—even the clothes of the noblewomen—
...re ragged and shabby. Their body odor, unmasked by perfume, is as odiferous as a
vat of Limburger cheese in mid-July.

And the living conditions are appalling. Even life in a castle is not as good as the
grimiest hotel in Vera Cruz. The first castles were constructed at the end of the ninth
century, built to defend the people of the manor from barbarian invasions. As the
castles are built of stone and surrounded by stagnant pools of deep water called
"moats," they are seemingly impregnable. Across the moats, cleated drawbridges lead
up to iron gates, or "portculli," that protect massive doors in the castle walls. The castles are cold, dark, and devoid of any comforts. Everything is covered with filth and
grime. And the beds are swarming with hundreds of bedbugs that really bite.

The food will make you retch. The meat is rancid, undercooked, and indigestible. The
bread is covered with mold. A favorite at feasts is a plate of eels boiled in broth, along
with helpings of frogs, toads, and snails. The most common meat is pork. Pigs eat the
garbage and people eat the pigs. Great sausages, stuffed
with blood, are a delight. When you bite into them,
the blood spurts from your mouth. You can't wipe it
away. Other delicacies are partridges, thrushes, pea-
cocks, and cranes. When you cut into them, you find
that they're poorly prepared and undercooked. There
are no potatoes, tomatoes, coffee, or tea. Dairy prod-
ucts, except for slabs of green cheese, are uncommon.
Salads are unknown and confections are rare. Everything is bland. In this world, there is neither sugar nor
spice nor anything nice.

And the people are woefully ignorant. There are no
books so no one reads. They know nothing of religion,
philosophy, art, science, or the outside world, so
there's nothing to talk about but local conditions.
People look very old but they're really very young. An
average girl of 17 has been married for three years and
has three children. She'll be lucky to reach age 25.

When we travel throughout Europe at the time of the
first millennium, our impression is of a vast wilderness,

Crosscurrent

Being a woman in the Middle
Ages was not easy. Civil and
canon law permitted and even
encouraged wife beating as a
means to establish domestic
harmony. A great advance for
feminism was made in the early
thirteenth century by the *Laws
and Customs of Beauvais*, which
stated that a man should beat
his wife only "for good reason."

virtually untouched by human hands. The population levels are incredibly low—less than a million in England and scarcely six million in France. Everywhere before us stretch dark, impenetrable forests, cutting off the scattered human settlements from each other and making each village a country unto itself. There are no towns, no schools, and no marketplaces.

The huts of the peasants are one-room hovels. They're constructed of rough wood or sod, and are wretched beyond belief. They have earthen floors, no windows, and a simple hole in the roof through which most of the smoke from the open fire can pass. Children, parents, and grandparents are crowded within the confines of these one-room structures, along with the few farm animals the family might possess. People live, die, have sex, and perform bodily functions in full and open view of one another.

There are no amenities. The beds are piles of straw that are infested with fleas and ticks. A table and a small stool might be found in the corner of such hovels, but there's little else to grace the living space except the implements of farm and domestic toil.

Christian Chronicles

Speaking of sex, people mate like dogs. The woman usually bends over and the man mounts her from behind. These creatures don't kiss and hug or engage in petting and exchange sweet talk. It's all business and the act is performed almost as quickly as you can say *"jackrabbit."*

Starvation vs. Serfdom

The peasants have hollow cheeks and bulging eyes. Their stomachs are swollen by starvation. Their bodies are deformed by rickets—a condition caused by severe malnutrition. Their teeth are green and worn to the gums, attesting to a diet that includes grass as a principal staple. Seeing this, you might think you've landed on an alien planet, but you're merely back in time on planet Earth, looking at the villagers. A common disease among these unpleasant and foul-smelling creatures is something called *holy fire,* caused by moldy rye in the bread. This disease makes the peasants break out in sores, vomit blood and bile, and foam at the mouth like rabid dogs.

It doesn't make sense that these people are starving to death. The forest is filled with wildlife—deer, boar, bear, pheasant, quail—but the peasants are not permitted to hunt. Such sport is reserved for lords and members of their households.

Let's look at the farm implements. They're simple, roughly crafted, and made of wood. Wood? That's right. Here in a medieval hamlet at the time of the millennium you have re-entered the age of wood. You're thinking: This can't be true. I know Europe entered the Iron Age around 500 B.C.E., and this *Complete Idiot's Guide* is supposed to be about the Middle Ages. But iron, in this year of 1000 C.E., is too valuable to be wasted on farm tools. It must be used for weapons so that the lords can protect the people from brigands, barbarians, and neighboring warlords.

The ploughs and hoes of the peasants scratch the earth and the earth scratches back, wearing down the points on which survival depends. That's the problem. The peasants can't create enough food for their lords, let alone themselves. Without iron tools, they can't plough the land. These guys don't even know the proper way to harness farm animals. Yokes are unknown. When they attempt to use an ox to till the soil, they harness the animal to a wooden plough by wrapping thick cords of leather around its neck. This makes rapid plowing and the plowing of heavy soils impossible, as the leather cord constantly cuts into the beast's throat causing a cutoff of blood to the brain—and strangulation. Faced with endemic starvation, many peasants have become serfs, but it is a harsh bargain: They are bound to the land, forbidden to do anything—even marry—without the lord's permission. In manors throughout France and England, lords claim the *ius primae noctis* or the "right of first night" with the serf's bride. On some estates, the serf is allowed to "redeem" his bride by paying a fee to the lord. In this form, the "right of first night" will survive in Bavaria until the eighteenth century.

Crusade Aid

In Medieval Europe, lords could not only strike but also kill serfs with impunity. But serfs were useful, and a nobleman's sense of economy usually controlled his brutality.

Working for the Lord of the Manor

The medieval world is a world without central authority. Lords are constantly at war with other lords. The possibilities for altercation are endless: a disputed boundary, a personal affront, a careless word, even a simple gesture. The lords want to expand their holdings in order to bestow gifts of land—or fiefs—to loyal vassals and members of their households.

But there are other enemies in this world: wandering bands of warriors who descend upon the countryside like locusts to destroy everything and everyone in their path. And there are the barbarians, especially the dreaded Norsemen, who periodically appear to rape, pillage, and loot every manor in Christendom.

For this reason, the lords surround themselves with paid or indentured warriors, relatives or friends of relatives, who are bound to them by oaths of fealty. These oaths are consecrated in church and sanctified by a bishop's blessing. To break an oath is the most serious of sins. It constitutes not only a breach of trust, but also a sacrilege. Oaths and only oaths hold this fragile society together.

Every lord claims the right of private war against any man not bound to him by feudal ties as well as the right to engage in "honorable robbery" of another noble's estate. When the lord goes to war, all his vassals and relatives to the seventh degree are obliged to follow and fight for him for 40 days. There is not a day in the eleventh and twelfth centuries when some part of what is now France is not at war.

The *knights* are trained for one purpose: to defend the lord and his holdings from the barbarians, from the bands of wild men, and from other warlords. The feudal aristocracy revolves around the use of the sword, shield, mace, and lance; around the proper fit of helmet and chain-mail (*hauberk*); around the breeding and selection of war-horses fit to bear armored warriors with speed and agility.

The lords and the knights live to kill. When they're not engaged in battle or preparation for battle, they spend their time wrestling, jousting, dueling, and of course, hunting. These guys love to hunt. Nothing is more entertaining than to spend a day tracking down a wild boar, to bring it to bay, to lay it low with arrows, and to hack off its head with a broadsword. Such game is brought to the castle for feasts.

Their low crop yields mean that there is never enough corn or fodder to feed the animals through the winter. They can only keep their cattle until late December when the animals are slaughtered and the people enjoy several days of feasting.

At feasts, hunting dogs wander over the long tables for scraps of meat. No one eats with knives and forks. People just rip into the poorly cooked meat with their incredibly dirty fingers and gorge themselves. To express pleasure at a medieval feast, guests belch loudly or expel gas. Flatulence conveys contentment. Neither napkins nor handkerchiefs have been invented. People blow their noses on their shirtsleeves, in their hands, or on the floor. No one at the table gives a thought to the starving peasants in the hovels.

Cattle and pigs that are slaughtered at Christmas-time have to be rapidly consumed as there is no means of refrigeration or other forms of preservation, such as curing with salt and spices.

Peasants cannot hunt. They cannot fish. They cannot forage. They could eat the corn that is stored in the shed, but it must be kept to provide seed for the coming year. If they eat it, there will be no chance for future survival. And so, they sit in their hovels and watch their children starve.

Warrior Words

Knights were originally servants. The word *knight* comes from the Old English *cniht,* meaning *boy.* When servants were granted land and property by the lord, they became part of the nobility.
Hauberk is a long coat of rings of armor that extends from the neck and shoulders to below the knees. It's slipped over the head and is incredibly heavy. Some hauberks weigh over 50 pounds.

Crusade Aid

The late-December slaughter of cattle provides the basis for the Christmas feast and the twelve days of Christmas. It's a time of great merriment and good cheer as the spitted ox slowly turns over the blazing Yule log.

Few animals survive the winter; those that do are apt to be sick, half-starved, and covered with mange. These are not very promising animals for spring plowing. This problem produces other problems. With unhealthy draught animals, the peasants must depend upon themselves to get the work done. For this reason, they strap their wives to the ploughs, so women serve as real "beasts of burden." It's all a vicious cycle. Without a healthy herd, there's a shortage of manure. Without manure, there's no fertilizer. And without fertilizer there are fallow fields.

Over 90 percent of the people farm simply to survive, and their level of efficiency is so low that it seems impossible to break from the chains of limiting circumstances that bind them to the manor and to the land. This economic fact is mirrored in medieval theology. The world, at this time, is presented as a vale of tears where men and women are doomed to misery because of the sin of Adam. There is no escape from endless drudgery, from the reality of want, from the wars and the rumors of wars, from plagues and pestilence, from famine and drought, from disease and death. This way of life, called manorialism, seems inescapable. But in order to live, people must have—if not bread—at least hope.

Christian Chronicles

Thank heaven for Sundays. On the Lord's Day, the serfs and peasants were not permitted to perform "servile work." After Mass, the peasants often gathered to sing and dance, or engage in a rough game of medieval football or bull baiting. Hilarity reached its heights on summer feast days when two blindfolded men, armed with clubs, tried to kill a chicken or a goose.

Faith, Hope, and the Church

Hope comes from the Church, from the promise of a better life—a mansion in heaven with an endless banquet and an end to all struggle and want. This life is only a preparation for the next life. There is hope for the future if only believers would resign themselves to the present scheme of things.

Because religion offers hope, their only hope, people of this age cling to it fiercely. If anyone seeks to call into question the hope of heaven, they're hacked to pieces or burned at the stake.

The ignorance and illiteracy of the age only serves to intensify the faith. The Devil is no figure of speech but a flesh-and-blood reality. He prowls around everywhere, suggesting temptations and creating all kinds of

Crosscurrent

Thousands of medieval men and women took flight from "the world, the flesh, and the devil" and entered monasteries and convents. Most were probably driven to do so not by religious fervor or from fear, but by the extreme disorder, insecurity, poverty, and violence of the times.

evil. The Devil can usually be sent packing by a dash of holy water or the sign of the cross. But he always leaves behind the telltale stench of burning sulfur. Satan has millions of cohorts, incubi and succubae, who hover around every soul, attempting to lure it to perdition.

These demons are very troublesome. They twist spoken words; they distort thoughts; they pollute prayer. They love to have sex with lonely or holy women when they fall asleep. They intrude audibly into conversations, cut holes in people's garments, and cast dirt at passersby. According to popular account, one day a demon became tired of tempting souls and sat on a head of lettuce, only to be inadvertently eaten by a nun.

Ignorance and Redemption

Strange as it may seem, the faith of the people is strengthened by their ignorance and illiteracy. Priests are seen as having miraculous power. They can say words over bread and water that transform these elements into the body and blood of Jesus Christ. If you eat this body, you can partake of Christ's holiness and his triumph over the grave. The Host is so sacred that no one is permitted to look at it. They must cast their eyes to the ground and beat their breasts, saying aloud: *Domino, non sum dingus* ("Lord, I am not worthy"). The words of consecration, *Hoc est corpus* ("This is my body"), become words of magic: *hocus pocus*.

The consecrated Host is the subject of a thousand tales of miraculous cures and events. One tale concerns a lecherous priest who wanted to seduce a beautiful virgin. Unable to win her consent, the priest kept the Body of the Lord in his mouth after Mass, hoping that if he kissed her, she would succumb to his desire by the power of the Blessed Sacrament. His plans backfired. When he attempted to walk from the altar, the priest grew so large that he banged his head against the ceiling. He removed the wafer from his mouth and buried it in a corner of the church. He confessed his sin to another priest. The two priests dug up the wafer and found that it had changed into the bloodstained corpse of a crucified man. Another tale concerns a woman who kept the consecrated Host in her mouth until she got home. She placed it in a beehive, hoping to reduce mortality among the bees. Several days later, she was stunned to discover that the busy bees built "for their most sweet guest—the sweetest of honeycombs, a tiny chapel of impeccable workmanship."

Since the Church alone offers hope for redemption, the most terrible of all punishments is excommunication, being cut off from the sacraments that bestow grace. If you're excommunicated, you have no means of obtaining forgiveness from sin and therefore the prospect of salvation. You'll pass from the horrors of this world into the eternal horrors of the next. You have to watch what you say, watch what you do, and watch what you think. Any priest can pronounce this penalty upon a believer for any reason whatsoever.

Crusade Aid

The doctrine of the real presence of Christ in the consecrated bread and wine was a medieval development. It was first voiced by Lanfranc, the Abbot of Beck, who wrote: "We believe that the earthly substance is converted into the essence of the Lord's body, while the appearance, and certain other qualities, of the same realities remain behind, in order that men should be spared the shock of perceiving raw and bloody things, and that believers should receive the fuller rewards of the faith.

Christian Chronicles

The monk Richland proclaims that the demons fill every inch of this fallen world. "The whole air," he says, "is but a thick mass of devils, always and everywhere in wait for us. It is marvelous that anyone should be alive. If not for God's grace, no one of us could escape."

This is an age of fear and trembling, of evil spirits in a sin-plagued world. It is an era in which 80 percent of babies die young, in which the starving masses eat grass, in which women are yoked to plows to replace animals lost during the winter, and in which barbarous men wage constant war upon one another. It is not an age of chivalry and courtly love, of knights in shining armor and high romance.

Welcome to the Dark Ages. There is no crusading cry here, but something is happening on the farm that will change the course of Western civilization and give rise to the cry, *Dieu li volt!* This cry, meaning "God wills it," will be uttered by a pope in Chapter 3, "The Pope Declares Holy War," and it will transform every aspect of the medieval world.

The Least You Need to Know

➤ The population of Europe was incredibly sparse at the time of the first millennium.

➤ Medieval people lived on the edge of starvation.

➤ Farm tools and agricultural techniques remained primitive.

➤ Peasants became bound to the land as virtual slaves or serfs.

➤ Agricultural conditions that created starvation gave rise to feudalism.

➤ In their despair, people turned to the Church for hope.

wn

ssance

...aterializes

➤ The ...

➤ The Code of Chivalry ...

➤ Ferocious warriors become crusaders

It's fifty years after the beginning of the first millenium (described in Chapter 1, "Welcome to the Middle Ages"), and you won't believe the difference. The fields are lush with crops; the storehouses are overflowing with grain; the population is rising; manors have marketplaces; and towns are popping up all over.

What happened? A new age has dawned, the result of several astonishing developments that cannot be overlooked by students of the Crusades. So, pay attention.

Technology Transforms Agriculture

The first development is the construction of the heavy plow with mould-board and wheels. This device can turn the moist and heavy soil of central and northern Europe into lush farmlands. It can pulverize the soil with each furrow so completely that cross-plowing of fields is no longer necessary. But there's a problem. Because of its considerable size and weight, it can only be used with draught animals. Oxen continue to be in scarce supply, and the method used to harness them hasn't changed, and still results in their strangulation.

The heavy plow, which offers such hope and promise, would work most effectively with horses. Horses have speed, and speed provides the best chance of increasing agricultural production. But guess what? Horses require great amounts of grain to get them through the winter, and it's just not available. And there are other problems. Their hoofs are tender and subject to injury, and their physiques make them even harder to harness than oxen.

The solution comes with the horseshoe, a simple device that is unknown in ancient times. In the history of human inventions, few are of greater significance. We don't know who invented the horseshoe, just as we don't know who invented the wheel. But the person who invented the horseshoe transformed the world. In fact, if it had not been invented, we'd still be eating grass, and hoping to reach the ripe old age of 30.

Christian Chronicles

With new techniques and equipment, peasants could cultivate more land. Gradually, they learned the three-field system in which land was put to the plow two years out of three rather than one year out of two. New crop rotations were introduced that gave rise to the sowing of one field of summer crops—the "oats, peas, beans and barley" of the Mother Goose rhyme—and another field for winter crops, especially wheat and rye.

With the horseshoe comes the development of the horse collar, transferring the strains of plowing from the animal's neck to its withers. The horse can now pull far greater loads, and without the risk of strangulation.

These inventions produce the following results:

➤ Greater harvests for less work

➤ More grain for more animals

➤ More animals for more protein in the human diet

➤ More manure for more enriched soil

With these innovations in cultivation come other technological wonders. Large mills are built with grinding stones powered by oxen and water wheels. They free the haggard women of the eleventh century from the utter drudgery of grinding meal and flour by hand. Women have time to dress, to brush their hair (if not their teeth), even to wash. They no longer look, smell, and act like jackasses. Suddenly, they're becoming sexy.

Other developments occur in rapid succession: gear trains, windlasses, and pulleys!

No previous historical era has seen the creation of so many labor-saving and civilization-producing devices.

Winds of Change

The population of the Western world begins to grow dramatically. At the millennium, the population of France was six million; by 1100 C.E., it has doubled. Everywhere, people are increasing in number and in vitality. The result is that ...

➤ No longer can peasants look forward to taking over their fathers' holdings; now there are too many heirs for their plots to support. For the first time in centuries, people are on the move, clearing new land and creating new settlements.

➤ Great advances have been made in sex education. People no longer copulate like jackrabbits; rather, the women lie on their backs in the "missionary position," which is sanctioned by the Church as the only way to have sexual intercourse as it is "most conducive" to conception. Don't think that this makes people salacious; they still keep their clothing on when having sex, and lust within marriage remains a mortal sin.

Everything is happening with breathtaking speed. With the increase in crops comes an increased demand for more workers on the medieval manor. With the increase in demand for workers comes an increase in the status of the serf. With an increase in status comes the formation of guilds and associations. With the formation of associations comes the demand for more rights: the right to property,

Crusade Aid

At the turn of the twelfth century, the serfs of Michel de Beauvais announced that they would marry any woman they pleased, and give their daughters to any man they pleased.

Similarly, the serfs and peasants of St. Arnoul-de-Crepy refused to pay death dues or the fines imposed for allowing their daughters to marry men from a different manor.

the right to lower taxes, and the right of people to marry whomever they liked. In other words, these folks are becoming unionized.

The Feudal Deal

A new relationship is established between the peasant and the lord. In exchange for protection, the peasant provides the following dues:

➤ Annual taxes on the money made from the sale of surplus crops

➤ A small rent (*cens*)

➤ One-tenth of his crops and livestock

➤ Several weeks of unpaid labor in such tasks as clearing woods and draining marshes

➤ The grinding of the lord's corn, the baking of his bread, the brewing of his beer, and the pressing of his grapes

➤ Service at call in the lord's regiment

The lord (or, in French, the *seigneur*), as his part of the bargain, offers the following services to the workers:

➤ The use of his ovens, presses, mills, waters, woods, and fields

➤ Military protection to all who inhabit his lands

➤ The organization of agriculture, industry, and trade on his lands

The lord is bound to an overlord who, in turn, is bound to a king. The king protects the lord and his property in exchange for the lord's loyalty (including military service) to the king. This system (a kind of protection racket) is known as feudalism. It persists until the eighteenth century.

The Middle Class Materializes!

With the surplus of crops comes the appearance of marketplaces. With marketplaces comes the rise of towns and villages and the rebirth of commerce. With the rebirth of commerce comes a new class of people called "merchants."

Merchants originally were peddlers, usually Jewish or Syrian in origin, who wandered throughout the various settlements of medieval Europe hawking their wares and bringing news of the outside world. In the new towns, these peddlers set up shops and stores to sell their goods. As Christians were prohibited from making money by charging interest (to make a profit by moneylending was labeled *usury,* a mortal sin that merited eternal damnation), Jews continued to be the medieval bankers and moneylenders.

The city-dwellers seek lordly protection from wandering bands of warlords and brigands. For this reason, they are willing to provide an ample percentage of their profits to the nobles and their knights. However, as part of this bargain, the merchants insist on independent town governments and a certain degree of private liberty. The merchants, being good businessmen, get the better part of the deal, and within a century or two, amass enough capital to buy nearly every estate in Christendom.

The Church Weighs In

The Church now imposes a tax on all *benefices* and *dignitaries*. Those who want to occupy a benefice or attain a church office must pay for it. Those who refuse to pay this ecclesiastical tax after obtaining an office are excommunicated. What you pay is what you get! If you're a cash cow, you get to be a cardinal. If you only have a few bags of silver shillings, you end up a bishop.

More Coins for the Coffers

Money comes into the Church from other sources, including a tax on every Christian in Christendom, fees for the granting of dispensations from canonical law (such as the permission to marry your first cousin or the annulment of your wedding vows), and the sale of *indulgences*.

Only a small percentage of Christians manage to completely atone for their sins on earth. The vast majority will have to endure thousands (maybe millions) of years of prison time in purgatory. The Church claims that it possesses the right to lay aside prison time in purgatory to any person who performs special acts of faith, such as assisting in the construction of a church, making a pilgrimage, draining a rancid swamp—or making a lump sum payment of money.

Think about it: You know when you die that you're headed for the fires of purgatory. And you know that you can escape all or at least some of this punishment simply by obtaining an indulgence. Small wonder that indulgences are so popular. And small wonder that hundreds of thousands

Warrior Words

Every church, diocese, monastery, convent, and cathedral is considered to be a **benefice**. And everyone in a church office, from the simple parish priest to the lofty cardinal, is considered to be a **dignitary**.

Warrior Words

An **indulgence** is a partial or full exemption from some or all of the hard time awaiting Christians in *purgatory* because they have sinned. *Absolution* in confession removes the guilt of sin (the *culpa*) that would condemn a sinner to eternity in hell, but it does not remove the punishment for sin (the *poena*), which must be endured in purgatory.

flock to the Crusade when the pope offers a *plenary* (or full indulgence) to everyone who takes up the cross and marches off to Jerusalem.

Throughout the Middle Ages, the popes send out "pardoners" who would sell plenary indulgences to the nobles and commoners. One such pardoner went about reciting this jingle:

> As soon as the money in the coffer rings
> A soul from purgatory suddenly springs.

The Peace of God

The new prosperity for the nobles, the clergy, the merchants, and the serfs requires a measure of peace and stability. Prosperity cannot continue under the old system of feudal anarchy with lords constantly at war with other lords for matters of trifle. For this reason, the Church issues a decree called the *Pax Dei* or the *Peace of God*. This decree imposes the excommunication of all nobles and knights who use violence upon noncombatants (such as priests, merchants, and serfs) in war. It also demands that all warfare cease during Lent, in times of harvest or vintage (August 15 to November 11), on holy days, and for a good portion of the week, from Wednesday evening to Monday morning. By 1095, when the first Crusade is proclaimed, feudal lords are allowed only 80 days a year to engage in private war. To them, the *Pax Dei* is a crying shame!

This restriction is of profound significance for the development of the Crusades. Because of the *Peace of God,* the aristocracy is in a very uncomfortable position. From earliest youth, its members have been trained to do nothing but fight. Few can conceive of any other life. But they are now prohibited from doing what they are meant to do by the Church, the only institution that can invoke fear and trembling within them.

Despite the advancements in technology and the issuance of the *Pax Dei,* the world at the time of the First Crusade was an incredibly violent place. Brutality was so common that it could and did become ritualized by the Church. In 1100, a knight from Gascony prayed at the monastery of Sorde that God would allow him to catch the murderer of his brother. The intended victim was ambushed; his face horribly mutilated; his hands and feet cut off; and his testicles were cut off and fed to dogs. Moved by gratitude for answered prayers, the avenging knight presented his enemy's bloodstained armor and weapons as pious offerings to the monks of Sorde. The monks accepted the gifts with praise and thanksgiving.

At first the nobles attempt to devise ways to skirt the Church's restrictions. As the Church prohibits "the spilling of blood" 280 days a year, the nobles come up with an ingenious weapon—the mace—that can crush an opponent's skull without spilling one drop of blood. It's a marvelous weapon, but soon it, too, becomes outlawed.

The Age of Chivalry

For fun, the knights begin to engage in mock combats, in tournaments, and in quests for legitimate combat against non-Christians. The Age of *Chivalry* has dawned.

Warrior Words

Chivalry is a moral system, a sudden outgrowth of eleventh-century socioeconomic conditions, that comes to govern all aspects of noble life. Knights are no longer barbaric thugs who rape, pillage, and hack to pieces anything in their path, but Christian heroes in the service of justice, piety, the Church, and the oppressed. A knight in the Kingdom of the Franks was called a *chevalier*. The word comes from *cheval*, an Old French word meaning *horse*. This makes sense because knights were mounted warriors. The code of conduct for a *chevalier* was aptly called *chivalry*.

A noble's man-at-arms becomes a knight not by the good old fashion method of baptism by blood but by a religious ceremony that consists of purification, confession, and Holy Communion. The relic of a saint is embedded in the hilt of the knight's sword so that the weapon of slaughter could become an instrument of righteousness. (This is good news for local merchants who find a lucrative market in selling phony relics to gullible members of the clergy and nobility.)

By the time of the first Crusade, chivalry has developed its own cardinal virtues:

➤ **Prowess**   A combination of courage, strength, and skill in battle

➤ **Honor**   A good name that has to be defended at all costs

➤ **Loyalty**   Defense of the lord's honor in all circumstances

➤ **Courtesy**   Behavior in a manner that best reflects the honor of the court

➤ **Largesse**   Open-handed generosity in gifts and hospitality

Christian Chronicles

As chivalry developed so did the ideal of courtly love. A knight became pledged to the service of a lady who gave him her colors to wear at a tournament. To the lady, the knight dedicated his feats of arms. It was her name he invoked in the thick of battle or at the moment of death.

Knights, as we know, are trained for one purpose: to engage in battle. Therefore, opportunities are created for knights to display their prowess in a civilized manner. These occasions are called *tournaments*.

Extreme Sports

Originating in France, tournaments consist of jousts between individuals and fighting exercises between groups with 40 knights to a side. The fighting exercises are conducted *a plaisance*, that is, with blunted weapons, or *an outrance* (with no restraints), in which case participants are severely maimed and often killed.

A tournament might last for as long as two weeks. Opening day is seeding the players, followed by days for jousts, melees, feasts, and "mock battles." These occasions are the great sporting events of the Middle Ages. They attract crowds of farmers, food vendors, merchants, prostitutes, and pickpockets. About a hundred knights participate in a typical tournament. Each knight is accompanied by two mounted squires, an armorer, and six servants in *livery* or distinctive dress.

A tournament includes ...

➤ **The joust** A single combat of rival knights. Wearing 30 to 40 pounds of chain mail, the knights crash into each other at full gallop while holding eighteen-foot lances, half the size of an average telephone poll. If either contestant is unhorsed, the other is required to dismount and to continue the combat with sword or mace until one or the other calls it quits, faints from heat and fatigue, suffers a serious wound (such as the loss of a limb), or gives up the ghost.

The combat is as real as an encounter between gladiators in the Roman Colosseum. Each knight is dead-set upon felling the other. By so doing, he gets to keep his opponent's horse and armor.

➤ **The melee or horseless contest** Consists of two knights hacking at one another with heavy (20- to 30-pound) broadswords. Few emerge unscathed. An injured knight, more often than not, ends up as a beggar in the marketplace.

➤ **The tourney** The climax of the festival, in which two groups of knights engage in so-called "mock" battle. But there is nothing phony about these encounters. At one *tourney* at Neuss, over 60 knights are killed in one afternoon.

Warrior Words

Tournament comes from the Latin word *tornus*, meaning *lathe*. It refers to the circular nature of these contests, with one group of combatants succeeding another. The servants and attendants of a knight were dressed in the knight's favorite or distinctive color. Their uniforms were called **livery** (from *livree*, the Frankish word for *deliver*) because they were delivered to the knight's entourage twice a year.

When all the contests are over, the survivors and the noble spectators join in an evening of feasting, song, and dance. The winning knights enjoy the privilege of kissing (but not fondling) the loveliest ladies, and hearing poems and songs recited in celebration of their victories. These guys are the sports celebrities of their time.

Training for Knighthood

By the end of the eleventh century, it's not easy for a young nobleman to become a knight. At seven or eight, he becomes a page, serving the lord at table, taking care of his clothes, and assisting him on the rare occasions when he decides to take a bath. During this time, the boy learns how to ride, to fight, to hawk, to play chess and backgammon, and to sing and dance.

At 14, the page becomes a squire. At this time, the training for combat intensifies. The squire learns how to wield a broadsword, how to smash through a shield with a battle-axe, how to unhorse an enemy with a lance, and how to crush a skull with a club-headed mace. He leads his lord's war-horse to battle or tournament and holds it when the fighting is on foot.

He assists in the business of the castle, keeps the keys to all doors, and carries his lord's purse and valuables on a journey.

The Knights of the Cross

At 17, the squire is ready to become a knight. He begins this ritual by taking a bath as a symbol of spiritual (if not physical) purification. For this reason, he can be called a "knight of the bath," as distinguished from a "knight of the sword" who distinguishes himself in battle. For a day he fasts; then he passes a night in church at prayer; confesses his sins to a priest in the morning; attends Mass; receives communion; hears a sermon on the knightly virtues, and solemnly pledges before the priest to uphold them. The candidate now is clothed in the knightly attire of hauberk, cuirass (or breastplate), armlets, gauntlets (armored gloves), and spurs. He bows before the lord, who lifts his sword and "dubs" the squire a knight. The new knight receives a lance, a helmet, and a sword. He adjusts his helmet, mounts his horse, brandishes his lance, flourishes his sword, and rides out of church (Yes, you read it right. Horses attend Mass with the knights). The new knight distributes lavish gifts to his attendants in the spirit of largesse and hosts a sumptuous feast for his fellow noblemen.

These knights will be the champions of the Crusades. They are young, haughty, reckless, and incredibly strong. They can wield heavy broadswords and battle-axes while wearing 40 pounds of armor along with 10-pound helmets. They are cold killing machines but they are unsophisticated in the art of warfare. Their means of going into battle is to charge into enemy forces with steeds and hack everyone and everything to pieces. They know nothing about gunpowder; it hasn't been invented yet. They know nothing about longbows that can pierce armor and kill soldiers at great range; they will not appear until the fourteenth century. They don't even use crossbows. Crossbows will not be developed until the end of the First Crusade. Such bows and arrows are in existence, but are only fit for serfs to use.

Crusade Aid

Nobles were distinguished from commoners by their ancestry or *gens*. For this reason, they were called "gentle" men. The term in the Middle Ages had nothing to do with kindness or refined behavior. Not all "gentlemen" were eligible for knighthood. Such honors were usually reserved for the eldest sons. Some younger sons remained squires until they carved out lands of their own or else purchased a "dignitary" from the Church and became archbishops, bishops, or abbots.

An anonymous medieval poet describes a knight going into battle as "a terrible worm in an iron cocoon." He rides on a saddle that rises in a very high ridge above the horse's backbone with his feet resting in extremely long stirrups. This means that he is virtually standing up as he rides. For this reason, he is able to deliver powerful blows from side to side with any one of his weapons. He begins battle by charging into the enemy's forces with his long and heavy lance. He has attached to his saddle a broadsword, a battle-ax fitted with a spike behind the curved blade, and a club-headed mace with sharpened, ridged edges. The war-horse carrying this heavy burden is itself covered with heavy plates of armor that protect its nose, chest, and rump. It is also fitted with a decorative drapery that often gets in the way of its legs. If the horse is felled, the knight, weighed down by armor and tangled in weapons, shields, and spurs, is likely to be killed or captured before he can rise to engage in hand-to-hand combat.

Since these guys are illiterate, they know nothing about military techniques and strategies. They insist on being first in battle because they relish the bloodshed. They form a long line and charge into battle at full gallop. The priests, bishops, abbots, and monks follow them, with the serfs in the rear. Chivalry demands that combat be personal and bodily. Missiles such as the arrow and the spear that permit combat at a distance are held in scorn and derision. An archer, according to a twelfth-century song, is a "coward who dares not come close to his foe."

Sure, the crusader image has been cleaned up in recent years. Crusaders uphold *noblesse oblige*—a pledge of martial valor and feudal fidelity, of unquestioning service to all knights, all women, the weak, and the poor. They are trained to sing and dance. But they remain rough and ready brutes. They still eat with dirty fingers, drink themselves into oblivion at night, and break into a violent rages if they're looked at cross-eyed. The Saracens, when they meet them, will be appalled by their cruelty and crudeness. Sir Bohemond, one of the greatest of the Christian crusaders, will express his contempt of the Eastern Emperor Alexis by sending to the imperial court at Constantinople several chests filled with the sliced off noses, thumbs, ears, and private parts of thousands of Alexis's subjects.

The Least You Need to Know

➤ The agricultural revolution of the eleventh century began with the invention of the horseshoe and the horse collar.

➤ Increased crops gave rise to a sharp increase in population.

➤ With the growth of cities came the emergence of a new class of merchants.

➤ Warfare between the feudal lords became regulated by the *Pax Dei*, or *Peace of God*.

➤ With the *Peace of God* came a new code of chivalry, but it by no means diminished the ferociously combative spirit of the crusaders.

Chapter 3

The Pope Declares Holy War

In This Chapter

➤ Pope Urban II rallies the knights

➤ Urban declares a Holy War on the Seljuk Turks

➤ The knights are spurred to defend Christendom—while adding to their wealth

➤ The pope's promise of salvation gains him an army of zealous fighting men

It is November 27, 1095. Pope Urban II has summoned the French nobles to a Church council in a field at Clermont. This is something unusual. A pope has never called a meeting like this. The field is crowded with thousands of lords, knights, vassals, and horses. A papal throne has been set up on a high platform. The pope is surrounded by cardinals, archbishops, bishops, and priests—all in full regalia. Behind the throne you can see the new church of Notre-Dame-du-Port, one of the grandest structures in Christendom. It seems a perfect backdrop for the dramatic occasion.

Pope Urban II Rallies the Troops

The pope rises from his throne with the help of his cardinals and blesses the assembly: *In Nomine Patris, et Filii, et Spiritus Sancti.* Everyone bows before the Holy Father. The pope is 60 years old, very old for a medieval man. He seems old and frail but his voice is vibrant and strong. He begins to speak not in Latin (as the crowd expects) but in French, and his words echo throughout the open field. The speech that he is about to deliver will become a masterpiece of oratory to rival the remarks of Antony over the body of Julius Caesar.

Pope Urban begins as follows:

> O race of Franks, race most beloved and chosen by God! From the confines of Jerusalem and the city of Constantinople a horrible tale has gone forth and very frequently has been brought to our ears that a race from the kingdom of the Persians, an accursed race, a race utterly alienated from God, has invaded the lands of Christians and has depopulated them by the sword, pillage, and fire.

This sounds serious—like another attack from the barbarians, only this time the barbarians are invading the holiest of cities, the very "navel of the world"—Jerusalem. The crowd is appalled.

The pope continues: "This horrible race of infidels destroy altars, after having defiled them with their uncleanness." Defile altars? What does the pope mean? Are they stripping them of the sacred relics of the saints? Are they performing heathen rites upon them? Are they eliminating bodily waste on a table sanctified for the miracle of the transformation of bread and wine? Good grief, what could be worse?

But there is worse, much worse news. The pope pauses, then says: "These infidels circumcise the Christians, and the blood of the circumcision they either spread upon the altars or pour into the vases of the baptismal font." All the lords, knights, and vassals flinch at the mere thought of having their members cut by pagan blades. Everyone in attendance is now riveted by every word the pope speaks: "When they wish to torture people by base death, they cut a hole through their navels and pull out the end of the intestines and nail it to the ground. Then they flog the victims, making them run around in circles, until all of their viscera gush from their bodies to the ground." Now chopping off an arm or a leg is one thing, but this is downright nasty and disgusting.

"Others," the pope says, "the Turks bind to a post and pierce with arrows." Arrows! The lords and knights are mortified. Bows and arrows are the weapons of common people, of lowly serfs and cowardly peasants. To be killed by arrows is most humiliating.

"Still others," the pope tells them, "are forced to extend their necks, and, then attacking them with heavy swords, the infidels attempt to cut through the neck with a single blow." Sure, the knights try to do the same thing when engaging in combat, but they would never cut off the head of a mere captive who is bound and gagged and defenseless. Such an act is completely un-Christian.

Crusade Aid

Pope Urban II knew how to address the French nobles, as he was a French noble. He had been born Eudes de Lagery and raised in his family castle near Chatillon-sur-Marne. An ancient portrait of Urban II depicts the pope as a robust and bald figure with a long beard and an unusually thick mustache.

Urban Declares a Holy War

"What shall I say of the abominable rape of women?" the pope asks. "To speak of it is worse than to be silent." Urban is not speaking about the rape of a serf by a lord, but of a Christian woman by a circumcised Saracen. The assembly shudders at the thought.

The pope now has the audience in the palm of his holy hand.

> On whom, then, rests the labor of avenging these wrongs, and of recovering this territory, if not upon you—you upon whom, above all others, God has conferred remarkable glory in arms, great bravery, and strength to humble the heads of those who resist you? Let the deeds of your ancestors encourage you—the glory and grandeur of Charlemagne—and your other monarchs. Let the Holy Sepulcher of our Lord and Savior, now held by unclean nations, arouse you, and the holy places that are now stained with pollution.

Christian Chronicles

The Holy Sepulcher, the tomb of Jesus Christ, was the holiest of all places in medieval Christianity. It was the place of the supreme miracle, the Resurrection of the crucified Jesus in historical time and place. The tomb was the destination of all pilgrims to the Holy Land. It was the relic of relics, the icon of icons. Here Jesus lay dead; here He threw off His linen wraps; here He sprang into eternal life—the life that is offered to all Christians.

The knights are standing now. They are raising their swords to the sky. They are seething with righteous rage and holy indignation. They are ready to kill every infidel on the face of the earth.

The pope holds the cross above his head to silence the knights. The crowd regains its composure as Urban continues: "Let none of your possessions keep you back, nor anxiety for your family affairs. For the land that you now inhabit, shut in on all sides by the sea, scarcely furnishes food enough for its cultivators. Hence it is that you murder and devour one another, that you wage wars, and that many of you perish in civil strife."

The pope has now appealed to their bellies. Not only will they get the chance to slaughter the Saracens, they will also obtain the possibility of gaining new lands, new

Crusade Aid

Although Urban II was not the first pope to go to war—that distinction rests with Gregory I, who took charge of the Roman legions to defend Rome against the Lombards—he initiated a highly original way of raising an army. Instead of pay, he offered paradise.

resources, and new wealth. Every knight in attendance will become a mighty landlord with a great fiefdom. Every lord will become an overlord with greater power, greater authority, greater prominence. Their imagination runs riot with thoughts of God, glory, and booty.

Now the pope's cry turns into a plea: "Let hatred depart from you; let your quarrels end. Enter upon the road to the Holy Sepulcher; wrest that land from a wicked race, and subject it to yourselves." It's amazing. The pope is calling for an end to feudal strife. He is calling for union of lord with lord, knight with knight, in one great quest for the glory of God. He is giving these Frankish lords who have quarreled and fought among themselves for centuries a sense of something they never had before—a sense of commonality as a people, a sense of nationalism. Tears are now running down the cheeks of many knights and nobles.

Ticket to Paradise

"Jerusalem," the pope says, "implores you to come to its aid. Undertake this journey eagerly for the remission of sins, and be assured of imperishable glory in the Kingdom of Heaven." Yes, you heard it right. The pope is offering forgiveness of sins—even the most grievous sins—to everyone who embarks on this Crusade. The nobles who go into battle against the Turks will be received in heaven to the acclaim of angels. They will receive glory, everlasting glory, in the court of the omnipotent Overlord who rules over all fiefdoms.

Through the crowd excitement rises until someone cries out: *Dieu li volt,* "God wills it." Now all the nobles are crying out the same thing with one voice, the voice of the Franks: "God wills it." The pope, too, takes up the cry, along with his clerical entourage.

After several minutes, the pope again holds up the cross. The cries subside and the great crowd becomes silent as the Holy Father says:

> Yes, indeed. Yes, it is the will of God. You today see the accomplishment of the word of our Savior, who promised to be in the midst of the faithful, when assembled in His name. It is He who dictated to you the words I have heard. Let these words be your war cry. Let them announce everywhere the presence of the God in His holy army.

The pope again flourishes the cross before the massive crowd, and the lords and knights in turn hold their swords to high heaven. There is a wild uproar. The chorus of voices is deafening as the pope retires to his throne.

Now there is a hush as Cardinal Gregorio dei Guidone, who will later become Pope Innocent II, pronounces a general confession. The nobles fall to their knees, beat their breasts, and confess their sins.

Crosscurrent

Don't think that the notion of a holy war originated with Urban II. The doctrine was developed by St. Augustine at the time of the fall of the Roman Empire (410 C.E.). St. Augustine said that a defensive war is always just, as it is conducted to protect the people. An offensive war, he said, is just when it is waged against a state that refuses to make reparation for wrongs committed or fails to return seized property.

Adhemar Leads the Charge

At the close of the ceremony, Adhemar of Monteil, the Bishop of Le Puy, bows before Pope Urban and asks that he be allowed to take the cross from the pope's hand in order to lead the good Christian warriors to the Holy Land. Adhemar has made a pilgrimage to the Holy Land before and he knows the way. The knights appear to be stunned by this brashness, not knowing that it had been privately agreed that Adhemar would serve as Urban's deputy in forming a base of papal authority in Jerusalem. The pope hands Adhemar the cross and blesses him.

Now something startling happens. Thousands of knights swear that they see the clouds part and an image of the Holy City appear in the sky. They fall to their knees in wonder, knowing for certain that God wills the Crusade.

The First Crusade is underway. For the next two years, the old but energetic pope travels to other

Christian Chronicles

At the close of the assembly in Clermont, white swaths of cloth bearing the Sign of the Cross were given to every crusader. The cloth was sewed to the right shoulder of a robe or mantle and fastened to the helmet. The symbol of the Crusade had been established, along with the slogan that would be screamed before the Turkish army: "God wills it."

cities: Tours, Bordeaux, Toulouse, Nimes, and Rome. By his authority, Urban II releases Christians from all commitments that might hinder the Crusade. He frees the serfs from fealty to their lord for the duration of the war. He confers upon all crusaders the right to be tried in ecclesiastical instead of manorial court. He guarantees the Church's protection of all private property during the course of the campaign in the Holy Land.

The Least You Need to Know

➤ At Clermont, the pope enjoins Christian knights to free the Holy Land from Seljuk Turks.

➤ The Crusades provide an outlet for the aggression of medieval knights.

➤ The Crusades offer new lands and riches for the nobles.

➤ The Crusades offer remission of the penalty of sin for all Christians.

➤ The Crusades represent a means of the unification of Europe.

The Lure of Byzantium

Pope Urban II's call for a Crusade comes in response to a cry for help from Alexis Comnena, the emperor of Byzantium. Byzantium is a different world. Sure, it's Christian and not Moslem, but it's not *Roman* Catholic—it's *Greek* Catholic! In 326 C.E., the Roman emperor Constantine, the first Christian Caesar, divided the Roman Empire in half with an eastern capital in Constantinople and a western capital in Rome. After his death, each empire elected its own ruler, adopted its own religious practices, and developed a totally different culture. By the time of the Crusades, the Catholic Church is not really "catholic," that is, "universal." It is torn in half between the East and the West.

East Is East ...

The major differences between the Eastern and Western forms of Christianity are ...

➤ The Eastern rulers and bishops look upon the pope, not as the Vicar of Christ and the Supreme Pontiff, but the first bishop among equals, with no more authority than any other bishop. In fact, the title "pope" or *papa*, meaning "father," had been applied in the first four centuries to every Catholic bishop. During the Middle Ages, the title became reserved for the Bishop of Rome.

➤ The Eastern Church has a different doctrine of the Trinity. It holds that the Holy Spirit does not proceed from both the Father and the Son (as the Roman Church says in its creeds), but only from God the Father. This may not seem like a significant issue at first glance, but it is an issue of utmost importance. It makes the Eastern and the Western Churches distinct, with different liturgies, different saints, and different theologies.

These disagreements came to a head in 1054, when the pope excommunicated the Bishop of Constantinople, and the Bishop of Constantinople excommunicated the pope.

Crusade Aid

Until the Turks seized Jerusalem from the Fatimids, Christian pilgrims had free access to the Holy Land. Pilgrims who had made the long journey were called "palmers," because they wore crossed palm leaves from Palestine.

Pope Urban II has no more love for the Greek Catholics than for the Moslems. They are heretics who refuse to uphold the Roman dogma of the Holy Trinity, schismatics who defy his divine authority, and defilers of true religion who make a mockery of the concept of "Catholicism."

Jerusalem isn't the pope's turf. It's 3,000 miles away. It hasn't fallen under Roman jurisdiction since the death of Constantine. For 300 years, the Byzantines ruled the Holy Land, until the Moslems conquered it in 638. The Roman pontiffs before Urban II had no real problem with this. The Fatimid Moslems, who ruled Palestine from Egypt, were extremely tolerant of other religions, giving Roman and Greek Christians a wide liberty of worship. In fact, when Al-Hakim ("the mad caliph of Cairo"), destroyed the Church of the Holy Sepulcher in 1010, the Fatimid Moslems contributed substantially to its restoration.

A Plea from the East

But now something monumental has happened. Alexis II, the emperor of the Byzantine Empire, is turning to Rome for assistance. He is submitting himself to the pope as a lord submits to an overlord. He is offering reconciliation, and the possibility of papal authority extending from West to East.

The terrible problem facing the Byzantine Empire is the Seljuk Turks. The Seljuk Turks are a horde of barbarians like the Mongol horde of Genghis Khan who come from the northern and central plains of Asia. They are nomadic warriors who live off the earth, setting up their tents wherever they please and taking pleasure in sacking cities, pillaging the countryside, and hauling men, women, and children off to slave markets. They are as destructive and unstoppable as a swarm of Tasmanian devils.

When they conquer Persia, the leaders of the Seljuk Turks convert to Islam. Their religious zeal only adds to their lust for conquest. In August 1071, the Turks confront the great and mighty army of the Eastern Emperor, Romanus IV, at Menxikert in Armenia. They rout the massive army and carry the emperor off in chains.

After this great victory, the terrible Turks set forth in all directions, spreading the fear of God among Greek Christians and Fatimid Moslems alike. They capture Jerusalem from the Fatimids; they seize Antioch from the Greeks; and they push on toward Constantinople, the great capital of the Byzantine Empire; and toward Cairo, the headquarters of the Fatimid Caliph.

The new emperor Alexis Comnena (who is a key figure in our story) needs help to defend his capital from the infidels. He turns to the Western princes and the pope with a desperate plea for help. In the plea, he writes:

> I am writing to inform you that the very saintly empire of Greek Christians is daily being persecuted by the Turks. They shamelessly commit the sin of sodomy on our men of all ages and ranks ... and, O misery, something that has never been seen or heard of before on our bishops ... Already there is nothing for them to conquer except Constantinople, which they threaten to conquer any day now, unless God and the Latin rite come quickly to our aid.

Christian Chronicles

Because of his humiliating defeat, Romanus IV was not only deposed, but also blinded and cast into prison by his subjects. He died of a broken heart one year later.

The Pope Takes the Bait

In his letter, Alexis Comnena goes on to speak about the great wealth of Byzantium that awaits the Christian princes of the West, and the pope:

> The churches of Constantinople are loaded with a vast treasure of gold and silver, gems and precious stones, mantles and cloths of silk, sufficient to decorate all the churches of the world ... And then, too, there are the treasures

Crusade Aid

The invasion of the Seljuk Turks was only one of the woes that befell the Byzantine Empire in the late eleventh century. The Empire also experienced an outbreak of the bubonic plague, a devastating drought, widespread rebellion, and the resurgence of leprosy.

in the possession of our noble men, not to speak of the treasures of the merchants. No words can describe this wealth of treasure, for it includes not only the treasuries of the emperors, but also those of the ancient Roman emperors brought here and concealed in the palace. What more can I say? What can be seen by human eyes is nothing in comparison with the treasure that remains concealed.

By the time Pope Urban II reads this, his tongue, no doubt, is hanging from his mouth and his eyes are spinning like saucers. Not only can he gain millions of new souls for the Holy Roman Church but wealth beyond measure, beyond imagination. The old pope keeps reading the words in a state of excitement that borders, perhaps, on hyperventilation.

Crusade Aid

At the time of the Crusades, the Roman Church was issuing decrees to enforce clerical celibacy. In 1059, Pope Nicholas II prohibited the faithful from attending Masses that were celebrated by priests who continued to live with their wives and concubines. In 1139, the Second Lateran Council ruled that all ordained members of the clergy must be celibate.

The Eastern Emperor, not knowing that the pope and members of the Roman clergy have opted for celibacy, goes on to speak of the "incomparable beauty of Greek women" who alone should be "sufficient reason to attract the armies of the Franks to the plains of Thrace." No, the pope is not interested in obtaining a girlfriend, let alone a wife. He is a Cluniac, for heaven's sake, which means that he spent his youth fighting temptation in a monastery. He is not about to relinquish his vows at 60, though he probably thinks that pretty girls are nice to have around, if only for decorative purposes.

After issuing his call for the Crusade, the crafty old pope distributes copies of Emperor Alexis's letter to the Christian princes and lords. What enticements! The Crusade offers everything imaginable: idealism, wealth, power, glory, remission of sin, and the prospects of connubial (if not carnal) bliss with the beautiful women of the East.

The pope sets August 15, 1096, as the date of departure of the Christian army. The First Crusade is ready to begin, and it's going to be one hell of a trip.

The Least You Need to Know

➤ Byzantine and Roman Catholics have different creeds, doctrines, and rituals.

➤ Byzantine Catholics do not acknowledge papal authority.

➤ Constantinople was the capital of the Byzantine Empire.

➤ Alexis Comnena, the emperor of Byzantium, sent an urgent plea to the pope for military help against the Seljuk Turks.

➤ The Seljuk Turks invaded Byzantium, occupied the Holy Land, and planned to invade Constantinople.

➤ The Crusade represented the pope's response to the Byzantine emperor's request.

Part 2
The First Crusade

Turn this page and you will begin the quest to save the Holy Sepulcher from the hands of the infidels. In these pages, the first Jewish holocausts will take place; Christians will rise against Christians; infants will be cooked over open fires; people will eat excrement; atrocities will occur in every paragraph. This part would be rated NC-17 if it were a movie. Consider yourself warned that when you enter this part of the book, it's hell inside.

The Crusade of the Poor

While great Christian armies are gathering in France, Germany, Italy, and England, a most peculiar man named Little Peter is wandering throughout the countryside calling the common people to engage in a peasants' campaign to drive the Turks from the Holy Land. How can commoners accomplish this task? They are not equipped with weapons. They possess no suits of armor, let alone armored war-horses. What's more, they are not trained in battle. They do not know how to wield and parry with a sword and shield. They don't know how to sit in a saddle and hold a lance. They can't even tell a mace from mail or a helmet from a hauberk. This doesn't matter, says Little Peter. They can succeed where mighty knights are doomed to fail, because they possess the most powerful weapon of all: the weapon of prayer.

Little Peter

Sitting in an easy chair with this *Idiot's Guide,* it may be hard to fathom how hundreds of thousands of peasants are carried off on a crazy crusade by an itinerant preacher. And in fact, the preacher himself is a bit of a puzzlement. Little Peter calls himself a hermit and yet he wears the robe of a monk. Which is he? Is he a solitary who set off to escape the temptations of the world by living alone in the wilderness? Or is he a cleric who assumed vows and lived in a monastic community? No one knows. He is ungainly, unkempt, and downright ugly. People swear that he looks exactly like the jackass he rides from place to place. He is round, short, dirty, and bald—in other words, not very appealing. And yet he is the leading charismatic figure of the day. From all regions of Christendom, people flock to hear him, to see him, and to receive his blessing.

Unlike the bloated bishops and cardinals of the Church, Little Peter refuses to live in pomp and luxury. He wears the same clothes day after day; he eats the same food—fish and wine—never a morsel of anything else; and he walks around barefoot even in the coldest weather. The people call him "Cucu Peter" for good reason.

Cucu Peter preaches a gospel of apostolic poverty. He speaks of Jesus as someone "kind and lowly," someone who cares for the poor and the dispossessed, someone who says, "The meek shall inherit the earth." The people have never heard such teachings. Christ, for them, was never a loving savior but the stern avenger of every mortal sin. He said, "I have not come to bring peace but a sword." (Matt. 10:34).

Christian Chronicles

Europe at the time of Little Peter was caught up in millenarianism, that is, the belief that the world was coming to an end. Clergymen began to preach that the assembly of Christian pilgrims in Jerusalem would hasten the return of Jesus. In 1065, a party of 7,000 believers gathered in the Holy City to welcome the Lord's return. Jesus didn't appear. The Seljuk Turks did.

What's more, the Lord taught His disciples that they should carry swords when they spread the "good news." (Luke 22:35-36). He was a figure who would appear at the Last Judgment to sentence the vast majority of mankind to everlasting suffering in a place of utter darkness. But the Jesus Peter speaks about is someone who chooses to identify with people just like them. This guy Peter, although his followers don't know it, is an evangelist, and they are becoming (like it or not) evangelical Christians.

Not only is Peter's message different, Peter is different. An early chronicler, Guilbert of Nogent, provides this description of him:

> Peter was very generous to the poor from the wealth that had been given him. He reclaimed prostitutes and provided them with husbands and dowries from his pocket; and everywhere, he restored peace and concord in places of strife. Whatever he did or said was regarded as practically divine, so much so that the people snatched whiskers from his mule as relics.

No other priest or preacher had ever been generous toward them like Peter was. The others always had something to sell—an indulgence, a relic—or take—a tithe, a tax. But Peter seeks only to give of himself and to share his earthly possessions. He seems to be a great saint, if not the Second Coming of Christ Himself.

Little or Cucu Peter (whatever you care to call him) tells the people that he has been commissioned by Almighty God to lead a Crusade of the Poor. For only the poor are the children of God and only God's children can rescue the Holy Sepulcher from the Turks. And the peasants, who had been held in feudal bondage, responded in overwhelming numbers. "All the common people, the chaste as well as the sinful, adulterers, homicides, thieves, robbers, all joyfully entered upon the great expedition."

Thousands follow the little hermit as he goes from place to place to recruit people for his army. As much as the poor people love him, the nobles dislike him. Who can blame them? Peter is calling their serfs from their manors for some cockamamie crusade. Yet, with all their might and manpower, the nobles are powerless to oppose him. They, too, think that Little Peter might be a holy saint, if not a divine angel.

While Little Peter is the undisputed spiritual leader of the Peasant Crusade, five knights, all belonging to the same family, serve as military leaders. These knights are Walter de Poissy and his four nephews: Walter the Penniless, William, Matthew, and Simon. When Walter de Poissy drops dead on the march, Walter the Penniless becomes the commander–in–chief of the untrained and unarmed army.

By the time Peter sets out on his march to Jerusalem, he has attracted well over 100,000 followers to his cause. The first Christian Crusade is underway. It is led not by a noble knight in shining armor, but a slightly crazy hermit in a monk's cowl.

The Crusade Produces the First Holocaust

The peasants have a problem. They lack the goods, provisions, proper clothing, weapons, and money for the 3,000-mile journey to Jerusalem. How can they come up with the cash to embark on the holy march? The answer is obvious. As true crusaders, they are committed to ridding the world of the enemies of Christ. And such enemies, with coffers of silver, are in their own towns and villages. The Jews! These are the people who crucified Christ, who cried out for blood. These are the people who have become prosperous by engaging in the hated practice of usury at the expense of all good Christians.

In 1096, the first massacres of Jews take place in the Rhineland. Count Emich of Leisengen, a noble who lost his holdings and served as a brigand, becomes inspired by Little Peter and, in a fit of religious ardor, burns a cross on his forehead. He leads a group of peasants to the town of Spier to hunt out the despisers of Christ.

To his dismay, Count Emich and his band find the small community of Jews protected by a Christian bishop. Nevertheless, he seizes a dozen Jews from the sanctuary and orders them to recant their Hebrew religion and undergo Christian baptism. When the stubborn Jews refuse to submit to this demand, they are hacked to pieces by the irate crusaders.

Crosscurrent

The systematic persecution and mass murder of Jews is such a prominent feature of European history that we are surprised to discover it is really an inheritance of the Crusades. Prior to the Crusades, Jewish communities were seen as economic assets, and Jews were allowed to own their own land, houses, and businesses. In 1048, the Bishop of Spier issued a charter that said: "Desiring to make a city out of the town of Spier, I have admitted Jews, knowing they will multiply one thousand times the honor of our community."

Emich and his band move on to Worms, where they storm a section of the town known as *Judengasse* or "Jews' Gate." They butcher every Jew in sight—every man, woman, and child, like reapers cutting them down with sickles. Every dwelling place is pillaged. Every article of value is seized. The synagogue is put to the torch, and the Torah is unrolled and ripped into small pieces that the crusaders toss into the streets like confetti. The rabbi, in an act of mercy, kills his child and his wife to spare them from the swords of the Christians. By the end of the day, in this prelude to the great Crusade, over a thousand Jews are massacred.

The roving band of peasant crusaders proceed north to Mainz. The Jews of Mainz try to appease the crusaders by casting coins and precious goods from their windows. The offering is not sufficient. The crusaders drag families from their dwellings and order them to submit to Christian baptism. The peasants with their scythes and sickles slice the throats of all who refuse. Over 900 suffer martyrdom.

Christian Chronicles

After the slaughter of the Jews at Mainz, the Bishop of Wurtzberg with the help of his prelates collected the bodies of the butchered Jews from the streets. The carts were filled with feet, hands, thumbs, fingers, and severed heads. The Bishop anointed these remains with holy oil and buried them in his garden.

Outbreaks of pogroms take place in other cities: Cologne, Trier, Metz, Prague, and Ratisbon. The anti-Jewish sentiment spreads throughout France and England. How many are slaughtered to provide provisions for the Peasant Crusade remains historians' guess. Some say 10,000.

The March to Jerusalem

Six months before the start of the Peasant Crusade, Little Peter and his army of the poor set out on their journey. They take the traditional pilgrim route through Hungary and into Byzantine territory. The peasant crusaders sing songs as they go on their merry way. It is an army unlike any other, consisting of the old and the young, women and children, petty nobles, and poor priests. The crowd stretches down the narrow pathways for many miles, and Little Peter leads the way on his jackass.

At first, all goes well. The motley crusaders are cheered and showered with gifts wherever they go. Their ranks continue to swell with more and more recruits from all regions of Christendom, including even guys in furry skirts who are called Scots. They march from Cologne to Oedenburg. At Oedenburg, the crowd shows signs of restlessness and begins to ask the age-old question: "Are we there yet?" Little Peter dispatches Walter the Penniless, his military commander, to lead an advance group of 5,000 crusaders to the city of Constantinople. From this time on, things begin to go terribly wrong.

Christian Chronicles

Emich, after running riot among the Rhineland Jewish communities, broke away from Peter's army in Hungary and tried to capture the fortress town of Weiselberg with a group of mercenaries. The outlaw crusaders were attacked by a garrison of the Hungarian army and disappeared from the pages of history.

Battles with Byzantine Christians

Walter and his soldiers arrive in the Byzantine town of Belgrade to the complete surprise of the local residents. They ask for food, but no food is available since it is not yet harvest time. Walter is irate. He and the men in his mangy company have traveled across Europe to help the people of Byzantium, and they are being denied food and drink. What ingratitude! The crusaders respond by pillaging the local countryside. There is a violent clash in which over 150 of Walter's followers are burned to death in a church.

The advance unit marches on to Sofia, and the Byzantine emperor Alexis Comnena sends out escorts to lead them to Constantinople.

The scene is now set for the first great battle of the Crusades. Walter and his unit of 5,000—minus those who had been burned in the church—are safe in Byzantium with the emperor. Little Peter and his massive entourage are traveling through Belgrade. The peasant crusaders see that a church has been burned to the ground; when they inspect the rubble, they find the bodies of Walter's men. Then all hell breaks loose. The peasant army storms Belgrade and overruns the Hungarian army. More than 5,000 Hungarians are put to the sword. They hack off the heads of hundreds of Hungarians as war trophies. The peasant army is elated. It is a great victory—the first victory of the Holy Crusade. The problem is that this victory is not over the Turks, but over fellow Christians. The Peasant Crusade, having achieved this marvelous success, sets the town on fire and marches on to Nish.

It would be nice to report that nothing terrible happens at Nish. But this is not the case. The Germans in the rear guard of Little Peter's army set fire to several country houses and steal a herd of cows. The governor of Nish is outraged and sends his well-trained army to teach Peter's army a lesson. The Byzantines attack Peter's rear guard and put many of the fire-starters and cattle thieves to death. In the midst of this melee, the townspeople of Nish and Belgrade appear to join in the fracas. Over 15,000 of Peter's crusaders are killed or led away into captivity until peace is finally restored.

By the time Little Peter and his army arrive in Constantinople on August 1, 1096, over a quarter of the enthusiastic members of the peasant Crusade have been killed or taken into slavery. Children are crying for their captured mothers. Wives are weeping for their slain husbands. Men in groups of hundreds abandon the holy march to return to their mean and arduous lives as serfs, without ever having entered Asia Minor or encountered a Terrible Turk.

The Crusaders Arrive in Oz!

The peasant crusaders are stunned by the magnificence of Constantinople. It is like the land of Oz, only better—more phantasmagoric. It is a vision from a dream, a glimpse of Utopia. Their jaws fall as they behold its massive walls and the magnificent dome of St. Sophia that looms above the shimmering city. This wonder is captured in an account of Fulcher of Chartres that dates from 1097:

> Oh what a great and beautiful city is Constantinople! How many churches and palaces it contains, fashioned with wonderful skill! How many wonderful things may be seen even in the streets or courts! It would be too tedious to enumerate what wealth there is there of every kind, of gold, of silver, of every kind of robes, and of holy relics. There traders at all times bring by boat all the necessities of man. They have, I judge, about twenty thousand eunuchs living there.

Crusade Aid

The enormous dome of St. Sophia rises 180 feet above Istanbul (the modern name for Constantinople). It measures an incredible 107 feet in diameter. Frescoes and mosaics once covered every inch of the walls. They were covered over when the ancient Christian cathedral became a mosque in 1453. The city of Constantinople in 1096 had a population of well over 300,000. Latin Europe had nothing to compare with it. The largest European city was Rome, with 30,000; Cologne had 20,000; and London and Paris less than 10,000 each.

Later crusaders such as Robert of Clari would say that the treasures of Constantinople surpassed those of Alexander and Charlemagne, and nothing approaching its wealth could be found even "in the 40 richest cities of the world."

Everything seems to shimmer with silver and gold and precious gems. The humblest dwelling places seem like magnificent palaces. The Blachernae, the home of the emperor, is a vast complex of mansions whose gardens contain menageries of strange and exotic beasts. Below St. Sophia is a huge sports complex called the Hippodrome that had been built by the emperor Constantine in the fourth century. In the center of the Hippodrome stands the Obelisk of Theodosius, the prototype of the Washington monument.

But the real treasures of Constantinople are not the mansions and palaces; they are the priceless holy relics. Here pilgrims can see the Crown of Thorns, the Seamless Garment of Jesus, the cloth of St. Veronica that contains an imprint of Christ's face, St. Luke's portrait of the Virgin Mary, and the severed head of St. John the Baptist in a coffin of solid gold.

As the crusaders gape at the wonders of Constantinople, the people of Constantinople gape with astonishment at the sight of the ghastly army.

When Emperor Alexis calls for help from Latin Europe, he expects an army of trained soldiers, equipped for battle, not countless thousands of peasants waving palms and crosses. It is the materialization of a nightmare.

Christian Chronicles

All that remains of the Blachernae Palace, where the Emperor Alexis received Peter the Hermit and subsequent crusaders, is a massive retaining wall that overlooks the northern reaches of the Golden Horn. In his chronicles, Odo of Deuil wrote this: "On its three sides, the Palace offers to its inhabitants the triple pleasure of gazing alternately on the sea, the countryside and the town. The interior is decorated with gold and the floor is paved with cleverly arranged marble."

In her chronicles, Anna Comnena, the daughter of the emperor, records her impression of Little Peter's army:

> Full of enthusiasm and ardor they thronged every highway, and with these uncouth warriors came a host of civilians, outnumbering the sand of the sea shore or the stars of heaven, carrying palms and bearing crosses on their shoulders. There were women and children, too, who had left their countries. Like tributaries joining a river from all directions, they streamed toward us in full force.

Crusade Aid

The Eastern Emperor Alexis I remains a key figure in the history of the Crusades. All the crusaders were obliged to visit his court and to submit to an oath of fealty. His daughter's account of his reign is an undisputed masterpiece of medieval history.

On to Anatolia

Emperor Alexis receives Peter and members of his entourage in court. Peter tells the emperor that he has heard a divine voice that urges him to organize a Crusade to save the Church of the Holy Sepulcher from the hands of the Turks. The emperor treats the hermit in a most courteous manner, advising him to wait until the papal Crusade arrives. He invites Peter to make camp for his army outside the city's walls, and agrees to provide food and provisions for the massive horde.

All would have been fine and dandy except for the fact that Little Peter's crusaders are totally out of control. They begin to steal everything in sight, breaking into houses and palaces, even stripping the lead from the roofs of the churches. Nothing or no one can contain them. Within five days, Constantinople is in a state of riot.

The emperor responds to the situation by transporting the army of the poor across the Bosphorus so they can go about their business as quickly as possible. On August 6, the first wave of Christian crusaders enters *Anatolia*, the land of the Turks, where things get really ugly.

A Bad End for the Poor

For the next two months, Little Peter's pilgrim horde raids the town of Nicea and its outskirts, stealing from houses, churches, orchards, and fields. Emperor Alexis, in an effort to alleviate the situation, sends shipments of barley, oil, wine, corn, cheese, and other provisions to the Crusade of the Poor, hoping that the pillaging of the locals, most of whom are Christians, will stop. But his efforts are in vain. The Christian horde responds to the emperor's kindness with unrestrained outbursts of cruelty. At one point, a band of crusaders invades a Greek village and, thinking it is Turkish, mutilates and kills without mercy—even roasting the bodies of infants on spits.

A force of several thousand crusaders, including priests and bishops, seizes a castle called Xerigordon. It is (unlike the castles in Europe) a very comfortable place, with elaborate tapestries and floor coverings. The storehouses are stocked with food and wine. In no time at all, the group of Franks make themselves right at home.

Warrior Words

Anatolia is the medieval term for the vast plateau between the Black Sea and the Mediterranean Sea. It was later called Turkey, as it was the land of the Turks.

Crusade Aid

King Arslan's name, along with that of Emperor Alexis, appears in subsequent chapters. In 1092, this powerful sultan conquered Anatolia and established his capital at Nicea (the modern Iznik), less than a hundred miles from Constantinople.

When King Arslan, the ruler of Anatolia, learns that the Christian army has invaded Nicea, the capital city of his province, and seized one of his favorite castles, he goes ballistic. He summons his army to surround the castle, which is perched on a hill, and to cut off all its sources of supplies and water. The strategy works like a charm. For eight days, the crusaders within Xerigordon are deprived of water. Dying of thirst, they suck the blood of mules and horses, drink their own urine, dip rags into the latrines and squeeze the filth and excrement into their mouths. Finally, the band of crusaders sends up the white flag. The terms of surrender are simple: either convert to Islam or have your head chopped off.

Conversion to Islam, as it turns out, is easy. All you have to do is utter the line: "God is great and Mohammed is his prophet," and then submit to circumcision. Few Christians are circumcised during the medieval period; the practice is reserved for Jews and Moslems. Despite that fact, many soldiers of the Crusade of the Poor withdraw their members, grit their teeth, and surrender their foreskins. Others are put to the sword and become Christian martyrs.

King Arslan then sends out word to the Christian camps near Civetot that a host of Franks has captured the city of Nicea and claimed all the loot for themselves. The crusaders at the camps feel betrayed. They have traveled thousands of miles, and now a group of Franks is keeping all the booty for itself. It is intolerable! Trumpets are sounded, and soon the great host of ragged Christian soldiers is on the march to Nicea—and into a trap.

Before they advance three miles down the road, the peasant crusaders are attacked by the Turkish army and mowed down, to the last man. Walter the Penniless is one of the victims. His chain mail has been pierced by more than twenty arrows. The carnage persists for several hours. By the time the sun rises on that morning of October 21, more than 20,000 pilgrims lay dead along the road to Nicea.

The Turks then storm the camp of the crusaders at Civetot to dispatch the remainder of the troublesome Christian intruders—the women, clergy members, and old people who lack weapons or feel too weak to march with the others. Some were slaughtered in their beds; others while performing their morning rituals. A priest who is celebrating the Mass is cut down at the altar. The Turks only spare pleasing-looking boys and girls who can be sold into slavery. About 3,000 of the Crusade of the Poor manage to survive by taking shelter in an old fortress by the sea until they are rescued by the Byzantine army.

Anna Comnena, the emperor's daughter, records that so many members of Peter's army are slain that a mountain of bones remains at Civetot: "Some men of the same race as the slaughtered barbarians, later, when they were building a wall like those of a city, used the bones of the dead as pebbles to fill up the cracks. In a way the city became their Tomb. To this day it stands with its encircling wall built of mixed stones and bones."

A Good End for Little Peter

But what of Cucu Peter? The little hermit manages to escape the slaughter. He makes his way back to Italy just in time to join the official Crusade, the Crusade of the princes. He is placed in charge of the peasant militia and becomes one of the first crusaders to enter the Holy City of Jerusalem. He later returns to France and the shelter of a monastery.

After his death in 1115, Cucu Peter is pronounced "Blessed Peter" by the Roman Church, and becomes venerated by future crusaders as a man who had been called by God. Few who engaged in these epic endeavors saw situations or people as they truly were.

The Least You Need to Know

➤ Little Peter led a Crusade of the Poor with over 100,000 adherents.

➤ The peasant crusaders were responsible for the first Jewish holocausts.

➤ The first battle of the Crusades took place between Christian forces in Hungary.

➤ Constantinople looked like a mythical kingdom to Latin Christians.

➤ King Arslan of Anatolia led the Turks against the Peasant Crusade.

➤ The peasant crusaders were slaughtered at Civetot.

Chapter 6

A Pride of Princes: The First Crusade

In This Chapter

➤ Meet the nobles who led the five crusader armies

➤ Follow the intrigue at the court of Alexis in Constantinople

➤ Learn about the questionable alliances of the leaders

➤ Get ready to follow the merged Christian armies to the First Crusade

The recruiting station for the First Crusade—the official Crusade—is set up at Le Puy in central France. In the midst of this town is the tiny chapel of Saint-Michel, poised on a pinnacle of lava over 275 feet above the countryside. It is a glorious sight to behold but if you want to visit the chapel you have to climb up an impossibly steep staircase that starts from a cluster of red-tiled houses at the foot of the rock. In one of these houses lives Raymond of Aguilers, a chronicler of the event we are about to discuss.

Throughout the spring and summer of 1096, Le Puy is a hotbed of activity. Lords and knights from throughout Christendom are appearing with their attendants and servants to enlist in the Holy War. The Crusade is set to start on August 15, 1096.

Meet the Holy—And Not-So-Holy—Crusaders

Le Puy is the *See* of Bishop Adhemar, who has been appointed by Pope Urban II to rule the Crusade in his stead. When the knights appear before Bishop Adhemar, they hold the cross, make their vows to save the Holy Sepulcher from the hands of the unholy Turks, pledge their loyalty to the pope and the bishop, and receive the bishop's blessing.

Renowned princes and knights of the Latin West have been appointed to lead the First Crusade. And it's now time for you to meet them.

Hugh: A Lot of Hot Air

Hugh, Count of Vermandois, is in charge of the first army. Hugh is the young brother of the King of the Franks, Henry I. Of all the nobles, he is the most proud and pretentious. To make matters worse, he is unskilled in warfare and a totally ineffectual commander. He demands that his servants and attendants bow and scrape the ground before him. A hint at the haughtiness of Hugh is found in a letter he sent to Alexis I to let the emperor of Byzantium prepare for his glorious arrival in Constantinople:

> Know, Emperor, that I am King of Kings, the greatest of all beneath the heavens. It is my will that you should meet me on my arrival and receive me with the pomp and ceremony due to my noble birth."

Get the picture? This guy is a real snob. He's a leader, but the least important.

Warrior Words

A **See** is the place from which a bishop governs all the churches in his jurisdiction. It comes from the Latin *sedes*, meaning seat, and is the town or village in which the bishop maintains his throne, or *seat*.

Godfrey: Strong and Saintly

Godfrey of Bouillon, Duke of Lower Lorraine, is in charge of the second Frankish army. This guy is a descendant of Charlemagne and one of the great medieval knights. He possesses incredible strength. Later, in Cilicia, he will wrestle with a huge brown bear and win. When an Arab sheik invites him to kill a camel, Godfrey will slice off the animal's head with one stroke of his broadsword. He is also deeply religious. He was so horrified by the sack of Rome in 1082 that he fell into a feverish swoon and remained incapacitated for several months. Godfrey prays so long before a meal that members of his company often complain that their meals are cold before they can eat them.

Crusade Aid

Charlemagne was the first Holy Roman Emperor. He was crowned temporal ruler of all Christians by the pope in 800.

Godfrey is the least pretentious of men, and therefore the polar opposite of the high and mighty Hugh. When Fatimid dignitaries come to meet him in his tent, they will find him sitting on the ground next to a sack of hay that serves as his bed. His tent, unlike those of the other nobles and princes, contains no carpets, no curtains, no silk hangings, and no furniture—not even a chair. The dignitaries asked Godfrey why he lived like this. "The earth serves well enough for a seat in life as it does in death," he answered.

Godfrey of Bouillon held the richest fief in Lorraine. He sold his estates on the Meuse to equip his army. He sold the city of Metz to its inhabitants for 100,000 gold crowns. He gave his holdings in Bouillon to the bishop of Liege, and the castle of Ramioul to the pope. He relinquished all his possessions to engage in the Crusade. He is about 35 when he sets out. He is a leading character in our story. Remember him. He takes his brothers Baldwin and Eustace with him. Baldwin is also a major character in our story, so you have to meet him. Eustace is a nice guy, but for our story, he remains a bit player.

The Baldwin Boy: Smart but Smug

Baldwin was trained for a career in the Church, but before assuming Holy Orders he decided that being a bishop might be boring so he dropped out of the Church and became a soldier. He wooed and wed a noble Englishwoman named Godehilde, who accompanies him on this Crusade.

This brings us to his weakness. Baldwin is a lover of women. He can't keep his hands off a pretty wench for the life of him. But don't get the wrong idea. This guy is no swashbuckling hero. Baldwin doesn't have much of a sense of humor. He rarely laughs, and is something of a scholar. That's right, he reads books, when most nobles don't read at all. This makes him a decent conversationalist and gives him a certain measure of sex appeal as a medieval knight.

Unlike Godfrey, Baldwin likes finery and never appears in public without a mantle draped from his shoulders. But he admires his oldest brother Godfrey almost to excess. He studies Godfrey's every move and speaks of him with deference and awe. But there is a real dark side to this guy—and he'll become a king!

Robert of Normandy: Comic Relief

A third army is led by Robert, Duke of Normandy. For some unknown reason, Duke Robert is called "Short Boots" by his friends. People like him. He's

Crusade Aid

In medieval times many wives accompanied their husbands on Crusades and battle campaigns. Women servants also went along to attend to the nobles and their families. In addition, there were many women camp-followers, including prostitutes who transformed tents into makeshift brothels.

gregarious and a great practical joker. He also is a lover of wine, women, and song.

Duke Robert is the son of William the Conqueror, the Norman who conquered England in 1066. He is the firstborn, and should have succeeded his father to the throne, but Robert's rebelliousness and hot temper had exasperated him so much that William handed the throne over to William Rufus, Robert's younger brother.

When we meet Duke Robert he's in good physical condition and gives no indication that he'll become grotesquely fat in his later years. He's a good warrior, who has distinguished himself in many battles and tournaments, but he's far from being a natural leader like Godfrey of Bouillon. Duke Robert is an interesting character, but he's not a leading character like Godfrey, Baldwin, and three fellows you're about to meet: Raymond, Bohemond, and Tancred.

Christian Chronicles

Too bad William the Conqueror refused to anoint his eldest son Robert as king. William Rufus, as it turned out, was a completely ineffectual ruler who ended up being struck down by an unknown assassin in the New Forest. Robert, it is said, laughed with merriment when he heard the news.

Stephen: The Wimp

Along with Duke Robert's noble companions is his brother-in-law, Stephen of Blois. Stephen is married to William the Conqueror's high-spirited daughter, Adela. To tell the truth, he's a bit of a nerd as a knight. He dislikes the idea of doing anything dangerous or adventurous, but his wife forces him to take up the sword and tag along with her brother Robert. Stephen of Blois is self-indulgent, incredibly rich, and for his time, incredibly uxorious. (In other words, he'd rather be in a castle knitting his chain mail than in a desert attacking screaming Turks.)

As we'll see, he later retreated from the First Crusade during the grueling siege of Antioch. When he returned to England, his shrewish wife, Adela, berated him as a deserter and a coward until he agreed to take part in the Second Crusade. He died in Jerusalem, defending the Holy City.

One-Eyed Raymond: The Oldest Crusader

Raymond IV, Count of Toulouse, leads the fourth army. At 56, he's by far the oldest of the leaders of the Crusade. Raymond feels that he doesn't have much time left and wants to die in the Holy Land. He only has one eye, having lost the other in single combat against the Moors in Spain.

Count Raymond, like Baldwin, is a great lover of women, but unlike Baldwin, he is affable and charming. He will become the crusader most admired by Alexis I. The count has been married several times and was excommunicated twice for marriages of consanguinity. (He married his first cousin, and later his niece.) His latest wife is Elvira, the beautiful daughter of Alfonso VI, the great Spanish king. Anna Comnena, the daughter of Emperor Alexis, will like the courtly Count of Toulouse more than the other leaders of the Crusade and say that he shines among the other crusaders "like the sun among lesser stars." He plays a key role in our saga.

Big, Bad Bohemond: The Complex Crusader

Now we come to the most complex leader of the First Crusade, a man of fierce ambition and ferocious temper named Bohemond, the Prince of Otranto. This guy is really interesting. Bohemond is a Norman prince who has gained vast holdings in southern Italy. He is a Norman through and through, with a Norman's cruelty and a Norman's belief that the world is his for the taking. When he hears the call for the Crusade, he sees a golden opportunity—a means of acquiring rich territories in the tottering Byzantine Empire. For this purpose, he summons a vast army of 2,000 knights, 14,000 foot soldiers, and 4,000 camp servants, and he spares no expense in buying armor, weapons, war-horses, and supplies. He is a man of great courage, and we'll see him conquer an entire city with 60 of his knights. He's also a bit of a skeptic. When miracles happen, such as the finding of the Holy Lance, he'll pass them off as sheer malarkey.

When Bohemond presents himself at the court of Constantinople several months later, his appearance will leave an indelible impression on Anna Comnena. In her memoirs, she'll note that he is a foot taller than the other crusaders; that he is perfectly proportioned, with broad shoulders and a narrow waist; that his hair is light brown and actually appears to have been styled; that his eyes are blue and lively; that he exudes a certain charm and a certain coarseness; and that his very laugh seems like a threat to others. He plays a leading role (a name above the title) in our epic.

Crosscurrent

Anna Comnena was not the only one to question the motives and character of Bohemond. Raymond IV, the Count of Toulouse, believed that Bohemond had entered the Crusade for all the mischief he could create and all the territory he could acquire. He remained at odds with Bohemond throughout the campaign.

Tancred: Our Teenage Hero

Bohemond is accompanied by his 17-year-old nephew, Tancred of Hauteville. Tancred is destined to become the great hero of our adventure and the epitome of medieval knighthood: handsome, fearless, gallant, and generous. He is also something of a thinker, and this gives him a measure of complexity. His biographer, Radulph of Caen, describes Tancred as a medieval Hamlet, torn between love of war and devotion to Christ:

Frequently he burned with anxiety because the warfare he engaged in as a knight seemed to be contrary to the Lord's commands. The Lord, in fact, ordered him to offer the cheek that had been struck together with the other cheek to the striker, but secular knighthood did not spare the blood of relatives. The Lord urged him to give his tunic and his cloak as well to the man who would take them away: the needs of war impelled him to take from a man, already despoiled of both, whatever remained to him. And so, if ever that wise man could give himself up to repose, these contradictions deprived him of courage.

Such contradictions will be resolved by the Crusade. The Holy War will give to Tancred and the other knights the right to kick butt and serve Jesus. Keep your eye on him.

Off to Constantinople

To summarize the preceding, the following five armies of the First Crusade will set off by different routes to Constantinople:

➤ The first army, led by Hugh, Count of Vermandois

➤ The second army, led by Godfrey of Bouillon

➤ The third army, led by Robert, Duke of Normandy

➤ The fourth army, led by Raymond IV, Count of Toulouse

➤ The fifth army, led by Bohemond, the Prince of Otranto

Warrior Words

A **liege man** is a vassal, a devoted follower. The medieval feudal system relied on the strength of oaths between knights and nobles, and nobles and overlords. Subjects were required to give their **liege** to their lord. Liege represented their word of honor that they would remain in loyal service.

Hugh's Humiliation

The arrival of the first army in Byzantium is anything but dignified. Hugh and his soldiers get shipwrecked on the eastern coast of the Adriatic. The haughty Hugh is rescued, but most of his men and munitions have been lost at sea. The bedraggled count and his remaining men are transported to the court of Alexis, where they are showered with gifts and lavish praises. The newly arrived crusaders are kept under such close scrutiny in the imperial palace that a rumor will spread that they are the emperor's prisoners. Hugh, however, doesn't seem to mind. He is placed in a luxurious apartment, and attendants cater to his every whim. Hugh feels so honored that he immediately takes the oath to be the *liege man* to Alexis. By taking this oath, Hugh swears to return to the emperor any lands that he takes from the Turks.

Godfrey and the Greeks

The second army to arrive is that of Godfrey of Bouillon. Godfrey isn't impressed by Alexis or his court. He thinks that the inhabitants of Constantinople are (as Bishop Liudprand of Cremona describes them) "soft, effeminate, long-sleeved, bejeweled and begowned liars, eunuchs and idlers." He refuses to take an oath of loyalty to Alexis until the other armies arrive. Alexis, in turn, refuses to provide food to Godfrey's army. First, the emperor cuts off the fodder for the horses, then fish and meat, and finally bread. The standoff continues for several weeks.

Infuriated that he's traveled halfway across the world to be treated with dishonor, Godfrey decides to launch a full-scale assault on the city. At the last moment, Hugh visits Godfrey and begs him to take the oath of loyalty to the emperor. He speaks of the dangers of continued resistance and the horrors of a full-scale war between Christians, when Christians should be united against the Turks. What's more, Hugh says, Alexis will give the crusaders everything they need: protection, provisions, friendship, and treasures. "Matters will turn out ill for us if we disobey him," Hugh adds.

At last, Godfrey reluctantly agrees to make the pledge of fealty to the Eastern Emperor, and peace is restored.

Now the army of Bohemond arrives. The giant warrior, hearing about the dispute between Godfrey and Alexis, wants to attack the city, lay claim to the Byzantine throne, and hack off the emperor's head. Godfrey refuses to join in this scheme since he has pledged his *liege* to Alexis, and a man (as we all know) is only as good as his word.

Christian Chronicles

Bohemond served as the Norman ruler of Sicily. He may have entered the Crusade to fight the Turks but he was no hater of Islam. Sicily had been ruled by Arabs until his uncle conquered it. Bohemond allowed Moslems freedom of worship and even used them to supervise his government. Once when Bohemond was urged to attack North Africa in order to Christianize it, the great Norman "lifted his foot and made a great fart, saying, 'By my faith, here is better counsel than you have given me.'"

Bohemond's Maneuvers

Questions now arise: Will Bohemond pledge his allegiance to the Byzantine Emperor Alexis? Or will he cast down his gauntlet in an act of defiance? No one knows. This

Norman is inscrutable and dangerous, capable of all manner of strategies to achieve his purpose.

When summoned to appear before Alexis, Bohemond strolls into court with giant strides and an unbowed head, in the manner of the lord of all creation. The emperor treats the great Norman with care and flattery, speaking of the Prince of Otranto's fame in battle against the Moors in Sicily. He diplomatically asks Bohemond what prompted him to take up the cross and travel to Byzantium. Bohemond smiles and says, "I come of my own free will as Your Majesty's friend." For the first time in history, icicles seem to form in the humid air of Constantinople.

Unlike the other crusaders, Bohemond is a fox. He knows exactly how to behave, which makes him infinitely more threatening than the others. At the emperor's request, beautiful servant girls accompany Bohemond to luxurious quarters. A sumptuous feast is presented before him. But the cagey Norman refuses to touch any of the food, fearing it is poisoned. The next day, the game continues. Alexis produces food for Bohemond's own chefs to prepare. The chefs prepare the food, but Bohemond won't touch it, even though his knights wolf it down without the slightest intestinal discomfort. Alexis is spooked. He then asks Bohemond to swear the oath or to state his true intentions. To the emperor's astonishment, Bohemond agrees to the oath and vows over the Crown of Thorns, the most sacred relic in Constantinople, that he will serve and protect the emperor. Everyone in court is shocked at the giant Norman's spirit of submissiveness. Something seems screwy.

Christian Chronicles

As the emperor of Byzantium, Alexis had many titles, including "Autocrat in Christ." He was, in the eyes of Orthodox believers, the representative of Christ on earth. He wore stiff brocaded gowns said to be copied after the gowns given by the angels to Constantine. He wore a cross in his crown. From the cross, ropes of jewels and pearls dangled to his shoulders. The ropes were intended to signify the radiance of Christ.

Alexis Pays Up

Alexis leads the Norman knight to a chamber that is filled with gold, silver, rich cloths, and other luxuries. "If I had such wealth," Bohemond says, "I would long ago have become master of many lands." Alexis answers by saying: "All this is yours today—a present from your emperor."

Alexis knows that the allegiance of Bohemond cannot be secured without payment—great payment—and so he gives to the troublesome prince a king's ransom. No other crusader will receive such gifts. But no other crusader is more frightening and more unpredictable.

Raymond Joins Alexis

Next to arrive in Constantinople is Raymond of Toulouse. The old Spaniard and Alexis become fast friends, probably because they are both suspicious of Bohemond. But Raymond has a problem: His overlord remains the pope, not the Eastern Emperor, and so he cannot pledge his liege to Alexis. Realizing that Raymond is a true Christian who (in the words of Anna Comnena) "values truth above everything," Alexis agrees to allow the one-eyed soldier the right to assume a modified pledge of fealty. Raymond simply swears on the Crown of Thorns to respect the life and possessions of Alexis. The two men embrace, and that's that.

Two days after the ceremony, Raymond leads his army to join the other armies at Pelecanum. Raymond's army remains vast, consisting of 4,000 knights, 18,000 foot soldiers, and 8,000 camp-servers, camp-followers, and auxiliaries. This is the best disciplined of all the armies.

Now there are approximately 150,000 crusaders ready to begin the long journey to Jerusalem, and the fifth army has yet to arrive.

Crusade Aid

The exact number of Christians who set out on the First Crusade remains unknown. Some say that over 300,000 went marching to Jerusalem to save the Holy Sepulcher; some say 100,000, but 150,000 is a good guess.

The Duke Gets Duped

Duke Robert, it appears, got sidetracked and decided to spend several weeks with his family in southern Italy. When he shows up in the court of Constantinople, Alexis greets Robert as the greatest of all the knights and the most noble of all crusaders. The emperor tells Robert (as Alexis no doubt told the others) that he is his special and most trusted ally. Robert falls for the emperor's flattery, hook, line, and sinker. Stephen of Blois is disgusted by this and writes a letter to his wife, comparing Emperor Alexis to Adela's father, William the Conqueror. "Your father, my love," Stephen says, "made many great gifts, but he was nothing compared to this man."

Bring On the Holy War

Now all the armies have been ferried to Asia, and the emperor is satisfied that the barbarians from the West are no longer at the gates of his city. He has acted with finesse and intelligence under severe strain; he has offered provisions and supplies; he has committed his own scouts and engineers to the venture; he has constructed elaborate siege engines so that the crusaders can attack the fortresses of the enemy; he has emptied his coffers to win their trust. Now Alexis can only hope they keep their oaths of loyalty and restore to him the lost provinces of his empire.

The war between Islam and Christianity is about to begin at Nicea. It is early May 1098, and the Holy War is falling behind schedule. Still, the crusaders expect to complete their campaign within a year. They are about to receive a very rude awakening.

The Least You Need to Know

➤ Adhemar, the Bishop of Le Puy, was appointed Ruler of the First Crusade.

➤ Five armies set out to rescue the Holy Land from the Seljuk Turks.

➤ All five military leaders were obliged to swear allegiance to Alexis, the emperor of Byzantium, who supplied them with everything they needed to do battle.

Chapter 7

The Siege of Nicea: The First Crusade's First Battle

In This Chapter

➤ The crusaders win their first battle with the Turks at Nicea

➤ The Christian army routs Arslan, the Red Lion

➤ The nightmarish march through Anatolia takes many lives

➤ Baldwin is crowned Prince of Edessa

The force that is assembled on the western edge of Asia is not a unified army under a single commander. It is an international gathering, divided by custom, language, and loyalties. The leaders of this host are as suspicious of each other as they are of the Turks and the Byzantines. The army in total consists of about 100,000 combatants. To this number must be added the families of the crusaders who intend to settle in the Holy Land; the old people who are making a pilgrimage to obtain the plenary indulgence; and the priests, nuns, monks, servants, attendants, merchants, prostitutes, and assorted strays, including a remnant from Little Peter's ill-fated venture.

But they are unified in one objective: to seize the city of Nicea, the capital of the sultanate of Kilij Arslan, the Red Lion. Here the sultan kept his treasure, his wife, his children, and his best soldiers. All the refinements of Byzantine design and engineering had gone into the building of Nicea's massive city walls.

The Crusaders Lay Siege to Nicea

When the crusaders arrive at Nicea, they are amazed by the huge wall around the ancient city. How are they going to attack it? They attempt to push their siege tower against the wall so they can raise the tower to the top of the wall, climb up to the top of the tower, lower a drop gate, and race out on the ramparts to kill the defending Turks. It doesn't work too well. The Turks are able to push the siege towers from the wall so that they topple to the ground. Even when the crusaders are lucky enough to get one tower in place, the knights must charge one at a time into a host of Turks who await their arrival with battle-axes.

Crusade Aid

Set among beautiful hills on the edge of a lake, Nicea looks as formidable today as it must have appeared to the crusaders in 1097. Most of the massive encircling wall, protected by a hundred towers, still survives. Iznik, as Nicea is now called, had been lost to the Byzantine Empire when the Turks swept over Asia Minor in 1071. Nicea was the site of the first ecumenical council of the Church, held in 325 to determine the nature of Christ's divinity. Was He truly man or truly God? Or was He some kind of demigod? The Nicene Creed, the first official creed of the Church, answered the question: Jesus was truly man and truly God, with two substances united in one Person.

For two weeks, they try to break into the city. Raymond, the Count of Toulouse, with his army attempts to dig huge holes under the foundation of the wall and to cut away at the stones. It's pretty pathetic. The garrison troop of Turks simply dumps vats of boiling oil on the heads of the invaders or mows them down with arrows.

One scene seems to come straight out of the Old Testament. Every day, a gigantic Turk stands on the battlements with a "bow of prodigious length" and kills every crusader in sight. Christian arrows always fall short of the giant, dropping at his feet. At last, Godfrey of Bouillon makes use of a newfangled contraption called a crossbow and looses an arrow at the Goliath's heart. Without a cry, the massive Turk falls dead to the ground.

Every few hours, a host of crusaders will attempt to break through the gates with battering rams. None of this is very effective. But the crusading army is so vast and the warriors so persistent that the Turks have to remain on constant guard against their antics.

The siege gets really grisly. When Christian soldiers are killed or wounded at the base of the wall, the Turks lower grappling hooks to seize the bodies of the dead and wounded. They raise the bodies to the top of the wall, strip them of all armor, weapons, and valuables, and then toss the naked bodies to the mud below.

But the crusaders, as it turns out, launched this attack at a perfect time. King Arslan, the ruler of Nicea, is away from the fortress with his main force, fighting his neighbor, Prince Danishmend. Arslan receives word of the attack on his capital, but assumes that the crusaders are yet another horde of untrained peasants who can be dispatched with little difficulty.

Crusader Tactics Win the Day

Arslan makes a hasty alliance with Danishmend, and returns to Nicea ready to create a new mountain of Christian corpses next to the stacked remains of the Crusade of the Poor. The Turks, according to the chronicler of the *Gesta Francorum*, are merry as they come down the heavily forested mountainsides, but their merriment is brief. As soon as they arrive in a clearing, the crusaders appear with battle-axes to chop off their heads.

Arslan assembles his Turkish soldiers to charge against the Christian army. This is the first clash between the Christian knights and the Turkish horsemen, and it would prove to be very instructive for both sides. The Christians go into battle by charging into the enemy's forces, hurling spears at them, and wheeling away. They regroup and, in tight formation, lead a second charge with their lances firmly wedged under their arms. This is called "pig-sticking," as the bodies of the opposing forces are often impaled at the end of the lance.

After the pig-sticking, the Christians withdraw their maces, battle-axes, and broadswords, and hack away—again in tight formation—to their hearts' content.

All European knights fight in this manner, riding in tight formation, galloping straight at the enemy, and crushing through the lines by sheer force. Anna Comnena, observing this manner of combat, will write: "A Frank on horseback could knock a hole through the walls of Babylon."

This means of doing battle is only effective against a stationary enemy, against knights who hold their positions by shield, battle-axe, and sheer

Crusade Aid

The Battle of Nicea was enlivened by the fact that the chargers of the Christian knights were stallions, whereas the Turkish archers rode mares. Moreover, since the battle occurred in June, many of the mares were in heat.

determination. But the Turks are different. When you charge, they move out of the way. This doesn't seem proper or fitting. They don't stand and fight like decent men. They ride long-legged mares that are carefully chosen for their speed and agility. What's worse, the slippery Turks don't fight in formation. They circle away from the stiff and straight attackers, and shoot arrows—like sissy serfs—with short and highly taut bows at the backs of the noble knights. This seems downright disgraceful to the Christians.

There is something else about the Turks. They wear little armor and carry small, light shields. This means that they are no match for fully armored knights with massive swords and shields in hand-to-hand combat. Once cornered, the Turks could be mowed down like cornstalks.

The real deciding moment of any medieval battle comes when the knights complete the pig-sticking procedure. If they remain on horseback, keep in tight formation, and use their swords as an armored group, the knights are almost invincible. They come at the enemy like a huge hacking machine. But if they break formation or fall from their mounts, they can be individually surrounded, cut to pieces with short swords, or turned into screaming porcupines by the relentless archers.

But the crusaders do not break rank. They stay in rigid formation and slaughter everything in sight. King Arslan makes a getaway with his remaining army. Everyone is in high spirits. The Christians have won the first great battle of the Crusade.

Après *Battle*

Following the conflict, the crowd of *varlets* (the serfs and servants of the great warriors) comb the battlefield on foot. They care for the wounded crusaders and carry the Christian dead from the battlefield so that their bodies can be blessed and buried. They dispatch the wounded enemies by smashing their skulls with battle-axes and clubs, and strip them of all their weapons and valuables. After they're slaughtered and stripped, their heads are severed from their bodies and tossed into carts. These heads will be very valuable. They can be catapulted over the wall of Nicea to spread even more terror among the besieged. For added measure, they toss beehives, firebombs, and huge rocks over the wall. It is truly a glorious day.

The crusaders return to their siege. The Turks within the walled city have no chance of relief, let alone victory. The army of King Arslan, the Red Lion, has been routed.

Still and all, the Christians cannot break through the gates or tunnel under the wall. There's only one thing to do; they must starve out the city. But this is not as easy as it sounds. Nicea is located on the eastern shore of Lake Iznik, and supplies—food, fodder, fish, wood, and building materials—keep coming into the city through its watergates. The Christians have no boats and no means of making a blockade.

Christian Chronicles

The crusaders used catapults to toss heads into the ancient city of the Christian creed and to spread "fear and trembling" among the inhabitants. At Nicea, they employed a medieval means of bacteriological warfare. They hurled not only severed heads and beehives over the walls but also the remains of diseased and rotting animals. The varlets eventually organized into a shock troop known as the Tafurs. These scavengers of the battlefield became the most daring of warriors, charging into the Turkish armies with knives, clubs, pointed sticks, axes, and scythes. They were known for their absolute indifference to danger.

Nicea Surrenders—To Alexis!

For six weeks, they can do nothing. Finally, Emperor Alexis arrives overland, with an army dragging an entire fleet of boats from the Sea of Marmara. The Byzantines, under the emperor's direction, place the boats in Lake Iznik and create a flotilla around the city.

Christian Chronicles

At dawn on June 19, 1097, the Turkish guards of Nicea, from their high towers saw the Byzantine fleet sailing across the lake and surrounding the city. Every ship was filled with soldiers. Drummers and trumpeters filled the air with their music. One chronicler said that the unexpected appearance of the ships did more than anything to strike fear in the defenders and to force their surrender.

Seeing this, the garrison at Nicea surrenders. Soon the Byzantine emperor's flag is flapping over the city. But no cheers are raised in the camp of the crusaders. The knights are downright livid. Alexis and his men are claiming the victory, and, by so doing, laying claim to the booty.

To make matters worse, Alexis attempts to be gracious to the captives, hustling King Arslan's wife and children off to Constantinople with all of their possessions, and showing mercy to the citizens. This is outrageous! He's protecting the Moslem infidels from righteous wrath while depriving holy crusaders of the sacred right of plunder!

Alexis tries to smooth over the situation by providing food and goods to every crusader and large gifts of gold to the leaders.

The March to Antioch

On the last day of June 1097, the crusaders set out in high spirits toward Antioch. "In five weeks' time," Stephen of Blois writes to his wife, "we shall be in Jerusalem, unless we are held up at Antioch." Little does he know that the 700-mile journey from Nicea to the Holy Land will take two years.

The crusading army decides to break into two parts since it is too large to travel through Anatolia as a single mass. The first army is led by Bohemond, Tancred, and Duke Robert of Normandy. The second army, lagging a day behind, is led by Godfrey of Bouillon and Raymond of Toulouse. This seems to make sense because Bohemond and Raymond are always vying to be the supreme commander of the Crusade. But the forces are now divided, and a near fatal mistake has been made.

Arslan Kicks Arse!

Don't forget King Arslan. Sure, he was driven from the battlefield at Nicea and fled into the mountains, but he's still alive and scheming. He joins forces with his new ally, Danishmend, and they await the crusaders in the narrow road to Dorylaeum, a city about 80 miles from Nicea. This is a perfect place to stage an ambush. The crusaders must make their way through a narrow valley where the Turks can massacre them without mercy.

Bohemond and his army pitch camp in a perfect place for a surprise attack. At the first light of day, Turks come screaming out of the mountains with swords in hand. Thousands of crusaders are slaughtered. Bohemond acts quickly. He orders his forces to form a tight but square formation. The knights plant their tall shields in the ground before Arslan's army. Behind the knights stand the infantry. In the center of the square remain the women and the noncombatants, around (as luck would have it) a pool of fresh water.

The fighting is fierce and the crusaders suffer enormous losses. Time and time again, the Turks charge toward the tight formation of Christians yelling the devilish words, *Allahu Akbar*, while showering the besieged crusaders with so many arrows that the sky darkens. As knights are killed in the front line, infantrymen quickly replace them. When infantrymen fall, women, priests, children, and old pilgrims take up swords and shields in the front line.

The savage attack continues for eight hours without let-up. But Bohemond's army never breaks tight formation. Still, the losses are staggering and all seems lost until the second army, under Godfrey and Raymond, appears on the mountain ridge. The second army comes storming toward the startled Turks, who panic and run.

But as they turn and run, the crusaders pursue them with clubs and battle-axes, not only the newly arrived troops of the second army, but also Bohemond's bold men who are now intent upon killing every Turk in creation. "We pursued them," writes Bohemond's anonymous chronicler, "killing them without let-up for a day and a night, and we took much booty: gold, silver, horses, asses, camels, oxen, sheep, and many other things about which we do not know."

The Crusaders Hold the Line

The battle at Dorylaeum is one of the great battles in the history of Christianity and a battle of monumental significance for the Crusades. The Christian army, under Bohemond, has managed to withstand a Turkish attack against all odds. The author of the *Gesta Francorum* guesses that King Arslan threw more than 360,000 of his troops into battle against 30,000 Christians, and yet the Turks were not able to penetrate the Christian defenses.

At the end of the day, Bishop Adhemar celebrates a Mass of praise and thanksgiving. Thousands of Christians lay dead in the narrow pass at Dorylaeum (including Tancred's 19-year-old brother William). But, now more than ever, the crusaders are convinced that God is on their side and victory lies within their grasp.

Little did they know that the Turkish Empire at the end of the eleventh century was in a state of chaos. Rulers such as King Arslan were more concerned with laying siege

Warrior Words

Allahu Akbar means "Allah be praised." Writing of the attack at Dorylaeum, one chronicler said of the distinctive Moslem war-cry: "These Turks began, all at once, to howl and gabble and shout, saying with loud voices in their own language some devilish word that I do not understand."

Crosscurrent

The defeat of King Arslan's forces at Dorylaeum dispelled the Turkish belief that the crusaders were pushovers, like Little Peter's peasants. During the long march of the Christian army across Asia Minor, the Turks remained unwilling to attack or ambush the Christian army.

to neighboring cities in a protracted struggle for power than with mounting a combined Turkish attack on the Christian invaders.

The Anatolian Nightmare

Before the crusaders stretches a waterless wasteland of 500 miles, and their supplies are running low. The journey across Asia Minor is a nightmare. It is mid-July and boiling hot. The temperature during the day often exceeds 110 degrees. The terrain is covered with great volcanic cones as high as the French Alps. There is nothing to drink except salty marsh water and nothing to eat except indigestible thorn bushes.

The march continues from July into August. By this time, many horses collapse and are devoured by the hungry crusaders; even the falcons and the hunting dogs of the great nobles are cast into the cooking pots. Women give birth by the roadside and abandon their infants. Old people are left behind in the remorseless desert. The crusaders walk with their mouths open, hoping to relieve their parched throats with the fresh air. And now a pestilence falls upon the army. Many break out in sores and boils. Raymond of Toulouse becomes so sick that the Bishop of Orange administers the Last Rites.

Occasionally, the crusaders come upon patches of sugarcane. They squeeze out the sweet liquid and drink it. They chew on the sugarcane as they travel, not knowing that their teeth will soften and decay before they return home.

Christian Chronicles

The friendly villagers of Iconium could not believe that the Christians had crossed the vast waterless salt desert without water bags. They showed them how water skins could be made from the intestines of animals, and the Christian army, from that time on, was never without them.

Bohemond's anonymous chronicler recorded that so many of the horses died during the march across Anatolia that "knights had to go as foot soldiers or use oxen as mounts."

Finally, in September, they reach the Cilician Gates and the fertile valleys of Iconium (modern Konya). When they reach a river, according to one chronicler, "many who had been weakened, along with beasts of burden, died from drinking too much."

Armenians inhabit this region of Asia Minor. They are Christians, and they care for the sick and starved crusaders. While the great army takes a rest, several nobles with their knights set out to make private conquests of estates, cities, and farmlands. Tancred and Baldwin set out for Tarsus, the ancient city of St. Paul, which is protected by a large Turkish garrison. After three days of fighting, the Turks slip away in the middle of the night, and the people of Tarsus come streaming out of the gates to welcome the crusaders.

After being crowned with garlands and showered with presents, Tancred and Baldwin have a terrible argument. Both lay claim to the city. Baldwin prevails because he has more soldiers, and Tancred marches east to seize for himself (not the Byzantine emperor) the Christian cities of Adana and Mamistra.

A Crusader Gets Crowned!

Baldwin's territorial ambitions are not satisfied. After rejoining the main Crusade to be at his wife's deathbed, he and 80 knights ride to the city of Edessa, almost 150 miles east of the Euphrates River. He's greeted with open arms and becomes the Crown Prince Baldwin of Edessa, the first Latin lord of the East.

This is incredible. Baldwin has penetrated more deeply into Asia Minor than any Westerner since the time of Alexander the Great. Located on an important trade route, Edessa is a very rich city, and Baldwin becomes its prince. His citadel is ornamented with Corinthian columns 50 feet high, and pools once considered sacred by the ancient goddesses of Mesopotamia. Here Baldwin will live in luxury with a harem of beautiful and willing women.

The dream of one crusader, at least, has come true.

The Least You Need to Know

➤ The first battle of the First Crusade occurred at Nicea.

➤ Frankish knights routed King Arslan's massive army.

➤ The crusaders won a second major victory at Dorylaeum.

➤ The march through Asia Minor was nightmarish.

➤ The crusaders seized Byzantine territory for themselves.

➤ Baldwin became Prince of Edessa.

Chapter 8

Autumn in Antioch

In This Chapter

➤ The crusaders lay siege to Antioch

➤ An Armenian enables Bohemond to conquer the city

➤ The Turks turn the tables on the crusaders

➤ The crusaders find the Holy Lance

➤ A miraculous victory is followed by endless disasters

The crusaders are now marching to Antioch through a mountain range known as the Anti-Taurus. It is a nightmare. The road through these steep mountains is only capable of bearing a small company of soldiers or pilgrims, not a massive Christian army of over 300,000. It is October and the mountain path has disintegrated under heavy rains and the weight of the crusaders and their baggage trains. The knights and vassals sink into the mud, weighed down by their armor and weapons. Some try to sell their military attire; others throw it away. The horses, mules, and loads of entire baggage trains slide over the precipices to the rocks below. But, lo and behold, they finally reach Antioch, the ancient city of Peter and Paul, where the title "Christian" was first applied to the followers of Jesus.

It is an amazing sight. The walls around Antioch stretch for 25 miles and contain over 400 watchtowers. The city has an excellent water supply from deep wells and running streams, and large areas of pasture inside the massive walls.

Intrigue at Antioch

Antioch, the most heavily fortified city in Byzantium, is ruled by a military commander called Yaghi-Suyan. When the crusaders appear, Yaghi-Siyan drives all the Christians from the city except for the Orthodox Archbishop, whom, to taunt the attackers, he dangles in a cage.

It took four months for the crusaders to reach Antioch from Nicea, and now they don't know what to do. They can't possibly attack the fortified city and they can't cut off its supplies of food and water. And so, they wait.

Crusade Aid

At the time of the First Crusade, Antioch was the richest and most powerful city on the Palestinian coast. The seaport at St. Symeon, 12 miles from the city, was always filled with ships, because Antioch was a vast trading center with merchants who came from North Egypt, Byzantium, and Central Asia.

Sometimes they attempt to attack the city with siege engines, but it's a waste of time. At other times they catapult firebombs, large rocks, and dead animals over the wall, but such acts are exercises in futility.

Incredible as it seems, the besiegers are worse off than the besieged. The weather is cold and the rain is persistent. What's worse, they're running out of food. Soldiers of the great Christian army begin to desert in droves. One such deserter is Little Peter (the Hermit), the leader of the ill-fated Crusade of the Poor. This is outrageous! The crusaders hunt him down and drag him back. Peter falls on his knees and apologizes for his sudden lapse of faith. "The devil made me do it," he says.

Another deserter is Stephen of Blois, who heads off in the middle of the night without so much as a "good luck" or "good-bye" to his fellow crusaders. He takes his knights with him. Stephen is convinced that Turkish reinforcement troops will arrive within a few days and the crusaders will be massacred without mercy. He heads off for home and Adela, his shrewish wife. The henpecked Stephen will live to regret his cowardly behavior.

Crosscurrent

When the crusaders first arrived at Antioch, they gorged themselves on the sheep and cattle they found in nearby villages; they captured many granaries; they ransacked the local mills and bakeries; but they failed to make provisions for the long winter ahead.

Meanwhile, Yaghi-Siyan manages to send messengers to the Turkish princes and emirs to ask for help against the Christian invaders. He also sends spies into the Christian camps to find out what the crusaders are planning. Many of these spies are Moslems disguised as Christian Armenians. Yaghi-Siyan seems to know everything the crusaders are doing and plan to do.

Bohemond the Barbarian

Bohemond becomes aware of the spy problem, and sets out to capture every spy in the Christian camp. He rounds up hundreds of them. The great Bohemond acts in accordance with his barbarian nature. He orders the spies to be placed before the main entrance to the city. He then orders his men to cut the throats of the prisoners, to skin them, and to ram huge cooking spits through their bodies so they can be roasted before the eyes of Yaghi-Siyan and his soldiers. All day long the spies are cooked over the open fires as the Turks watch with horror.

An Armenian's Revenge Is Bohemond's Victory

Bohemond has his own spies among the Armenian Christians within the city walls. One such spy by the name of Firouz is in charge of a section of the wall around the Tower of the Two Sisters. The scene is now set for one of the greatest incidents in the history of the Crusades.

Firouz was an Armenian armor-maker who had converted to Islam but was unhappy with his position as a guard in the Tower of the Two Sisters. His commanding officer had fined him for hoarding grain and had seduced his wife. On June 3, in the dead of night, Firouz slings a rope ladder from the Tower of the Two Sisters, near St. George's Gate. Bohemond and sixty of his men climb up the ladder and open the gates to the city. The crusading army storms into Antioch, killing every Turk in sight. By the end of the day, not one infidel remains alive—not even Yaghi-Siyan, whose head is presented to Bohemond as a trophy.

The scene inside the city is unbelievable, as the author of *Gesta Francorum* reports:

> All the streets of the city on every side were full of corpses, so that no one could endure to be there because of the stench, nor could anyone walk along the narrow paths of the city except over the corpses of the dead.

On top of the conquered city flies Bohemond's red flag, as proof to all crusaders, Greeks, and Turks that Antioch belongs not to the Byzantine Emperor—but to him!

The Besiegers Are Besieged

On the very next day, a large army of Turks under Kerbogha, the *Emir* of Mosul, arrives to come to the relief of Kerbogha's pal, Yaghi-Siyan. If Kerbogha had arrived just 24 hours earlier, he would have crushed the crusaders, and the course of human history would have been forever altered. But he is one day late. Still, Kerbogha and his soldiers

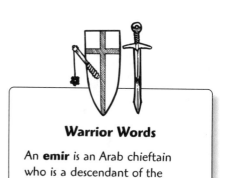

Warrior Words

An **emir** is an Arab chieftain who is a descendant of the prophet Mohammed.

surround the city. The tables are now turned. The besiegers become the besieged. The wild elation of the Christians descends into deep despair. They cannot hold out in the city. They have no food or water, and the stench of the dead is insufferable.

The crusaders' only hope is that the emperor will come to their rescue with his Byzantine army. And sure enough, Alexis is on his way. But now another terrible misfortune occurs. The advancing emperor meets the retreating Stephen of Blois, who reports that Antioch is lost and that the Christian army, by now, must be completely decimated. Alexis is crestfallen by this account and retreats to Constantinople. Little does he know that over 30,000 half-crazed and starving crusaders are crying out to high heaven for deliverance.

The Holy Lance

At this point in our story, the strangest of all the weird events surrounding the Crusades occurs. Peter Bartholomew, a dirty peasant with a reputation for drinking and whoring, begs for an audience with Count Raymond and Bishop Adhemar. When the two nobles reluctantly agree to a meeting, the peasant says that St. Andrew appeared to him in a vision and told him that the Holy Lance that pierced the side of Jesus is buried in the Cathedral of Antioch. If they can locate the Holy Lance, Peter says, it will dispel the Turkish army. This sounds crazy, but the crusaders are so desperate they'll do anything—even dig up the floor of the church in search of a mysterious relic at the request of a madman.

Crusade Aid

The Holy Lance became the talisman of the crusaders. Wrapped in brocade, it was solemnly unwrapped for the benefit of all the lords and knights who wished to venerate it. It was shown on hundreds of occasions to the faithful. It was carried into battle in order to spur on advances against the enemy. Raymond of Toulouse was particularly devoted to the Holy Lance and kept it on the altar of his private chapel.

On July 14, hundreds of soldiers excavate every square inch of the great cathedral, but nothing is found. They're about to give up when Peter Bartholomew leaps into the pit, clad only in his shirt, tells everyone to pray, and then with a flourish pulls out a length of iron from the rubble. It is the Holy Lance. The crusaders break out in prayers of joy and thanksgiving. With this Lance, Christ had been killed. Now, with the help of this Lance, the crusaders will destroy the infidels who had taken possession of the Holy Sepulcher.

Bishop Adhemar orders a three-day fast to begin on June 24 in preparation for battle. Hey, a fast isn't difficult for the crusaders; they have nothing to eat anyway. They've managed to survive by chewing leather and boiling tree bark.

At the crack of dawn on June 28, the starving crusaders confess their sins, attend Mass, and receive Holy Communion. Soldiers open the gates of Antioch, and the Christian army marches out to meet the enemy. They have no mortal chance to survive. They have only a hundred remaining horses, and no strength. They are haggard and weak. Bohemond leads the army, along with Bishop Adhemar and a funny-looking peasant holding up the small spear. Behind the soldiers come priests in white robes chanting prayers and holding up crosses.

As Bohemond and his troops approach the great Turkish army, there appears from the heavens "a countless number of men on white horses," whose banners are gleaming white. St. George and the heavenly host are accompanying the Christian army into battle. The crusaders call upon the name of God, and charge. Bohemond wisely uses one of his squadrons of knights to stop the Turks from outflanking the Christian forces.

The turning point in the battle comes when several of Kerbogha's emirs, fearing that victory would only strengthen Kerbogha's stranglehold on their lands, begin to flee the battlefield. By the end of the morning, the incredible battle is over, and the mighty Kerbogha has fled in the direction of Mosul, leaving behind his treasures and his stores of food and provisions.

Against all odds, the crusaders have withstood siege on both sides of the great walls of Antioch for over eight and a half months. They've put to flight the most powerful army that a Moslem ruler could assemble. They've recovered the Holy Lance, and now they turn their eyes toward Jerusalem and the end of their adventure.

Crosscurrent

Kerbogha was playing chess when he heard that the Christians were pouring out of Antioch. He was advised by his fellow emirs to attack at once. Instead, he continued to play chess, stating that he wanted the whole Christian army to appear from Antioch so that he could destroy it with one blow.

Plague, Chaos, and Famine

Another calamity now befalls the crusaders. In July, a strange plague spreads throughout Antioch. The diseased show strange black swellings about the size of eggs in their armpits and groins. The swellings ooze blood and pus and are followed by boils and blood blotches on the skin. The sick suffer severe intestinal pain and begin to cough up clots of blood. Everything that issues from their bodies—breath, sweat, bloody urine, and blood-blackened excrement—smells rancid. After five days of agony, they finally die.

The dead are buried in mass graves. The plague even grips Adhemar, the papal-appointed ruler of the Crusade. He dies on August 1. Without a ruler, chaos breaks out among the military commanders, each vying for supreme command. The squabbling becomes so intense that Hugh of Vermandois, the first of the great lords to leave Europe, gathers his forces and begins the long march home to Normandy.

Hugh of Vermandois spends several months in the imperial palace at Constantinople before returning to France. During this holiday, the pompous Hugh shows little concern over the fate of his fellow crusaders and the plight of the Holy City. The Count of Vermandois once said that he would not come home until the Holy City was in Christian hands. Upon returning to France, he is treated with contempt by his fellow nobles until he is finally goaded to take part in the Second Crusade.

Raymond of Toulouse argues that Antioch must be handed over to Emperor Alexis, as they had pledged loyalty to him. Bohemond disagrees and says that the emperor failed to come to their aid in their darkest hour, and therefore, had forfeited all rights to the city. This city, Bohemond says, belongs to him. By November, five months after the miracle, the dissension among the princes is reflected in a breakdown of law and order between all factions within the Crusade. Knights engage in bloody battles with other knights; vassals with other vassals; peasants are murdered in their sleep; serfs steal from serfs; women are sexually violated in the streets.

Crosscurrent

The situation in Antioch became so severe that the soldiers met on November 1 and threatened to elect their own leaders and march on to Jerusalem without the bickering princes. But since the army, too, was divided into factions, a suitable leader could not be found.

Now famine again besets the crusaders. Princes and knights begin to forage the local countryside. Hunger becomes so acute that incidents of cannibalism occur. When Raymond and Bohemond raid Ma'arrat-an-Nu'man, the soldiers "cut pieces from the buttocks of dead Saracens, which they cooked, but when it was not yet roasted enough by the fire they devoured it with savage mouths."

As the plague and the famine abate, Raymond of Toulouse tries to negotiate with the other leaders—Godfrey of Bouillon, Robert of Normandy, and Bohemond—to serve under him. They refuse. This forces Raymond's hand, and on January 13, 1099, the Count of Toulouse, barefoot and penitent, sets out with his soldiers on the 400-mile march south to Jerusalem. Raymond says that he wants to enter the city where Jesus died with a spirit of piety and humiliation. The other lords now feel shame over their squabbling and pettiness. They gather their troops and follow the courtly Count of Toulouse in a pious procession. But Bohemond doesn't join them. He stays behind with his troops to consolidate his position as ruler of the principality of Antioch.

An Ironic End to the Final March

The final march of the First Crusade is underway but without the armies of Hugh and Bohemond. They have experienced every misery known to man. The vast army of 150,000 now numbers less than 20,000.

And now, just at the point of triumph, the utmost irony occurs. Word comes that the Seljuk Turks have been driven out of Jerusalem by the Fatimid Moslems. After all this time and trouble, the Holy City really doesn't need to be delivered. The Fatimids, who are friendly to Christians, offer Western pilgrims a clear road to all the holy places, with the stipulation that the crusaders abandon their plans to "liberate" the city.

The crusaders are still on the march as Emperor Alexis is negotiating a neutral policy with the Fatimid Caliph in Egypt. He asks the Holy Army to cease and desist the campaign. But it is too late. On June 5, 1099, the crusaders behold an eclipse of the moon. It is another sign from heaven that victory is within their grasp.

The Least You Need to Know

➤ Antioch was the most heavily fortified city in Byzantium.

➤ Bohemond captured Antioch by the action of an Armenian spy.

➤ The crusaders became trapped in Antioch by Turkish armies.

➤ Finding the Holy Lance was the key to Christian victory.

➤ The Fatimid Turks preempted the Holy Army's plans by reclaiming Jerusalem from the Turks.

The Conquest of Jerusalem

It's the eve of the Christian army's assault on Jerusalem. The Seljuk Turks have been expelled from the city by the Christian-friendly Fatimid Moslems, but the Christian army is unwilling to abandon its plan to regain control of the Holy Sepulcher. What was to have been an attack on the Turks has escalated into a war against all Moslems—a Holy War.

The Eve of the Siege

We've reached the seventh inning of the First Crusade. It's time for a stretch. Some of our leaders have left; some have died; and some remain for the assault on Jerusalem. As so much has happened, let's recap the positions of our principal players on the eve of the siege of Jerusalem:

➤ The Seljuk Turks are gone. The Fatimid Moslems have made an alliance with the Eastern Emperor Alexis I. There's no need for the crusaders to conquer the Holy Land. All Christians have been granted permission to visit all the holy places. But the crusaders have suffered much misery on their journey to Jerusalem, and they're bound and determined to complete their mission and lay claim to the Holy Sepulcher.

➤ Bishop Adhemar, the ruler of the Crusades, has died in Antioch of the plague. In his absence, there is a power vacuum at the heart of the Christian army.

➤ Hugh of Vermandois, the haughtiest and most obnoxious of the military leaders, has turned from the Holy War in disgust and returned to Normandy with his soldiers.

➤ Godfrey of Bouillon remains at the head of his Frankish army. His brother Baldwin, who has become Prince of Edessa, remains with him for the final battle.

➤ Duke Robert, the eldest son of William the Conqueror, remains on the outskirts of the Holy City with his Norman forces.

➤ The one-eyed Spanish count, Raymond of Toulouse, who holds the Holy Lance, stands at the head of his Frankish army. He has become by force of will the titular head of the Christian army.

➤ The brave and barbaric Bohemond remains in Antioch, where he will reign as Prince until the time of his death. His brave and bold nephew Tancred now stands in the service of Raymond of Toulouse.

➤ The emperor Alexis, who now is freed from the menace of the Seljuk Turks, has fallen out of favor with the leaders of the Crusade since he failed to come to their aid at Antioch. His plea for help from the Latin West has backfired.

Holy War

The Christian army is no longer facing Turks who commit sacrilege and threaten the Byzantine Empire. The Turks have been vanquished. They face Fatimid Moslems who are ruled by a Vizier (Moslem governor) in Egypt. The Fatimids have been cooperative with the crusaders. They sent ambassadors to the leaders of the Christian army and explained that, while the crusaders were recapturing Byzantine lands from the Turks, they, too, had been busy doing battle with them to recapture lost Fatimid territory, including the city of Jerusalem. Jerusalem was ours, the ambassadors explain, until the nasty Turks took it from us in 1070. Now, they say, we want it back, and our vizier is willing to honor the Christian army for its efforts. "We shall restore the Holy City and the Tower of David and Mount Zion to the Christian people," they are happy to say.

But the crusaders have gone too far to turn back from their goal when it stands before them. They are bound and determined to rid the Holy Land not only of the Turks but also of all Moslems, whom they call Saracens. They have now declared war not on an Islamic horde, but on Islam itself. The crusade has now reached a new stage. It has become a monumental war, not between two warring factions, but between two religions, and the fate of the world hangs in the balance.

At Last, Jerusalem

And now, on June 7, 1099, the crusaders catch sight of the place they had been dreaming about since they had gathered on that cold day in November 1096 to hear Pope Urban's call for a Holy War. This is the "Navel of the World" for medieval men and women. They call it the "navel" because they think it's the center of the earth, just as your belly button is the center of your body.

The members of the Holy Army can see the honey-colored stone buildings and the magnificent Dome of the Rock—a massive golden dome that covers the rock upon which Abraham prepared to sacrifice Isaac and from which the prophet Mohammed ascended into heaven—and the al-Aqsa Mosque that stands on the site of Herod's Temple.

Jerusalem's city wall is protected by a lower outer wall, because the valleys and ravines offer no natural protection. Behind the outer wall is a dry moat that is 62 feet wide and 23 feet deep. Behind the dry moat stands the massive wall, over 50 feet high.

The Armies Prepare

The Egyptian garrison, commanded by General Iftikhar al-Daula, has prepared for the Western invaders. The countryside has been stripped of livestock and crops; the wells outside the city have

Crusade Aid

Why do the crusaders refer to Moslems as Saracens? Before Mohammed, Arabia did not exist as a political unit. The Greeks, with their careless nomenclature, referred to all inhabitants of the Arabian peninsula as *Sarakenoi* or Saracens, from the Arabic *shar-qiyun,* meaning Easterners.

Christian Chronicles

General Iktikhar al-Daula served as the Fatimid governor of Jerusalem. His greatest problem was manpower. Many Moslems had fled when the Seljuk Turks arrived. Others had been massacred when the Moslems rebelled against the Turkish rule of the Holy City in 1076. General Iktikhar had killed or expelled the Seljuks when he gained control of Jerusalem the previous year.

been poisoned; the trees on the hillsides have been chopped down; and the city has been well provisioned for a long siege. But the Moslems do not expect a long siege. They already have called for reinforcements from Cairo.

As added security, the Moslems have expelled all the Christians from Jerusalem for fear they might betray the city to the crusaders.

For the first five days, the Crusaders pore over maps and plan the attack. The heat is incredible and the choking dust is relentless. The Christians must bring water from springs four or five miles away. Small fortunes are paid for a mouthful of it.

Now, on June 12, a strange hermit who has lived for years in the hills of the Holy City meets the Christian princes at the Mount of Olives. The hermit seems to be a prophet, a messenger of God. He speaks to them of a miracle. "If you attack the city tomorrow on the ninth hour," he says, "the Lord will deliver it into your hands." This sounds crazy. The siege engines and towers have not been constructed, let alone the scaling ladders. They have no tackle, nails, iron bolts, or leather hides. The hillsides have been stripped. They have no timber. "But these things," the hermit insists, "do not matter. What matters is faith, faith in God, faith in His promises, faith in His miraculous power."

Miracles! The crusaders do have faith in miracles. They've experienced the Miracle of the Holy Lance. The princes are so impressed with the prophecy that they prepare an assault for the ninth hour of the next day.

A Disastrous Assault

When the time comes, thousands of crusaders fling themselves at the outer wall of the city, without siege equipment. The Christians fight fiercely. Some, against all odds, reach the parapets, when the princes call retreat. The Moslems are puzzled. These Christians are acting crazy! Are they delirious from the sun and the heat?

The trumpets sound and the Christians withdraw. Hundreds lie dead or dying at the foot of the wall. And now comes another wave of Christians with knives, clubs, and pointed sticks. Many of them are naked—stark naked; others clad in rags. They're covered with sores, filth, and battle scars. They have hollow cheeks, burning eyes, ragged beards, and wild hair falling to their shoulders. The wretched mob flings "Greek fire"—a medieval form of napalm made from sulfur and resins—over the walls. It is madness. The Moslems unleash a torrent of arrows, and the Tafurs, "the poor people of Christ," fall in a heap.

The crazy assault ends as suddenly as it began. The Moslems scratch their heads in bewilderment. What the heck triggered that act of lunacy? They watch the crusading army retire to the hills.

Crusade Aid

The Tafurs were the holy savages of the First Crusade. *Tafran* is Arabic for "penniless." They comprised primarily Flemish followers of Peter the Hermit, who believed that the poor were destined to inherit Jerusalem as "a sign that the Lord God does not care for presumptuous and faithless men."

The Christians fall into deep despair. Some say the hermit is a crackpot, and want to lynch him. Others say that the hermit is a real prophet, and blame the knights for their lack of resolve after reaching the parapets.

Divine Intervention

But now two things will happen that will change the outcome of the Crusade. First, Tancred will experience extreme diarrhea, and second, Bishop Adhemar will return from the dead.

Tancred becomes afflicted with a nasty case of dysentery. He can't go a mile without running off to a bush or a cave. Most medieval men wouldn't mind dropping their drawers and doing their business on the road, but Tancred is different. He requires a certain degree of privacy.

Tancred's Miraculous Find

Several days after the calamitous first attack, Tancred and his men set off in search of some wood for siege towers. They search for hours and only come up with a handful of sticks. Then Tancred feels the turmoil in his intestines and heads for the hills. The chronicler Radulph relates the rest:

> Tancred had almost given up the search when the accustomed trouble struck again. So he pulled away from the others and dismounted. He hoped he would be able to avoid the gaze of his companions, but on looking back he saw he had not done so. He therefore sought concealment further away, but again he could see a few men wandering about, so he changed his position a third and a fourth time, until in a deep recess beneath a hollow rock, surrounded by trees and bristling shade he found peace. While relieving himself in this secluded spot, he found himself facing a cave where four hundred timbers lay open to view, enough timber to construct a siege tower.

It is an astonishing miracle. The discovery of the timber is followed by the arrival of six English ships at Jaffa, bringing much-needed supplies. Since there is such a need for wood, two of the ships are dragged to shore and dismantled board by board. Now the construction of several siege

Christian Chronicles

Aboard the English ships were several Genoese sailors who joined the crusaders. As luck (or miracle) would have it, these sailors were skilled engineers and carpenters, who knew how to construct great weapons of medieval warfare, including the huge battering ram that was used at the Siege of Jerusalem.

towers got underway under the supervision of Godfrey and Raymond. The army became transformed into a massive carpentry shop, building siege towers, scaling ladders, battering rams, and catapults at a furious rate.

The Crusaders' Crazy Parade

A second miracle occurs three weeks after the ships arrive. Bishop Adhemar, the late leader of the Holy Army, appears to the priest Peter Desiderius in a vision and imparts a message for all crusaders. The dearly departed Bishop tells them to free themselves from all the filth of the world, put sin behind them, and walk barefoot around the walls of Jerusalem. If the army obeys these instructions, then the city, at the end of nine days, will fall into their hands. If the crusaders fail to obey these orders, then their miseries will increase a hundred fold.

General Iftikhar watches another strange spectacle on the morning of July 10. Over 20,000 of these crazy crusaders are now marching around the walls of Jerusalem in underwear and white robes. They are barefoot and sing hymns as they step on sharp stones and assorted rubble. The trumpeters blow their trumpets and priests swing censers. The Moslems on the walls make fun of them by making obscene gestures with makeshift crosses and showing their naked backsides to the priests, who lead the procession carrying a collection of holy relics. What's the story with these crusaders? Have they gone loco after chewing on the local weeds? Finally, the long parade comes to an end, and the crusaders return to the Mount of Olives where they hear a rousing sermon from (you guessed it!) Cucu Peter.

The Siege

On July 14, 1099, the final siege begins. The crusaders have built a massive battering ram from a tree trunk that is suspended by massive chains. The head of the ram is made of iron and weighs 30 pounds. It takes 60 soldiers to swing the gigantic ram that is capable of smashing through the stoutest mortar and masonry. The ram begins to pound against the outer wall at the crack of dawn. When Moslem defenders attempt to ward off the attackers with "grenades" (pots filled with Greek Fire), they are kept at bay by a mighty barrage of stones that hail from a host of newly constructed Christian catapults.

In no time at all, the crusaders smash through the outer wall. Upon orders from Raymond of Toulouse and Godfrey of Bouillon, they feverishly work to fill in the dry moat with the rubble. The Moslems on the Great Wall could mow them down with arrows but they are protected by the umbrella of thousands of shields. By late afternoon, the crusaders complete their work of filling in the ditch.

Now, as it grows dark, the crusaders continue their siege by turning their catapults upon the inner wall of the Holy City. As huge rocks fly through the air, hundreds of soldiers drag the two gigantic siege towers along with the massive battering ram toward the Great Wall. The Moslems attempt to ward off the attackers with arrows, spears, darts, rocks, and, of course, the newfangled grenades. The air is thick with smoke and the stench of sulfur. The Christians are protected from the projectiles by their suits of armor and the heavy shields which, held by an arm, can create an instant ceiling. Inch by inch, the great battering ram and the siege towers approach the Great Wall. Time and time again, the ram and the siege tower blaze into flames and the crusaders scramble to extinguish the fire with pails of water and vinegar.

In the midst of the mayhem, two Moslem women appear on the wall and attempt to cast a spell over one of the Christian catapults. While they weave their magic, a massive stone from the catapult the women are cursing hurls through the air and crushes them against the battlements like two black bugs. The crusaders cheer with delight.

Crusade Aid

Two Flemish knights, Litold and Gilbert of Tournai, were granted the honor of being the first to cross from the siege tower to the battlements. They were followed by Godfrey of Bouillon, his brother Eustace, and Duke Robert of Normandy.

High Noon for the Saracens

On the morning of July 15, the battering ram is in place and the pounding begins, with a devastating rhythm, to smash against the inner wall. In desperation, the Moslems attempt to cushion the blows of this monstrous machine by suspending bales of straw and mattresses stuffed with cotton from the walls. But the cushions soon catch on fire, sending huge columns of black, billowing smoke over the battlements. The Moslems cannot breathe or see. The thick clouds of smoke are blinding and the incessant crash of the battering ram deafening.

Finally, above the thick smoke, the Moslems see the large, gilded figure of Jesus that adorns the siege tower of Godfrey of Bouillon. Before the Moslems can scream in alarm, crusaders leap from the tower to the wall. It is noon on Friday, July 15, on the ninth day prophesied by Bishop Adhemar, and the crusaders are aware that they're entering Jerusalem at the very hour in which Jesus died on the Cross.

The Holy Army Breaks Through

As the first wave of crusaders sweeps down the north wall, thousands of Moslem defenders retreat to the Temple area and seek shelter in the Dome of the Rock. But Tancred and his troops break down the doors, hack the Moslems to pieces, and lay claim to all the treasures within the magnificent mosque.

In the center of the Holy City, the dead are everywhere—headless, armless, legless. The crusaders rush over the mutilated bodies as though they represent a welcome carpet. Raymond of Aguilers, the great chronicler, sees the bloodletting and says, "This is the day the Lord hath made. Let us rejoice and be glad in it."

The Moslems who escaped from the Dome of the Rock are now bottled up in the al-Aqsa Mosque. They bar the doors and take refuge on the roof, hoping to make a last stand against the invaders. But Tancred's shock troops break down the door and come upon the Moslems with such speed and force that they have no recourse except to surrender. The infidels agree to provide Tancred with a large ransom for their lives, and the gracious knight agrees to spare them. The Moslems are permitted to fly Tancred's banner over the mosque as proof that they are under his protection.

While Godfrey and his men ransack the north of the city, Raymond of Toulouse and his forces run amok in the south of the city. In an unexpected act of chivalry, the old count suddenly halts his attack and proposes safe conduct for Iftikhar and members of his court if they agree to surrender the Tower of David. Having no alternative, the governor surrenders to the Franks, and Raymond stuns the Arabs by keeping his word. The governor and his men become the only Moslems to escape from the Holy City with their lives.

Ethnic Cleansing, Crusader Style

The next day, the carnage continues. The crusaders ignore Tancred's protective banner and slaughter all the Moslems in the al-Aqsa Mosque; men, women, children, and "a large number of Imams (religious leaders) and Islamic scholars, devout and ascetic men who had left their homelands to live lives of pious seclusion in the Holy Place."

Crosscurrent

Chroniclers who were eyewitnesses to the conquest of Jerusalem told of women being stabbed to death, of babies snatched from their mothers' breasts and flung over the walls, of children snatched by the legs and smashed against stone walls.

The Jews who've remained in Jerusalem are treated in a similar manner. They remain in the chief synagogue, where they plead for shelter and protection. The crusaders respond by burning the synagogue to the ground with the Jews inside. No one questions this action. Jerusalem is to become a Christian city.

But the bloodletting continues even though all the infidels are dead. The crusaders slice open the bellies of the corpses and extract the intestines in search of gold coins the Saracens might have swallowed.

The Crusaders Go to Mass

At sunset, the victorious crusaders gather at the Church of the Holy Sepulcher in a spirit of praise and thanksgiving. The Mass is celebrated, and the priests chant the Office of the Resurrection. Knights in chain mail stand before simple soldiers in the half-darkness of the high-vaulted sanctuary. They've triumphed over tremendous odds. They've suffered nearly every calamity known to man, and yet they've survived. A feeling of Christian brotherhood sweeps over the congregation—a feeling that has not been stirred for hundreds of years.

Remembering the Mass within the Church of the Holy Sepulcher, Fulcher of Chartres wrote:

> Oh time of times most memorable! Oh deed before all other deeds! They desired that this place, so long contaminated by the superstition of the pagan inhabitants should be cleansed of their contagion.

But so much for sentimentality! There's another problem that merits immediate attention. The corpses are beginning to swell and stink, and a method must be devised for immediate disposal. Count Raymond suggests the digging of a massive grave. But, Duke Robert argues, these bodies do not require a decent burial. They are not the bodies of Christian soldiers that will be resurrected at the end of time. They are the remains of infidels who have defiled holy shrines, who have sodomized bishops, and who have circumcised good men without mercy. They deserve to be burned. The other princes agree. It's hard to argue against such impeccable logic.

What's more, there are so many bodies—70,000 in all. It would take weeks to dig a pit deep and wide enough to contain them. And so the scene is set that later will be recalled by a Frankish chronicler:

> They also ordered that all the corpses of the Saracens should be thrown outside the city because of the fearful stench; for the whole city was full of their dead bodies. The Saracens who were still alive dragged the dead ones out in front of the gates, and made piles of them, as big as houses. Such a slaughter of pagans no one has ever seen or heard of; the pyres were like pyramids.

The Least You Need to Know

➤ At the end of the First Crusade the rulers of Jerusalem were not Seljuk Turks but Fatimid Moslems.

➤ The crusaders called the Moslems "Saracens," from an Arabic word meaning "Easterners."

➤ The ghost of Bishop Adhemar provided the blueprint for victory.

➤ The key elements in the Christian victory at Jerusalem were the creation of the world's largest battering ram and the construction of two huge siege towers.

➤ The crusaders massacred 70,000 Moslems and Jews in Jerusalem.

Part 3

The Formation of the Latin East

The crusaders have conquered Jerusalem and a new age is about to dawn in the Middle East. The Christians will become rich, fat, and indolent, while the Moslems will become filled with righteous rage. Assassins will spread widespread terror; Saracens will unite under the slogan of jihad; and monks will form military orders. It is one of the weirdest and wildest eras of world history. To enter this era, which is filled with sex, drugs, and violence, turn the page.

Chapter 10

Life in the Latin East

In This Chapter

➤ Godfrey becomes king of Jerusalem

➤ Christians defeat and massacre Egyptian Moslems

➤ Emperor Alexis is denied a share of the spoils

➤ A new pope precipitates new waves of the Crusade

➤ Crusader states get rich and get along with the Moslems

➤ The Franks get Easternized and take Syrian wives

The crusaders have attained (sort of) their goal. They have rescued the Holy Tomb from the Saracens, even though the Saracens, unlike the Turks, are friendly toward Christians, and even quite supportive of the Holy Army. But why worry? A Moslem is a Moslem! And the Christian army has won a tremendous victory against all odds. They have survived the most grievous miseries that can be inflicted on mortal man. They have been forced to battle mighty armies, to suffer desert heat and relentless rain, to relinquish their most prized possessions, and to endure outbreaks of pestilence and plague. They have been compelled to butcher their war-horses (even their hunting falcons), to commit unspeakable atrocities, to drink blood and urine, to use severed heads as catapult cannonballs, and to eat a fair share of human flesh.

Still, in Jerusalem some problems have to be solved without delay. A huge army of Egyptian Moslems has been sent by the Vizier to destroy them. The leader of the army, a general named Al-Afdal, vows to massacre all the Christian soldiers, to destroy all Christian churches, and to cast all Christian relics (including the Holy Lance) into a fire. This last bit of news particularly incenses the pious crusaders, that is, the crusaders who remain in the Holy City.

Most of the crusaders are gone. They leave Jerusalem immediately after celebrating Mass at the Church of the Holy Sepulcher. They believe that they have fulfilled their holy obligation and are eager to return to the missionary position of their wives and the questionable comforts of their castles. After all, during the course of the Crusade, they had to act as penitents; they were bound to uphold the virtue of chastity.

The Last Hurrah

The vast Moslem army is only a week away and the crusaders have to unite and prepare for battle. But who will be the commander-in-chief? Bohemond remains in Antioch. Henry of Vermandois has headed back to England. And the remaining three princes cannot agree about places at the dinner table, let alone issues of life and death.

The leaders of the Christian armies gather in council and squabble over everything: Who should take up residence in the governor's palace? Where should the soldiers and priests be quartered? Some knights and commoners have placed their names on various houses; is this enough to claim ownership? And speaking of ownership, should Tancred really be allowed to keep all the treasure from the Dome of the Rock, including the eight hanging lamps of solid silver? It doesn't seem fair that this young upstart should become the richest of all Christian knights.

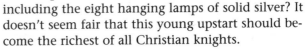

Crosscurrent

The crusaders came to one immediate decision. They decided that the Orthodox Greek Christians, the Georgian Christians, the Armenian Christians, and the Jacobite Christians no longer could hold services in the Church of the Holy Sepulcher. Only the Latin rite could be celebrated in Jerusalem.

The Crusaders Get a King

Squabbling continues until it is decided that someone has to be appointed the Supreme Leader over all others or all will be lost. The crusaders need a king. But who should be crowned? There are three candidates:

➤ Raymond, the Count of Toulouse, is the richest and most powerful of the princes. He led the Christian army on its long march to Jerusalem, but he was not the most heroic in the final battle. What's more, he actually permitted the Moslem governor of Jerusalem to walk away scot-free, without so much as a severed toe, let alone complete castration.

➤ Duke Robert of Normandy is the son of William the Conqueror and an able warrior. But he has never displayed the cunning of Bohemond or the courage of Tancred.

➤ Godfrey of Bouillon has all the right credentials. He is a descendent of Charlemagne; he was the hero of the final siege; and he is very religious.

The choice is easy. Godfrey is elected by popular acclaim. He refuses the title "King of Jerusalem," saying that no one wears a crown of earthly glory in a city where our Lord wore a crown of thorns. He rather opts for the modest title "Advocate of the Holy Sepulcher."

Far from being a magnanimous monarch, Godfrey's first act is to order Count Raymond to vacate the Tower of David on the pretense that it is needed for defense. Raymond is incensed. He gathers his followers and marches out of Jerusalem in a huff. The old count heads for Jericho because he wants to be baptized in the River Jordan.

After being dunked in cold water, Raymond comes to his senses and returns to Jerusalem to join the other crusaders in the battle against the great Egyptian army.

Crusade Aid

The title that Godfrey of Bouillon chose displayed his humility. *Advocatus* means "friend" or "witness" and had the force of "protector." His successors were not nearly so humble. All, including his brother Baldwin, wore a crown and insisted on being venerated as kings.

Egyptian Moslems Are Defeated

On August 11, the entire Christian army under Godfrey marches out of Jerusalem, leaving behind a meager garrison. Little Peter and the other priests keep vigil at the Holy Sepulcher, chanting hymns and offering fervent prayers for victory over the Saracens (Egyptian Moslems).

The prayers are heard. Al-Afdal and his vast army are camped at Ascalon. The Egyptians have completely underestimated the strength of the crusading army. They have heard that the leaders are quarreling, that soldiers are deserting, that the horses are scrawny and poorly fed, and that the army is an unorganized and undisciplined rabble. They do not expected an attack.

The attack comes at dawn. Al-Afdal awakes to the sound of the Christian army's trumpets and horns.

Christian Chronicles

The Christian army returned to Jerusalem with vast herds of camels, cattle, and sheep from the Egyptian army. Exactly one month after the fall of Jerusalem, they celebrated in the Church of the Holy Sepulcher a solemn Mass in honor of their second victory.

Within minutes, the crusaders descend upon the Egyptians with their broadswords and battle-axes. It is another massacre. Tens of thousands of Moslems are hacked to pieces without mercy. Others retreat to the sea and sail home in Egyptian ships. Knowing they need divine assistance to crush the Egyptian army, the crusaders carry the Holy Lance and the True Cross into battle with them. Count Raymond is partial to the Holy Lance and holds it high above every Saracen head that he severs with his broadsword. Al-Afdal's tent is captured. It is filled with wonderful treasures: chalices of pure gold, chests of precious jewels, ceremonial swords of crafted silver, helmets decorated with gold inlays, and a dozen of his delectable concubines.

The battle at Ascalon is the last hurrah of the First Crusade. Duke Robert and Count Raymond remain too proud to serve under Godfrey. Duke Robert sets sail for Constantinople, where he is well received by Emperor Alexis before heading home. Count Raymond, who vows to spend the remainder of his life in the Holy Land, ventures north into Syria, where he carves out the County of Tripoli in the narrow strip of land between Mount Lebanon and the coast.

The Kingdom Comes Together!

The Latin East has been created. Bohemond remains as the ruler of the Principality of Antioch. Baldwin returns to his throne in Edessa. Count Raymond governs the County of Tripoli. Godfrey holds the title of Advocate of the Holy Sepulcher, although he is really King of Jerusalem. And Tancred sets about to lay claim to Galilee, Tiberias, and Beisan.

Crusade Aid

Alexis I Comnena, the Byzantine Emperor, reigned until 1118. He was succeeded by his son John Comnena, much to the dismay of his daughter, Anna. Anna conspired to assassinate her brother, was detected and forgiven, retired to a convent, and chronicled her father's career in *Alexiad*.

On Christmas Day of that fateful year, Bohemond, Tancred, and Baldwin travel to Jerusalem to pay tribute to Godfrey in order to strengthen the Christian position in the Latin East. They pledge their loyalty to Godfrey, and Godfrey in turn officially recognizes Bohemond as Prince of Antioch, Tancred as Prince of Galilee, and Baldwin as Prince of Edessa. In the noble spirit of nepotism, Godfrey also appoints Baldwin as his successor to the throne. All seem happy and content.

Emperor Alexis Gets Dumped!

The Christians have sworn their allegiance to Alexis I and have not lived up to their word. They have vowed to return all the lands they conquer to the Byzantine Emperor. But guess what? Alexis gets the shaft. The only one who maintains some sense of loyalty to him is Count Raymond of Toulouse. He returns to

Constantinople and says that he is willing to accept the Eastern Emperor as his sovereign lord. The other Christian nobles feel that they have been betrayed by Alexis at Antioch and tell him, in effect, to buzz off, as they are claiming the conquered lands for themselves.

By the following Christmas, Godfrey will die of typhus and be buried next to the Holy Sepulcher, Bohemond will be locked in a Turkish dungeon, and Baldwin will be king of Jerusalem.

Crusader Power!

Despite their vulnerability, the fledgling crusader states manage to take root and flourish. How can this happen? There are only a few thousand crusaders left in the East. Why aren't these Christians wiped out by the millions of Moslems? It doesn't make sense. Are the Moslems afraid of the Christians? The answer to this last question is yes. The Franks scare the living hell out of them. The crusaders have managed to terrify everybody, including the Byzantine emperor. From neck to waist, and from thighs to toes, the Frankish knights are encased in chain mail made of iron links on a foundation of leather. They wear incredibly sharp spurs with iron rims and iron bosses. Their helmets are round, flat-topped boxes of steel that cover the entire head, with slits for the eyes, perforations for the nostrils, and a small opening for the mouth. They are intended to look terrifying. They have marched across Asia Minor and won every battle against the Turks: Nicea, Dorylaeum, and Antioch. They have defeated the mighty Egyptian armies at Jerusalem and Ascalon. These warriors seem like raving wolves with a lust for blood that no amount of slaughter can satisfy.

To the Arabs, the Crusaders seem unwashed, uncouth, and downright uncivilized. The Moslems pride themselves on their culture, their learning, their refinement. They have established colleges throughout the Middle East, where scholars and students pore over the writings of Plato, Pythagoras, Aristotle, and other Greek philosophers. These works, by and large, are not studied in the West. The Latin world has come to believe that all the writings of Aristotle have been lost. Nevertheless, the crusaders are a power to be reckoned with.

Christian Chronicles

A tally of Godfrey's forces at the time of his death showed that he had only 300 knights and an equal number of foot soldiers to defend his kingdom. If one adds to this the settlers elsewhere in Palestine and in the north around Antioch and Edessa, there could not have been more than 3,000 Europeans in the region at that time.

The New East

Disarray in the Arab world, a new pope, more Crusades, and more Turkish assaults. But a new and prosperous East emerges.

Crazy, Beautiful Baghdad

Baghdad is the largest and most civilized city in the Eastern world. It enjoys free hospitals, public baths, a postal service, a water supply, a sewage system, and financial institutions—banks—with branches in China.

The Arabs also have made great advancements in science, while Europe remains lost in the Dark Ages. Albanius has calculated the exact distance from the Earth to the Moon, and Jabir bin Hayyan has reasoned that if an atom can be divided it will release enough power to destroy the great city of Cairo.

They establish the first apothecary shops and dispensaries, found the medieval school of pharmacy, and write great treatises on pharmacology.

In medicine, the Arabs are specialists in eye surgery, breast cancer, epilepsy, preventative medicine, and hygiene. They know the importance of sterilization and cleanliness. They have even developed a form of anesthesia from hashish, opium, darnel, and belladonna.

But the rough and tumble warriors from the West have no such sophistication. They are covered with lice and stink to high heaven. And they are capable of unspeakable atrocities—including genocide and cannibalism.

Apart from being afraid, the Arabs could stamp out the new Christian states if they would unite. But this is not the case. Baghdad remains the Islamic center of authority, but in name only. It is still the home of the Caliph, but the city is in the hands of the Seljuk Turks and the Turkish overlord assumes the title of "Sultan." And the Turks aren't Arabs at all.

Crusade Aid

Malik Shah was one of the greatest of the Seljuk sultans. He saw himself as the sovereign of all the Middle East and, with his general Suleiman, conquered Asia Minor. His conquest of Nicea, less than a hundred miles from Constantinople, sparked the First Crusade.

The chaos within the Arabic world is best reflected by the chaos in Baghdad. In the three years after the capture of Jerusalem, Baghdad changes hands eight times, as the sons of Malik Shah fight for supremacy. The Turkish rulers are more concerned about the capital city of their empire than the plight of Jerusalem and other towns on the western edge of their world.

There is another problem that prevents the Moslems from stamping out the crusader states: The crusaders keep coming, wave after wave, year after year. The Turks and other Moslems are too busy warding off new invaders to turn their attention to the situation in Syria and Palestine.

New Pope, New Pitch

Pope Urban II never receives the story of the success of the First Crusade. He dies less than a week before the news arrives in Rome. But the news brings a new bout of "crusader fever." As soon as he ascends to the throne of St. Peter, the new pope, Paschal II, begins to preach the need for the formation of a new Christian army to fortify the crusader states. The response to Paschal II's call is phenomenal for two reasons:

Christian Chronicles

Urban II, who called for the First Crusade, is in heaven. He was beatified by the Roman Catholic Church in 1885. The eternal fate of his successor, Pope Paschal II, remains in doubt.

➤ People are intoxicated with the possibility of fame and fortune that await them in the Holy Land. Common people, it is said, come back with great riches. Nobles have gained vast holdings and rule as kings. And there is the glory. Overnight, Bohemond, Godfrey of Bouillon, Count Raymond of Toulouse, and Tancred have become folk heroes and are hailed as the greatest of knights.

➤ The pope has threatened to excommunicate any able-bodied soldier who fails to head off to the Holy Land.

Historians estimate that nearly as many Christians—over 300,000—set out on the second wave of the First Crusade. The armies come from France, Northern Italy, England, Scotland, and Germany. Among the nobles are Stephen of Blois and Hugh of Vermandois, the two leaders who had abandoned the first expedition at Antioch. They will both die in battle, and thereby receive full forgiveness of their many sins.

New Crusaders, New Disasters

The new crusaders travel to Constantinople, where they are met by Count Raymond of Toulouse who agrees to serve as an adviser and to repeat the grueling march across Asia Minor. Everybody, Greeks and Romans alike, is in high spirits.

Count Raymond urges the leaders of the new army to follow the same route taken by the First Crusade. But something happens. The crusaders are informed that Bohemond has been captured by the treacherous Turks and tossed into a rat-infested dungeon in the Turkish castle at Niksar. This is outrageous! The new crusaders cannot allow this great hero to rot in chains. And so, they set out to rescue him.

The whole enterprise is a disaster! The Turks assault the Christian army day and night as they march across the waterless, high plateau. More than three quarters of the new army perishes and the slave markets of the East become saturated with captured Christian men, women, and children.

Crusade Aid

Following the debacle of the second wave of the First Crusade, Count Raymond of Toulouse returned to his castle called Mount Pilgrim, outside Tripoli. He died on February 28, 1112. His province in the Latin East was claimed not by Emperor Alexis but by Baldwin, the King of Jerusalem. From this time on, Baldwin would rule three of the four Christian kingdoms: Tripoli, Edessa, and Jerusalem. The counts of Tripoli and Edessa were appointed by King Baldwin and remained his personal vassals.

Still another Christian army, this one led by the Count of Nevers, meets a similar fate, but year after year the crusaders keep on coming. One army is led by William IX, Duke of Aquitaine, the great-grandfather of Richard the Lion Heart. His army, like the others, runs out of supplies in the vastness of Asia Minor and falls prey to Turkish mounted archers.

Prosperity Breaks Out

Some of the new crusaders, however, actually make it to the Holy Land and serve to bolster the Latin East. More help comes from the Armenian Christian population, who welcome the arrival of each and every new army from the West.

The fledgling crusader states take root and begin to thrive. The Franks, unlike the gentry in Europe, do not farm any of the land themselves. For this reason, the labor services of serfs and peasants are not needed for the grand manor. Instead, the overlord in the East takes a share of the harvest, something between a quarter and a third, which he uses to construct new castles and to fortify old ones.

But agriculture in the East, unlike that of Europe, is not the mainstay of the economy. The crusader states grow prosperous from the caravans that come from Damascus and beyond to the ports of Tyre and Acre. The caravans carry silks; sugar; spices: pepper, ginger, cloves, and cinnamon; and exotic fruits: melons, lemons, peaches, cherries, dates, and Damascus plums (better known as apricots). They also bring tapestries, rugs, dyes, powders, scents, and gems to adorn and sweeten feudal castles and flesh. Such trade brings incredible wealth, and the Latin Christian nobles rake off a good percentage of the profits from the caravans as well as from the Pisans, Genoese, and Venetian merchants who are given "trading estates" in the main ports.

Everyone prospers—Christian and Moslem alike—and an amazing thing happens: They begin to get along together, to tolerate each other, even to work together. Money, not faith, becomes the real source of brotherhood. A Moslem writer, Ibn Jubayr, when traveling through Palestine is very impressed at what he sees: "We passed through a series of villages and cultivated lands all inhabited by the Moslems, who live in great well-being under the Franks." Ibn Jubayr also notes that Moslems are paying less tax under the Christians than they were under the Turks and Fatimids: "One of the great tragedies of the Moslems is that they have to complain of injustices of their own rulers, whereas they cannot but praise the behavior of the Franks, their natural enemies. May Allah soon put an end to this state of affairs."

Christian Chronicles

The Latin West was so desirous of attracting Western settlers that the reigning princes and monarchs offered freedom to serfs on the promise that they act as tenants in carefully planned settlement areas, such as Qubeiba.

The Franks Go Eastern

The fierce Franks suddenly begin to act like medieval socialists. In order to attract more people from the West, they offer all new Christian settlers a house in a specially constructed new town and 150 acres of land. Not a bad deal for a serf in Saxony who owns nothing but his wife. Many European peasants, no doubt, are attracted to this utopian Levittown of the eleventh century. Archaeologists recently excavated a dozen of these settlements around Jerusalem. The two-storied houses (infinitely nicer than the squalid huts on a medieval manor) are arranged on a main street that ends in a town square with a courthouse, a tower, and a church.

Crusade Aid

In times of peace, the Frankish nobility found a lot in common with their Moslem counterparts: They enjoyed hunting, flying falcons, and playing dice and other games of chance in the miles of orchards and gardens that flourished outside towns and villages on the fertile coastal plain.

All is going great. The Franks, in fact, are even going Eastern. Many of them marry Syrian Christian women and begin to eat seasoned food and misshapen things called dates. Some dress in a turban and an Oriental dress. They decorate their homes with carefully woven draperies and tapestries. The Franks even begin to sit around the public bathhouses and gossip. It is downright decadent. In 1135, James of Vitry, Bishop of Acre, complains that the third generation of the great Frankish warriors have become complete sissies: "They were brought up in luxury, soft and effeminate, more used to

Christian Chronicles

After the battle of Dyrrhacium, Bohemond was captured and brought before Emperor Alexis in chains. In defeat, he remained superbly insolent. Anna Comnena wrote of the radiance shining from him and said that he appeared like a god standing among mortals.

baths than battle, addicted to unclean and riotous living, clad like women in soft robes." Bohemond, Tancred, Baldwin, and Godfrey of Bouillon must have been turning over in their graves.

The Fate of the Great Heroes

By 1118, the first generation of heroes has gone to their reward.

➤ Bohemond, the fiercest crusader, was finally ransomed in 1103. He returned to Europe and managed to whip up support for a Crusade against the Byzantine emperor. In October 1107, he attacked the Byzantine fortress of Dyrrhacium with an army that included Turkish mercenaries. His force was soundly defeated and he returned to his estates in Southern Italy where he died in 1111.

➤ Tancred, who became the hero of Tasso's epic poem "Jerusalem Delivered" remained "Prince of Galilee" until 1112, when an outbreak of typhoid carried him off to eternal glory at the age of 36.

➤ Baldwin, who ruled the Latin East, became one of the mightiest kings in medieval history. In the spring of 1118, he led an expedition to Egypt, where he crushed the Egyptian forces at Pelusium and Tanis. One day, as he was walking along the banks of the Nile, he came upon some knights spearing fish with their lances. He joined them for a fish fry and immediately became desperately ill. The soldiers carried him to a chapel at al-Arish, where he died. His vassals cut out his intestines, salted them liberally, and placed them in his coffin, which they carried to Jerusalem. On Palm Sunday, he was buried next to his brother Godfrey of Bouillon in the Church of the Holy Sepulcher.

On Baldwin's tombstone is written: "This noble King was a second Judas Maccabaeus, whom Kedar and Egypt, Dan and Damascus dreaded." He is succeeded by his nephew, Baldwin of Le Bourg, who happens to arrive in Jerusalem on the day of his funeral.

More and more pilgrims are coming to the Holy Land. There is only one problem: These good Christians need protection from the Turks and Saracens who are still intent upon the elimination of all Western intruders.

Something has to be done to protect them, especially as the great crusaders have all passed away.

The Least You Need to Know

➤ Godfrey of Bouillon became the first King of Jerusalem.

➤ The crusaders defeated the great Egyptian army at Ascalon.

➤ The barbarian Christians were greatly feared by the civilized Moslems.

➤ The Arab world at the start of the twelfth century remained in profound chaos.

➤ Trade brought wealth to the crusader states.

➤ New settlements were established to attract peasant farmers from Europe.

➤ The Frankish knights took Syrian wives and adopted Middle Eastern lifestyles.

Chapter 11

The Knights Templar and the Hospitallers

In This Chapter

➤ The Knights Templar become the first order of warrior knights

➤ Templar wealth leads to moral corruption

➤ The Hospitallers exchange their bedpans for battle-axes

➤ Both orders are sworn to protect pilgrims, which escalates into attacking Moslem outposts

➤ A third military order, the Teutonic Knights, is on the horizon

You probably think that all monks are either in a cave or a monastery. If they're in a monastery, you figure they're spending their time illuminating manuscripts, growing herb gardens, performing acts of penance, or counting their beads. You can't conceive of a monk as a warrior in chain mail, swinging a mace at the face of a Turk and giving glory to God by hacking off a head. It seems incredible, but it's true.

To protect pilgrims from the marauding Turks, Hugh of Payens, a knight from Champagne, and eight of his friends establish the Order of the Knights Templar. They present themselves before St. Bernard of Clairvaux, a fiery preacher and the most influential churchman of his time, and dedicate themselves to poverty, chastity, and obedience (like all good monks). Then they add a fourth vow: to offer military service to the Roman Catholic Church for the defense of the Holy Land. St. Bernard gains approval of the new religious order and draws up a set of monastic rules by which the order's monks are to be governed.

Hugh and his knights next meet with King Baldwin of Jerusalem and place themselves at his service. Baldwin is so delighted with the notion of military monks that he gives the guys an entire section of his imperial palace, a section that was said to have been part of the Temple of Solomon. This becomes their headquarters and they become known as the Templars.

Christian Chronicles

The Templars were not your average red-blooded Franks. They were distinctly odd. St. Bernard wrote: "They have a horror of chess and dice; they hate hunting; they despise mimes, jugglers, story-tellers, dirty songs, performances of buffoons—all these they regard as vanities and inane follies."

Crusade Aid

Some European patrons of the Templars gave money to the order as a substitute for going on a Crusade. All donors gave as a means to obtain divine favor in this world and the next. The names of the patrons were included in the daily prayers of the military monks.

The Knights Templar

The Templars spend their days in prayer and meditation; they sleep in barracks where lights burn all night; they never speak during a meal for fear they will miss a word of sacred scripture. These guys are straight arrows. They are also somewhat smelly. St. Bernard has advised them to "wash seldom" and to keep their hair closely cropped for lice control.

The Monks Make a Mint

Money pours into the Templars' coffers from estates throughout Europe. The nobles, knights, and merchants look upon these military monks with awe and admiration. The monks really *do* something. They don't spend their time saying prayers, performing acts of penitence, and planting herb gardens in a cloister. They police the passageway from Jaffa to Jerusalem, where evil Saracens remain in wait to attack small groups of Christians, confiscate their goods, cut their throats, and cast their bodies into mountain caves. They make the world a safer place.

With their newfound wealth, the Templars (never mind their vow of poverty) begin to build spectacular castles throughout Palestine and Syria. The financial records for the construction of Safad, one of many fortresses along the Jordan River, show that the Knights of the Temple shelled out the equivalent of $100 million for the undertaking.

To Slay Is to Pray

To many of us this religious order doesn't make sense. We have monks sworn to vows of poverty living in incredible castles with Gothic chambers and Romanesque chapels, mosaic floors, marble paneling, vaulted ceilings, elaborate tapestries and wall hangings, and magnificent fountains.

But the Templars still retain a simple and chaste communal life; their breeches are tightly laced; they are never permitted to see each other naked; and they fast, pray, and chant the canonical hours when they aren't busy protecting pilgrims and killing the enemy.

Still, the Templars, in their white robes on war-horses, seem "walking contradictions." These guys are not "blessed peacemakers" who espouse the belief that those "who live by the sword shall perish by the sword." They are ascetics who believe that they are praying by slaying. "The Christian who slays the unbeliever in the Holy War," says St. Bernard, "is sure of his reward; more sure if he himself is slain. The Christian glories in the death of the pagans, because, by such acts, Christ is glorified."

The Templar knights, by the order of their Rule, are forbidden to engage in such activities of secular knights as hawking and hunting. Unlike other monks, they are permitted meat, but only three days a week. The fasts they are subjected to are far less rigorous than those in other monasteries, as it is important to keep the brethren strong enough for combat.

The Templars negate every teaching of the Sermon on the Mount. They don't turn the other cheek; they brandish the battle-axe. They are totally incorrect—politically, theologically, and morally. But they don't view matters that way. They know that the great heroes of the Bible—Joshua, Samson, and David—were not pacifist preachers but mighty warriors. The twelve disciples did not refrain from the shedding of blood; they carried swords and they were dangerous. At the time of the arrest of Jesus, Peter drew his sword and cut off the ear of the servant of a high priest. Looking at the Knights Templar through the looking glass of the past, we shake our heads in indignation at them, not knowing that if the looking glass were a two-way mirror, they would be shaking their heads at us.

The Templars are obedient only to the pope. For this reason, they often act independently of the king of Jerusalem. They are governed by a grand master, who is venerated as a representative of the Holy Father in Rome.

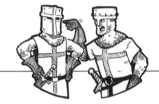

Crosscurrent

The Templars were not without Christian critics. The English Franciscan Roger Bacon was opposed to the notion of consecrated monks killing Moslems. His argument, however, was one of expediency rather than principle. He believed that military activities impeded the conversion of the infidels.

Greed Leads

As so much cash flows into this order, the Templars become experienced money managers. (Eventually, they enter the banking business and serve as treasurers for the king of France.) They begin not only to construct castles but also to build ships that can transport pilgrims and goods to and from Italy to Palestine. This is not to say that they live lavishly. They still wear uncomfortable hairshirts, sleep in dormitories, and rarely speak to one another. They are rich, and in time, their riches will give way to corruption. By the thirteenth century, several ships of the Order of the Knights Templar will change course and dump their cargo of Christian pilgrims in the nearest slave market.

Crusade Aid

The Templars, unlike the Hospitallers, were under no obligation to care for the sick or wounded—not even to provide hospitality. However, they were expected to dispense alms regularly. This duty was partially fulfilled by giving to the poor a tenth of the bread baked at Templar monasteries.

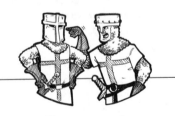

Crosscurrent

The military orders did not remain confined to the Holy Land. The Templars and the Hospitallers took up arms in Spain and central Europe. This extension opened new avenues for conquest, income, and recruitment.

The Hospitallers

The Templars give rise to a second order of military monks called the Knights of St. John. This order sprouts from a hospital in Jerusalem that was in service before the First Crusade. The members of the order take care of pilgrims who become destitute or ill. Their hospital, which is just around the corner from the Church of the Holy Sepulcher, is an incredibly large facility that can provide care to over 2,000 patients. Existing hospital records show that it had four surgeons, four physicians, and nine "sergeants at service" to attend to the patients in the wards. Each patient has a bed to himself (a novelty in a medieval hospital), fresh meat several times a week, and white bread (to prevent an outbreak of the horrible disease known as "holy fire").

The first grand master of the Knights of St. John is Gerard of Jerusalem, a Benedictine priest, who escaped from Jerusalem at the time of the Turkish invasion. Gerard provides the crusaders with valuable information and falls into the good graces of the Christian princes. As soon as the Latin Kingdom is established, Godfrey of Bouillon endows Gerard's order and rebuilds his hospital.

As the Knights of St. John work in a hospital, the order becomes known as the Hospitallers. Like the Templars, at first they seek to protect and nurse pilgrims on the torturous passageways from port cities to Jerusalem, and later evolve into shock troops that attack Moslem outposts.

When Raymond of Le Puy becomes the new grand master in 1118, he decides that the members of his order should not only protect pilgrims but defend them. Why, he wonders, should the Templars get all the earthly and heavenly glory? His monks are fully capable of exchanging bedpans for battle-axes. He sends a petition to Rome, saying that the pilgrims need not only medical care but also military protection. The pope agrees and a second military order comes into existence. In no time at all, the Hospitallers, like the Templers, turn from policing the passageways to attacking Moslem outposts.

The rule of the Hospitallers is less strict than the rule of the Templars. They are permitted to shave their beards, to speak to one another, and even to embrace their mothers and their sisters. They wear black robes with a white cross on the left sleeve. Next to the Templars, who wear white robes with a red cross on the mantle, they seem rather colorless. Nevertheless, the Hospitallers also become wealthy beyond measure and build breathtaking fortresses in the snow-covered Amanus Mountains of Turkey, the coastal plain of Palestine, and the middle of the Syrian desert.

Laws unto Themselves

The two orders naturally hate each other. They violently clash, often turning their lances against their fellow monks after doing battle with the Saracens. The military orders come to represent uncontrollable states within the Christian Kingdom of Jerusalem. William of Tyre, a chancellor of the Kingdom, writes: "They have taken away titles and first fruits from the Church, have disturbed its possessions, and have made themselves exceedingly troublesome."

The success of these two orders gives rise to a third when German forces in Palestine form the Teutonic Knights and establish a hospital at Acre.

Crusade Aid

The Hospitallers opened convents for women in Jerusalem, Santiago, and Calatrva. The Hospitaller nuns did not engage in military activities or care for the sick. They were not allowed to leave their convents and spent their days and nights praying for the conversion of the Moslem infidels.

The Least You Need to Know

➤ The Order of the Knights Templar became the first military order of the Roman Catholic Church.

➤ The Templars were monks who lived under strict monastic rule and were obedient only to the pope.

➤ The Knights of St. John, or Hospitallers, who arose from a hospital in Jerusalem, became the second military order.

➤ The Hospitallers cared for sick pilgrims and patrolled the passageway between Jaffa and Jerusalem.

➤ Both orders attracted the support of wealthy nobles and spent lavishly on fortresses and castles.

➤ The Templars and the Hospitallers vowed to offer military protection to Christian pilgrims.

➤ Eventually, the orders became adversarial, and disdainful of the laws of the Christian Kingdom of Jerusalem.

The Wild, Wild East

When the crusaders arrive in the Holy Land, Syria and Palestine become like the wild, wild West, in which range wars are endemic. There is not a time in the twelfth century when the Christian princes are not besieging a castle, raiding a Moslem caravan, or repelling a Moslem counterattack. Of course, it is only going to be a matter of time until the Moslems finally come to their senses, gather their intestinal fortitude, and retaliate against the Western invaders. They only need one victory over the Franks and the entire Christian Kingdom of Jerusalem will be in serious trouble. The victory comes in 1119 when Frankish forces under Prince Roger of Salerno, the cousin of Tancred, set out to attack the army of Ilghazi, Emir of Mardin.

The Moslems Fight Back

Having no heirs, Tancred, on his deathbed, bequeaths the principality of Antioch to his kinsman Roger. Roger, in turn, becomes bound and determined to expand his

Crusade Aid

Bohemond was the first Prince of Antioch. He was responsible for the conquest of the city in 1098. Bohemond died a broken man at his estate in southern Italy in 1111. He bequeathed the principality of Antioch to his nephew, Tancred, who was also the Prince of Galilee. Tancred, who died of typhoid in 1112, gave the principality to Roger.

holdings in Syria until he becomes fabulously wealthy. In 1119, he hears that the Turkish army is traveling to Aleppo, where Ilghazi has been appointed Vizier. This sends Roger into a tizzy. By defeating Ilghazi's forces, he can gain control not only of Aleppo but of Mardin as well. With his Frankish head spinning with dreams of conquest (and Ilghazi's legendary harem), poor Roger makes a really stupid mistake: He decides to send Arabic messengers to inform King Baldwin II of his plans. The messengers are spies who inform not only Baldwin II but Ilghazi.

Baldwin II urges caution, but Roger is completely overcome with covetousness. He sets out with seven hundred knights and two thousand foot soldiers to engage the Turkish army of forty thousand. Talk about foolish pride! Roger believes that the Turks will be terrified by the sight of him and his knights in shining armor, and immediately scatter to the four winds. It doesn't happen that way.

Emir Ilghazi Ambushes Roger

Fifteen miles from Aleppo, the Turks pop out of a fierce desert wind (known as a *khamsin*) and ambush Roger and his men. It isn't just a defeat; it is a humiliation. The Christian knights and infantrymen are methodically—almost ritualistically—put to death like sheep in a slaughterhouse. Ibn al-Qualanisi, an Arabian chronicler who observes the massacre, writes: "In less than an hour, the Franks were lying dead. Their horses bristled like hedgehogs with arrows sticking out of them."

The battle is a medieval version of Custer's Last Stand. The Turkish army actually encircles the Christian forces with thousands of archers on horseback. Round and round Roger's camp they ride, until no knight is left standing. Poor Roger, unlike Custer, is one of the first to fall. A handful of Christians are taken prisoner and dragged through the streets of Aleppo, naked and in chains, as part of a triumphant procession. Ilghazi watches with amusement as his soldiers display ingenious means of torturing them before cutting off their heads.

Indeed, Ilghazi is so busy celebrating the first victory of the Turks over the crusaders that he neglects to seize Antioch as it stands completely defenseless. The celebration goes on for weeks. Every time the victorious sultan makes an appearance, the people break out in wild cheers and sing this ditty: "After Allah, it is Ilghazi whom we trust."

The party only comes to an end when the new hero becomes too ill to quaff another goblet of wine. Upon regaining his strength, Ilghazi goes back, not to battle but the bottle, and remains totally incoherent for several months.

By this time, King Baldwin II is bound and determined to kick this Turk's butt. Two months after the rout of Roger, he leads his forces against Ilghazi at the curious battle of Tel-Danith. Neither side can claim a decisive victory; both are badly bruised. When the fighting ceases, Baldwin II, who lacks the nerve of his uncle Bohemond, retires to Antioch to lick his wounds. Ilghazi, however, takes pleasure in tying Christian prisoners to stakes and using them for target practice.

Returning to Mardin, Ilghazi throws another victory party, drinks himself into a stupor, and chokes to death on his own vomit. The great emir dies in 1122, and there is anguished mourning throughout the Moslem world. Ilghazi was not only a great general but also a terrific party animal.

The Raging Dragon Captures the King

Ilghazi has sparked a flame within Islam that will not be extinguished. A new hero arises from the Turkish ranks: Balak, the "Raging Dragon." Balak is Ilghazi's nephew but unlike his uncle, he is a sober character who refrains from the excesses of wine, women, and song. His sole focus is to rid the Moslem world of the Christian princes and knights.

Balak is really ballsy. In 1122, he ambushes the forces of Joscelin, King Baldwin II's cousin, who has been appointed Prince of Edessa, and casts him into a dungeon in the castle of Kharput. Far from being sympathetic to his cousin's plight, Baldwin II ridicules Joscelin for his stupidity in allowing himself, a Christian prince, to be caught and carried off by a tribe of Turks. Joscelin, the king decides, deserves to rot in the dungeon, so he refuses to cough up one dinar for ransom. Instead, Baldwin II assumes the regency of Edessa and acts as though the embarrassing situation has never occurred.

Several months after arriving in Edessa, King Baldwin II goes on a hunting expedition. He rides with his falcon on his wrist and his knights at his side through a valley in the lower Euphrates. Out of nowhere, Balak's troops surround the king and his entourage and place them under arrest. The king and his company are hauled off to Kharput,

Crosscurrent

The situation within the crusader states was becoming increasingly bizarre. King Baldwin II and Count Pons had a bitter dispute in Antioch, as Pons refused to acknowledge Baldwin as his sovereign. When Pons returned to Tripoli, Baldwin II sent a small army against him.

Crusade Aid

King Baldwin II was quite unlike his worldly and sensuous uncle, King Baldwin I. He was cautious, systematic, and a scrupulous administrator who earned the nickname "the Goad." He had no liking for the trappings of royalty. He spent so much time in prayer that his knees were covered with calluses.

where they are cast into the dungeon with Joscelin, who has been cooling his heels in chains for more than two years. It isn't a very joyous reunion.

News of the incident spreads far and wide. The King of Jerusalem is the prisoner of an emir, along with the Count of Edessa. The Arab world rejoices. Allah is with them!

Christian Chronicles

While the Turks kept King Baldwin II and Count Joscelin of Edessa in dungeons, an Egyptian (Saracen) fleet attacked the port city of Acre. The Venetian Christians dispatched vessels that were decoyed to look like ships used for the transportation of pilgrims. Exulted at the prospects of booty, the Egyptians attacked the decoy ships only to find themselves in the hands of the crafty Venetians. Every Egyptian ship was captured and every Egyptian sailor put to the sword. It was the greatest naval battle in medieval history.

The Moslems Fight Each Other

Meanwhile, Balak receives word that a small army of Franks are laying siege to Tyre, the last seaport north of Ascalon still in Moslem hands. Upon arriving at the scene, Balak conducts a tour of inspection in order to concoct a battle plan. In the midst of surveying the troops and terrain, the Raging Dragon is struck in the chest by an arrow shot from his own camp. He wrenches the arrow from his body, spits in the air, and says: "This blow will be fatal for all the Moslems." Then he falls dead before his soldiers.

The Sunnis and the Shiites

The arrow was fired by an Assassin. The Assassins are mystic Shiite Moslems who believe in the divinity of the seventh Imam, Ismail ibn Jafar.

The great majority of Moslems, estimated at 85 percent, are Sunnis, while 14 percent are Shiites. For the Sunnis, an imam (leader) is simply the man who leads others in prayer on Friday. For the Shiites, the imam is the true deputy of the prophet and they developed the notion of the "hidden imam." This leader, who is not recognized by his contemporaries, will one day return as a messiah to restore the Caliphate to its true nature.

The Turks, during the time of the Crusades, are Sunnis, while the Fatimids in Egypt are Shiites. The vizier in Egypt, who considers himself a Caliph, ignores the Caliph in Baghdad, because Baghdad has fallen under the control of a Turkish governor or vizier. This takes us to the Assassins.

The Assassins

The founder and grand master of this extremist sect is a poet named Hasan as'Sabah, who has established his headquarters in the mountain fortress of Alamut (Eagle's Nest) in Northern Persia. From this stronghold, 10,000 feet above the sea, Hasan launches his campaign of terror against all Sunni Moslems. His favorite weapon is political murder. These murders have to take place in the most public of places (such as a mosque after Friday prayers) before the greatest gathering of people. Upon completion of the execution, the Assassin is expected to take his own life. Every mission, therefore, is a suicide mission.

Ismail believed that all Moslems should share their wealth and live in a state of true communism. The Assassins come to think that they can only accomplish this goal by putting to death all Sunni Islamic leaders. The Turks are Sunnis, and so they have to go along with all their accomplices, including the Caliph in Baghdad. It gets even crazier. Any Shiite leader who gets friendly with any Sunni also has to go. Islam has to be purified from the top to the bottom.

As the *Assassins* are expected to act as kamikazes, they are transformed by Hasan into an army of zombies before performing their daring deeds. Hasan has arranged his fortress like the Prophet's Paradise. In the center is a perfumed garden where naked nymphs cater to every whim of chosen candidates of the secret society. After several weeks of feasting and frolicking in Paradise, the candidates are given potent potions of hashish to drink; they are then removed from the garden. When they ask to return to the garden of pleasure, they are told that they will be readmitted to it forever, as long as they kill in the service of the grand master.

Crusade Aid

The Sunni/Shiite split within Islam arose after the prophet Mohammed's death. The Prophet's son-in-law, Ali, was the fourth Caliph or "successor" of the Arab world. Ali was murdered by Muawuya, who founded the Omayyad dynasty. Shiite means "the party of Ali." They looked upon the Sunni Caliph in Baghdad as corrupt because his power was based on the shedding of sacred blood.

Warrior Words

The youths who went out on these missions were called *hashshasheen*, or "drinkers of hashish," hence, the term **assassins**.

113

The Assassins are incredibly successful, and serve to personify the internal division within Islam. They are so opposed to Sunni Moslems, including the Turks, that they become close allies of the crusaders. Richard the Lion Heart meets with the grand master of the Assassins, "the old man of the mountain," on numerous occasions and arranges "hits" of Sunni leaders, including Saladin. Now you know who killed Balak, and you also know that Moslem sects are supportive of the crusaders. It's kind of crazy, isn't it?

When Balak is killed by an Assassin, Fulcher of Chartres, the great Christian chronicler, writes: "We all praised God because Balak, the raging dragon who had oppressed and trampled on Christianity was suffocated at last."

The Christians Recoup—And Go Native

Upon the Raging Dragon's untimely death, Tyre immediately surrenders to the Franks. The Christian army regains control of the Mediterranean coast from Egypt to Antioch. Balak is succeeded by Emir Timurtash, Ilghazi's nineteen-year-old son, who immediately releases King Baldwin II for a ransom of twenty thousand dinars. Fearful of Frankish retaliation, Emir Timurtash treats Baldwin II to a banquet, where he gives the Christian king a royal robe, a gold cap, and embroidered bushkins, like those worn by the Byzantine emperor. The Moslems again are acting like lap dogs before the Christians.

Christian Chronicles

At times, there emerged a remarkable degree of tolerance between Moslems and Christians in the Kingdom of Jerusalem. A Syrian aristocrat by the name of Usamah ibn-Munquidh wrote that Templars, whom he calls his friends, allowed him and other Moslems to worship in the al-Aqsa Mosque. On one occasion, Usamah says, a Frank turned his face to the east, saying that this was the proper direction to pray. The Christian knights apologized for the Frank's behavior by saying: "This is a stranger who just arrived from the land of the Franks and has never seen anyone praying except eastward."

The crusaders are back in control. Everything goes back to normal, with money pouring into Moslem and Christian coffers from trade markets. New generations are growing up: Franks who have been born and raised in the Middle East, who have Syrian mothers and olive skin, who live in palatial palaces in a manner that their European counterparts could not imagine. They take baths, they wear turbans, they smoke water pipes, and they act not like fierce warriors but effete Byzantines. It is shameless. When pilgrims meet the sons and daughters of the crusaders, they call them *pulani,* or "chickens."

Oh, the shame of it! The mighty crusaders have been transformed into clucking chickens. Fulcher of Chartres affirms this fact by writing:

> We, who were once Westerners, are now Easterners; a Roman or a Frenchman in this country becomes a Galilean or a Palestinian. He, who was from Rheims or Chartres, has become a citizen of Tyre or Antioch. For we have already forgotten the lands of our birth, which are unknown to many of us and never mentioned among us. Some already possess homes and households and tenants by inheritance. Some have taken wives not only of their own people but also of Syrians and Armenians or Saracens who have been granted the grace of Baptism. Those who were poor in the West, God had made rich in the East. Those who had little money there have innumerable bezants here, and a man who did not even have a house in the West now possesses a city. Why return to the West when there is an Orient like this?

It is a good question. The Kingdom of Jerusalem seems to be heaven on earth. But the days of wine and roses are coming to a blood-soaked end, and this end, weird as it may seem, will begin with an idea.

The Least You Need to Know

➤ Emir Ilghazi led the Turks to victory over Christian forces at Aleppo.

➤ Balak, Ilghazi's successor, kidnapped the king of Jerusalem and cast him into a dungeon.

➤ The Moslems are divided into Sunnis and Shiites.

➤ Balak was killed by Assassins, a Shiite terrorist group within Islam.

➤ Assassins drank hashish before committing political murders.

➤ Moslem Assassins served Christian kings.

Jihad!!!!

Zengi wants

You!!

Help to Drive out
The infidels!

Chapter 13

Jihad: Holy War Against the Franks

In This Chapter

➤ The Christians take Beirut

➤ A *jihad* against the Franks is led by Zengi

➤ Zengi is thought by many Moslems to be the *Mahdi*, or "Deliverer"

➤ Zengi lays siege to Montferrand

➤ Christian forces help the Damascus Moslems rout Zengi

➤ Edessa falls to Zengi, and the pope calls for a Second Crusade

The idea of *jihad* or "holy war" originated with the Arabs rather than the Turks. The Arabs saw the invasion of the Franks in theological rather than socioeconomic terms. Arabs had conquered the Byzantine Christians' lands in Syria, Persia, and Palestine in the "jihad," the Holy War for Islam, in the seventh century. Now the Christians were turning this idea against them. The Franks were recovering by war what the Moslems had obtained by war. Surely, there must be a new "jihad" against these invaders, a Holy War led by a Mahdi, or "Deliverer."

Soldiers of Allah vs. Soldiers of God

The Prophet Mohammed has said that the world must be subjected to Allah so that true believers (a.k.a. Moslems) can live in true brotherhood. Unbelievers who refuse to submit to the teachings of the Koran are to be put to the sword. "Take not the Jews and the Christians for friends," the Prophet teaches. "Choose not your fathers nor your brothers for friends if they take pleasure in disbelief rather than faith." Every able-bodied man is obliged to take part in the Holy War. Mohammed says: "Lo, Allah loveth those who battle for his cause. I swear by Allah that marching about, morning and evening, to fight for religion is better than the world and everything in it. Verily, the standing of one of you in the line of battle is better than supererogatory prayers performed in your house for sixty years."

Crusade Aid

In 610, at the age of 40, Mohammed was meditating in a cave when the angel Gabriel appeared and revealed to him the word of God. Several visitations followed. He began to recite what had been revealed to him to the people of Arabia. The Arabic word for "recite" is *Qur-an*, or "Koran." The Koran, the holy book of Islam, represents a collection of Mohammed's recitations.

The crusaders uphold their own notion of "jihad." They believe they are involved in a war for the glory of Jesus Christ. They wear red crosses on the right shoulder of their mantles to show they are religious warriors. They storm into battle screaming, "God wills it!" They hold the cross before the crescent, and turn mosques into Christian shrines. To many Arabs, it seems that the Christians have been sent by Allah to humiliate them for their weaknesses and failures.

In 1109, the crusaders under King Baldwin have stormed through the streets of Tripoli at the end of a siege that lasted five years. The great library at Dar al-Iim is pillaged and over a hundred thousand books are put to the torch. The contents of these works are lost forever. The Moslem inhabitants of this Syrian city are sold into slavery or exiled in the wilderness.

St. George's Arm Goes Back to Beirut

A year later, the Christians overrun Beirut, the city where St. George had killed the dragon. This time, carrying the petrified arm of St. George (a favorite relic) into the besieged city with them, they massacre the people of Islam without mercy because they have offered stubborn resistance to the Christian army.

News of the slaughter in Beirut spreads far and wide. When the crusaders appear at the gates of Sidon, the people bow before them and beg for mercy. Within eighteen short months, the Moslem world has experienced a blitzkrieg, as three of the most famous Moslem cities fall into the hands of the infidels. Observing this, Imad ed-Din, chronicler of Zengi, writes:

> I do not know whether it is pasture for wild animals or my house, my birthplace. I turn to it, my voice full of tears, my heart torn with suffering and love, and ask: "House, why did destiny pronounce such an unjust sentence on us."

The Arab world is filled with mourning and weeping. Damascus and Aleppo become crowded with refugees, who leave everything behind to flee the advancing Franks. One refugee from Maarat writes: "I come from a town that God has condemned. All the inhabitants perished. The Christians passed their blades through old men and children."

Zengi Preaches Jihad

The refugees gather in the Great Mosque of Baghdad and demand that a Moslem army be raised to rid the realm of Islam of all Christian invaders. The Caliph, who is torn between Sunnis and Shiites, is powerless to heed their pleas, but they are heard by the young slave-born Prince of Mosul, Imad ed-Din Zengi. Zengi, by the way, is a Turk, not an Arab (an Egyptian Moslem); and a Sunni, not a Shiite. Though jihad is an Arab, not a Turkish, concept, Zengi is its leader.

At Mosul, Zengi founds the Atabeg ("Father of the Prince") dynasty and seeks to extend his rule over all of Mesopotamia. He is a simple, austere soldier who can be found sleeping on a straw mat more often than in a soft bed in one of his palaces. He is a hard drinker but he demands total abstinence from his troops. He speaks of religious truth but practices political treachery. He is merciful or cruel depending on which way the wind is blowing. And he inspires fear in everyone he meets.

Zengi is also a charismatic preacher. He attracts vast masses of Turks from many princedoms with the idea of a Holy War against Christians that will bring about the utopian vision of the Prophet Mohammed. Many come to look upon him as the Mahdi even though belief in the Mahdi arose from a secret society of Shiites known as the Ismailites. The Ismailites come to believe that a Mahdi or Redeemer will be sent to unite the people of Islam and to establish a regime of justice and brotherly love on earth.

Crusade Aid

Zengi first came to prominence by crushing an uprising in Baghdad led by the Caliph, who wanted to free himself from his Seljuk overlords. As a reward, the Turkish Sultan gave Zengi control of Mosul, along with permission to lay siege to Aleppo.

Christian Chronicles

Count Fulk of Anjou was a distant kinsman of Baldwin and Godfrey of Bouillon. Baldwin chose him to be the husband for his eldest daughter, Melisende. Fulk agreed only with the stipulation that he be appointed Baldwin's successor as King of Jerusalem.

Zengi Goes on a Rampage

In 1131, King Baldwin II of Jerusalem falls ill with typhus and knows he is dying. He summons his son-in-law, Count Fulk of Anjou, to his side and anoints Fulk to serve as his successor. Having accomplished this, Baldwin II sheds his royal gowns, dresses as a common monk, and prepares to meet his Maker. In this habit, he is buried beside Godfrey and Baldwin I in the Church of the Holy Sepulcher.

Meanwhile, Zengi continues to preach the "jihad" and amass more and more Moslems to his cause. In 1137, he attacks King Fulk's army and, though Fulk knows a great deal about warfare, forces the king and his soldiers to seek shelter in the castle of Montferrand outside Tripoli. The Moslem army forms a tight ring around Montferrand and patiently waits for the Christians to starve to death.

Franks Eat Their Falcons

King Fulk manages by some miracle to smuggle out of the beleaguered fortress an urgent appeal for help to (get this) the emperor of the Byzantine Empire, John Comnena, the son of Alexis I, whose father had been denied a share in the crusader victory that installed Baldwin I as king of Jerusalem.

The wait drags on. King Fulk and the other Franks are forced to eat their horses and their falcons. The situation is becoming interminable. It is made worse when Zengi begins to bombard the castle with huge rocks and stones. The castle shakes continuously day and night without let-up. The noise is unendurable, and all the famished Christians are going stark-screaming crazy. King Fulk is unable to send out other messages and he has no idea that help from Constantinople is on the way.

Zengi, however, keeps soldiers on the lookout for relief forces and they inform him that the emperor of Byzantium is indeed on his way with a huge army. Knowing this, Zengi offers the Christians terms of surrender.

Christian Chronicles

John Comnena, emperor of Byzantium, was called "Kalojohn" by the people of Constantinople. *Kalos* means "good" or "beautiful" in Greek. He was one of the greatest of Byzantine emperors, as he regained most of Asia Minor from the Turks through a series of hard-fought campaigns that took him to the gates of Antioch, the city that Bohemond had refused to relinquish to John Comnena's father, Alexis I.

King Fulk and his knights can't believe their luck. They will agree to anything to get out of the castle. Zengi's terms are generous. They can go free as long as they pay 50,000 dinars. It seems a bargain. The Christians pay up and are allowed to leave unmolested.

Several days later, King Fulk is cursing himself for being a fool. The emperor John Comnena has arrived with a large army that could have zapped Zengi and his men like a swarm of pesky insects.

Zengi Eyes Damascus

As soon as John Comnena and his army withdraw from the area, Zengi turns his attention toward Damascus with hopes of adding the ancient city to his expanding kingdom. The vizier of Damascus, an old Turk named Unur, is not at all happy about Zengi's plans. He isn't about to turn over the keys to the city to an upstart who had been a Kurdish slave. The people of Damascus are not too pleased with the thought of a takeover either. They are happy and content under Unur, and the caravans are making oodles of dinars. Their anxieties are increased when Zengi lays siege to the nearby town of Baalbek. Zengi, having sworn on the Koran that he would spare the lives of all the defending soldiers if they surrendered, upon gaining control of the town crucifies all the soldiers and has the commander burned alive. This guy is not a man of his word, and no one in Damascus wants to be set on fire or crucified.

Franks Help Turks Foil Zengi's Plan

Unur has a *huge* problem: Where is he going to turn for help? The Moslem world is uniting behind Zengi, even proclaiming the Kurd as the Mahdi. Unur is in a terrible fix, and so are the people of Damascus, so he does something really incredible. Unur calls upon King Fulk for help. That's right. A Moslem ruler calls upon a Christian king to save himself and his citizens from the so-called Savior of Islam. It kind of makes you scratch your head. Unur offers King Fulk twenty thousand bezants a month, the restoration of a confiscated castle, and an offer of alliance in return for his help in chasing Zengi once and for all from his city. King Fulk, who has recently been fooled by Zengi, is only too happy to oblige. He immediately sets out for Damascus, and Zengi heads for the holy hills.

The weirdness of the alliance between the Moslem vizier of Damascus and the Christian king of Jerusalem is noted by William of Tyre, who writes:

> Then might have been witnessed a strange and novel sight, a hostile people encouraging their enemy to the fiercest warfare, and, as an ally, actually in arms for the destruction of a common foe, Christians and Damascenes were equal in courage and united in purpose.

Crusade Aid

Baldwin III was the first king of Jerusalem to be born in the Holy Land. His four predecessors: Godfrey of Bouillon, Baldwin I, Baldwin II, and Fulk came from the West and retained Frankish habits and prejudices.

Unur is properly grateful for the help, and, in celebration of this strange alliance, King Fulk invites Unur to attend his court. It is the first time a Moslem ruler enters the court of the king of Jerusalem. There are festivities, ceremonial exchanges of silly gifts, and formal speeches. A rather simple-minded Knight Templar, hoping to convert the old Turk to the true religion, asks Unur if he would like to see God as a child. The Vizier says that he would welcome such a sight. The knight leads Unur to a painting of the Virgin Mary with the infant Jesus on her lap. "Here," the Templar says, "is God as a child." The old Turk smiles and says nothing.

The alliance lasts longer than King Fulk. In 1142, he falls from his horse and fractures his skull. He dies several days later, leaving the throne to his 13-year-old son, Baldwin III.

Zengi, of course, has not gone away. He is just waiting for the right moment to win Damascus. But this is difficult since the Turks and the Franks remain united. Finally, he comes up with an ingenious plan. He will attack the weakest Christian outpost, Edessa. The Christians will have to hurry to save their province and then he can turn around and snatch Damascus from that old ogre Unur.

Zengi Takes Edessa

The perfect time has come to attack Edessa. The two Christian princes, Joscelin of Edessa and Raymond of Antioch, are at odds with one another to the point that "each rejoiced in the distress of the other and exulted over any untoward mischance." This means that Raymond will not come to Joscelin's aid, even though they are supposed to be Christian brothers.

In December of 1144, Joscelin leaves Edessa with his army to go on some cockamamie goose chase. The city is now defenseless. Zengi's army appears out of nowhere, sets siege engines in place, and hurls huge boulders against the massive walls of the city. It is a nightmare. The native inhabitants of Edessa, according to William of Tyre, are "utterly ignorant of the use of arms and familiar only with the business of trading. The protection of the city is entirely in the hands of mercenaries."

This would have been all well and good except for the fact that the mercenaries haven't been paid in months, and many have left the city. The soldiers are supposed to be paid by Hugo, Archbishop of Edessa, but Hugo, in the spirit of the Christian hierarchy, simply keeps the money for himself. William of Tyre notes this by writing: "Although he was said to have amassed great riches, which he might have used to pay troops for defending the city, Archbishop Hugo preferred, like a miser, to store up his wealth rather than to consider his perishing people."

Zengi has been right in his assessment of the temperament of the Christian nobles. Receiving word of the siege, Prince Raymond of Antioch refuses to come to the aid of the people of Edessa. Joscelin has personally offended him and has refused to apologize.

But Zengi has been wrong in his belief that he could take possession of Edessa in a few days. The walls are thick and impregnable. The boulders bounce off them like ping-pong balls. A siege that should have taken four days has taken four weeks and the walls are still standing.

Finally, Zengi orders that massive tunnels be furrowed beneath the walls. After great mounds of dirt are removed, the tunnels are fortified by wooden props and beams. On Christmas Eve, the support posts are covered with animal fat, sulfur, and naphtha and set on fire. The props and beams collapse, along with portions of the great protective walls, and Zengi's troops pour into Edessa.

The desperate citizens seek support in a citadel, but Archbishop Hugo has the doors locked against them. In the panic that follows, women and children are trampled to death. The remaining citizens are rounded up by the invading Moslems. The Latin Christians are separated from the Byzantine Christians and put to death in accordance with Zengi's orders. Among the victims is the ignoble Archbishop. Hugo's attendants and priests are hacked to pieces as they chant prayers and hold up relics of the holy martyrs.

Count Joscelin, according to Archbishop William of Jerusalem, is a small man with an "evil" face ravaged by pockmarks. He has bulging eyes and a monstrous nose and is "licentious, dissolute, and often drunk." While Zengi is attacking his city, Joscelin remains in a faraway fortress, where he spends his time drinking wine and playing dice.

Crusade Aid

Although Prince Raymond of Antioch adamantly refused to come to the aid of Edessa, Queen Melisende, the wife of dearly departed King Fulk, sent a sizeable army to ward off Zengi's attack, but it arrived too late to do any good.

Crosscurrent

The people of Damascus blamed the Archbishop Hugo for the Christmas Eve massacre. William of Tyre wrote this: "An unsavory reputation will ever be affixed to the memory of Archbishop Hugo. For terrible are the words of Scripture concerning men of his sort: 'Thy money shall perish with thee.'"

Eastern Christians Spared

Every Latin church in Edessa is sacked, pillaged, and set ablaze, but the Armenian, Jacobite, and Greek churches are left untouched. In this way, Zengi makes it clear that the jihad is directed against the Franks and not all Christians.

To show his magnanimity toward Orthodox Christians, Zengi drapes his robe around an old bishop of the Jacobite Church who is being dragged naked from the city by a rope. Asked about his future loyalty, the bishop says that anyone who could be loyal to the Franks could be loyal to anyone. Zengi then invites the bishop to serve in his administration.

Zengi's Triumph Rocks the Latin World

Zengi becomes hailed as the righteous arm of Allah. In minarets throughout the Arab world, his name is honored and his deeds memorialized. Overnight, he accumulates over a hundred titles. The chronicler Ibn al-Qalanisi verifies this by writing: "Imad ed-Din Zengi, the champion of Islam, the emir, the general, the just, the servant of God, the triumphant. The unique, the pillar of religion, the cornerstone of Islam, the protector of Allah's creatures, the associate of the dynasty, the auxiliary of defense, the ornament of Islam, the grandeur of nations, the honor of kings, the supporter of sultans, the victor over infidels, the commander of Moslem armies, the victorious king, the king of princes, the sun in the deserving ...."

In Jerusalem, the Christian nobles cannot believe that a Moslem upstart has conquered a mighty Christian city. They speculate that Zengi must have Frankish or Teutonic blood flowing through his veins. Stories begin to circulate that Zengi's mother had been Ida, a famously beautiful Germanic princess who had been kidnapped while bathing in the river Eregli and cast into the harem of Zengi's father.

The news of the fall of Edessa rocks the Latin world. Pope Eugenius III immediately sends out a call for the Second Crusade. One of the great debacles of the Middle Ages is about to unfold.

The Least You Need to Know

➤ The concept of "jihad" originated with the Arabs, not the Turks.

➤ Moslem refugees in Baghdad cried out for retaliation against the Christian invaders.

➤ Zengi, the son of a slave and a Turk, became the leader of the "jihad," and many Moslems looked upon him as the Mahdi, the Redeemer of Islam.

➤ Zengi trapped King Fulk of Jerusalem in a castle at Montferrand and received a kingly ransom.

➤ The rampages of Zengi compelled the vizier of Damascus to form an alliance with the Christian King of Jerusalem.

➤ Zengi conquered the Christian Principality of Edessa, but killed only the Latin Christian population.

➤ The fall of Edessa led to the Second Crusade.

Part 4

The Second Crusade: A Dream of Kings

This is not a rerun of the First Crusade. It's a true sequel, with a stunning ending. This section, for sheer sensationalism, will feature raw sex, black magic, oodles of blood and guts and, believe it or not, an honest-to-goodness medieval romance. It will relate the genesis of modern Middle Eastern problems, the unification of Sunni Turks with Saracen Egyptians, the promise of jihad, the formation of the Assassins, and the rise of a remarkable Kurd called Saladin. Want to go off on another adventure? Read on.

Chapter 14

A Medieval Million-Man March

In This Chapter

➤ A prosperous Europe has reason to march to the Holy Land

➤ St. Bernard sells the Second Crusade

➤ Two kings lead almost a million Christians to the East

➤ Turks crush the Christians at Dorylaeum and Antalya

➤ The Eastern Emperor leaves the crusaders stranded

➤ Prince Raymond and Queen Eleanor play house in Antioch

➤ The Christians decide to attack their only Moslem ally

It is the middle of the twelfth century. The news that Edessa is lost strikes the Latin world like a thunderbolt. Pope Eugenius III sounds the alarm. All able-bodied Christians are needed to come to the aid of the Holy Land. But the pope is unable to drum up much support for his campaign. He is enmeshed in a terrible revolt within Rome. A group of rabble-rousers under a troublesome priest called Ademar insist that the Catholic cardinals and bishops should relinquish their riches and return to the ideal of apostolic poverty. Everyone laughs at these crazy demands until the trouble-makers seize St. Peter's Cathedral, turn it into a people's palace, take possession of the Vatican and its treasures, and levy taxes on all priests and pilgrims. The frazzled pope has to flee to Pisa, while commoners inhabit the Lateran Palace.

All hell is breaking loose within Christendom: rebellion in Rome and upheaval abroad. Eugenius III pleads with the nobles to come to his aid and to help him restore order and decency to the Holy Roman Empire. He also urges them to embark on a Crusade to save Edessa.

High Times Back at Home

The pope's words fall on deaf ears. Small wonder. The nobles are becoming fat and complacent. The idea of trekking off to kill Turks is no longer tantalizing to them. Trade in Europe is flourishing and the quality of life on the manor is improving at a dramatic rate. Even the damp, drafty castles are becoming quite comfortable. Tapestries hang on the walls, and in some of them, carpets cover the floors. Many of the nobles sleep on feathered pillows. They wear shirts of white linen with showy collars and cuffs, leather tunics, capes with cowls, robes lined with ermine, and velvet hats. Well-born ladies wear long linen chemises, covered by full-trimmed robes that reached to the floor. They also walk about with jeweled girdles, silk purses, and chamois-skin gloves. Often the ladies wear flowers in their hair, or bind their tresses with fillets of jeweled silk. They're becoming fashion plates.

After banquets, the lords and ladies are entertained by jugglers, tumblers, minstrels, and fools. Some of the fools are really funny and tell risqué stories about other members of the nobility. At the end of the evening, musical vagabonds called troubadours sing songs. Everyone is having a jolly good time. The nobles take baths on a regular basis and sprinkle their bodies with perfume. Believe it or not, they actually smell good. It's unfortunate that they don't bother to brush their teeth.

The food is better. It is widely believed that pork causes leprosy, but that doesn't lessen the taste for it. Lordly hosts have whole pig roasts brought to the table to carve before their hungry guests. Along with pork, the medieval lords and ladies regularly dine on mutton, lamb, partridge, quail, peacock, and crane. Everything is tasty because cooks use spices and seasonings such as mustard, sage, savory, anise, garlic, and dill—thanks to the Crusades. Cookbooks are beginning to come into vogue.

With prosperity comes, sad to say, a rise in promiscuity. Pederasty (another word for homosexual activity), which had been effectively repressed by the Roman Church, suddenly crops up as a problem within medieval Christendom. This, no doubt, is a result of many factors: the Crusades, the influx of Eastern ideas, and the unisexual isolation of nuns and monks. Henry, the Abbot of Clairvaux, surveying the moral situation in France, writes: "Ancient Sodom is springing up from the ashes." The Knight of La Tour-Landry mourns

Christian Chronicles

Plucking up his courage, Pope Eugenius III returned to Rome in the garb of a humble penitent. He regained his throne, confined himself to spiritual functions, and began giving away a great deal from the papal treasury to the poor. In this way, he regained the support of the people.

about the prevalence of fornication among aristocratic youth. He says that knights and squires openly fornicate "in church, nay, even on the altar." This good knight also tells of "two queens who took their foul delight and pleasance within the church during a divine worship service."

St. Bernard Plays Barker

Times have definitely changed. People are becoming permissive and indolent. For this reason, the Second Crusade would never have happened except for the appearance of a master salesman by the name of Bernard of Clairvaux.

St. Bernard is an ascetic. He fasts so long that the abbot of his monastery must command him to eat. His residence is a cramped cell at Clairvaux with a pile of hay for a bed and a cut in the wall for a chair.

This guy is an incredible preacher. He can hold vast crowds in the palm of his hand for hours. What's more, he can perform miracles. For this reason, epileptics, paralytics, and other ailing Christians seek him out wherever he speaks.

St. Bernard of Clairvaux cares nothing for science or philosophy. The mind of man, he teaches, is too infinitesimal to comprehend the whole of creation. He scorns the silly pride of schoolmen who speak of the nature, origin, and destiny of the universe. He says that true wisdom is to walk unquestionably and gratefully in the miracle of revelation.

Eugenius III, recognizing talent, turns to Bernard to pitch the Crusade. On March 31, 1146, the loquacious monk mounts a stage in a field outside Vezelay in Burgundy and delivers his first Crusade sermon to a large crowd. Bernard tells them that the situation is dire; that the Latin Kingdom is falling apart; that Edessa has been captured by Turks; that Christians have been slaughtered in the streets; that Christian altars have been defiled; that holy relics have been tossed into a fire; and that soon the Holy City of Jerusalem will be in the hands of the infidels. Immediate action, he says, is required. All true believers must respond to the call to arms. They must turn from their homes and hearths and march off to Jerusalem.

Crusade Aid

London in the twelfth century had rows of bordellos, or "stews," near London Bridge. They were officially licensed by the Bishop of Winchester and sanctioned by Parliament. An act of Parliament in 1161 forbade brothel keepers to maintain women suffering from the "perilous infirmity of burning." This is the first known legislation against venereal disease.

Christian Chronicles

Despite St. Bernard's flair for graceful speech, he cared little for worldly beauty. He covered his eyes for fear they would take too much sensual pleasure from the lakes of Switzerland. His abbey was bare of all ornamentation except the crucified Christ.

There is no time to waste. The fate of Holy Mother Church is at stake. Islam has a death grip on the Bride of Christ. What could be more horrible? Anyone who fails to respond to the Crusade incurs the grievous sin of omission and the penalty of everlasting suffering. Never in the history of the Church has the situation been more perilous, not even during the time of the early persecutions, not even when Urban II preached the First Crusade.

His words are electric. Women swoon, old people weep, children cry, and young men enlist. So many mob the stage to take up the Cross that Bernard, as a grand and highly dramatic gesture, rips off his robe and cuts it into cloth crosses for the new recruits.

Everywhere Bernard travels the effect is the same. It's almost as if the monk can create mass hysteria by means of mass hypnotism. When he arrives at a town or village, "mothers hide their sons and wives hide their husbands." But this is to no avail. Through Bernard's words, crusader fever sweeps over all of France and spreads to England.

The Offer No One Could Refuse

Of course, the sales pitch wouldn't work without sensational offers, and Bernard is a master in presenting them. He tells the crowds: "If you are a prudent merchant, if you are a man fond of acquiring the world's goods, the Holy War will provide great markets and great opportunities." But this is only part of the package. The real bargain is instantaneous salvation. The crusaders will inherit not only the world and all of its riches but also the Kingdom of God. "God," he said, "will award to those fighting for him the richest of wages: the remission of sins and everlasting glory."

If you see things properly, Bernard argues, the fall of Edessa is not just a setback for the Church; it's a rare opportunity for believers. "This," he says, "is a plan not made by man, but a plan that comes from heaven and that proceeds from divine love." No doubt about it! This is a once-in-a-lifetime deal, guaranteed by God Himself. You can't afford to refuse.

Bernard whips up support for the Second Crusade not only from peasants, merchants, and local nobles, but also from mighty kings and queens. One king, who had fallen under Bernard's spell several months before the sermon at Vezelay, is Louis VII of France.

Christian Chronicles

Louis VII was devoutly religious and attended all church services as though his very life depended on it. He seemed more like a priest than a king. He liked to talk familiarly with his subjects and played the part of a "man's man." But the role was not very convincing. People found him stiff and artificial.

Louis VII: A Loser

Louis VII comes to the throne in 1137 at the age of sixteen. By that time, he is already married to Eleanor of Aquitaine, one of the great medieval women. Eleanor is witty, intelligent, lovely, and almost totally unscrupulous. The marriage is not a match made in heaven. Louis is her polar opposite. He's dull, stolid, unattractive, gravely absorbed in affairs of state, and he hates to dance. To make matters worse, Louis is somewhat "simple-minded."

This last quality becomes evident by a quarrel he has with Count Thibault of Champagne. The king invades the count's territory with a large army and, during a windstorm, sets Thibault's castle on fire. The fire quickly spreads to the village and then to the church where the villagers have sought refuge. The roof collapses and thirteen hundred of the king's subjects burn to death. Louis VII falls into deep despair and becomes physically ill. Bernard is called to heal him. The saint does heal him, but he also tells Louis that he must perform an act of profound penance for his sin. And what could be a more suitable display of faith and repentance than a glorious Crusade?

Another King Takes the Bait

After gaining support for the Crusade throughout Burgundy, Lorraine, and Flanders, Bernard heads off to Germany to recruit the Holy Roman Emperor, Conrad III. Not only does Bernard use his standard sales pitch, but he also informs Conrad that the Holy Crusade will be a great way to unite his divided kingdom. Conrad III falls for the pitch, hook, line, and sinker.

What a coup! Bernard, a lowly monk, has recruited two great kings to lead his Crusade, and he's amassed the largest Christian army ever assembled! Hundreds of thousands of nobles, knights, merchants, workers, peasants, and priests have joined the ranks of the Holy Army. "Cities and castles are empty," Bernard writes to Pope Eugenius, "there is not left one man to seven women, and everywhere there are widows to still living husbands."

Christian Chronicles

According to William of Tyre, King Conrad of Germany melted before one of St. Bernard's harangues. Bernard assumed the voice of Christ and thundered this question in Conrad's ear: "Man, what could I do for you that I have not done already?" Not able to come up with an answer, the king burst into tears and took the Crusader's Cross without further hesitation.

The First Million-Man March

At Easter of 1147, King Conrad III and the German army set out for Constantinople. At Pentecost, King Louis VII and the French follow, not sure if the Turks are really worse foes than the Germans. News of the approaching Christian armies fills the Arab world with fear and trembling. Ibn al-Qalanisi writes in his chronicles:

Reports kept coming in—from Constantinople, from the territory of the Franks, and from neighboring lands, too—that the kings of the Franks were on their way from their countries to attack the land of Islam. They had emptied their own provinces, leaving them devoid of defenders, and had brought with them riches, treasures, and immeasurable material. They numbered, it was said, many a million foot soldiers and mounted knights, perhaps even more.

But this first million-man march (it's really several hundred thousand) is not without women. Hungry for adventure, Queen Eleanor accompanies her dull husband on the grand march to Palestine. Eleanor and her attendants don male and martial costumes and become the first medieval cross-dressers.

Crosscurrent

Before setting out for Jerusalem, the German Crusaders again massacred hundreds of Jews and stole their possessions. Their actions were prompted by one of Bernard's monks, a fanatical anti-Semite. Bernard was summoned to restore order. Many German nobles joined Conrad III on the Second Crusade. One was the young Frederick of Swabia, who would become Frederick Barbarossa, a leader of the Third Crusade.

The queen and her ladies are not the only women in the large army. The counts of Flanders and Toulouse also bring along their countesses. The baggage train for the French women is heavy with trunks and boxes of apparel and cosmetics to ensure the loveliness of the ladies in all kinds of climes.

There is also an army of women within the regular army, and this army is more dangerous in the eyes of prelates than the combined forces of the Turks and Saracens. "The Crusaders," writes Albert of Aix, "had in their ranks a crowd of women wearing the habit of men; they traveled together without distinction of sex, trusting to the chances of a frightful promiscuity."

This Crusade is not a response to a call from the emperor of Byzantium. The Byzantines had quite enough of the crusaders with the first group; they look upon the arrival of the new army with trepidation. As expected, the crusaders do not disappoint them. In the Byzantine city of Philippopolis, a local magician tries to make an honest buck by performing some tricks for the Germans. He is so convincing that King Conrad and his men believe he's a warlock, and set a torch to the suburbs of the peaceful little town.

Déjà vu *All Over Again?*

(Stop! you're thinking. This Crusade is a mere rerun of the First Crusade: the same stirring sermon, the same assembly of a grand army, the same massacre of the Jews, the same misbehavior in Byzantium. Be patient. This Crusade is a real, honest-to-goodness sequel, and in a page or two, it will get really ugly.)

At Constantinople, Emperor Manuel, like his grandfather Alexis I, wines and dines the German troops with great opulence in an effort to persuade Conrad to move on to Nicea without waiting for the arrival of the French. As an incentive, the emperor pledges back-up support, supplies, and his crack guide, Stephen, who will lead them through Asia Minor. Conrad, anxious for conquest, packs up his army, crosses the Bosphorus, and heads off for the Holy Land. Manuel is greatly relieved.

When the Germans near Dorylaeum (the site of the first great battle between the Christians and the Turks), Stephen, the sneaky Greek guide, deserts them. The Germans are fit to be tied. They rant and rave about the deceitfulness of the Byzantine emperor and make plans to sack Constantinople. According to William of Tyre:

> It was common talk, and probably quite true, that these perilous wanderings were devised with the knowledge and at the command of the Greek Emperor who has always envied the successful advance of Christians. For it is well known that the Greeks have always looked with distrust on all increase of power by the western nations, especially by that of the Teutonic nations, as rivals of the empire. They take it ill that the King of the Teutons calls himself the Emperor of. the Romans. For thereby he seems to detract too much from the prestige of their own Emperor.

The Turks Turn Up Everywhere

Lost in the wilderness area of Dorylaeum, the Germans are ambushed by a large Turkish army. The Germans are tired and thirsty; the Turks fresh and alert. Weighed down by their oppressive armor, the Christians are unable to engage the Turks in close combat. In no time at all, "the great Christian army, whose arms and strength, courage and number, seemed beyond compare, suddenly collapsed." Less than one tenth of the mighty army escape with King Conrad. Several weeks later, after much pain and suffering, the remains of the army finally straggle from the desert to the city of Nicea.

At Nicea, King Louis VII catches up with what remains of the German army. Conrad III is delirious (not with happiness to see the French King, whom he despises, but with a high fever) and has to be shipped back to Constantinople, where Emperor Manuel, who is skilled in medicines, treats him and restores him to health. Knowing the emperor's

Crusade Aid

Tens of thousands of German crusaders were slaughtered by the Turks at Dorylaeum. The German booty, including the possessions taken from massacred Jews, was sold in the bazaars of the Near East for many months. The women and children were sold into slavery at a premium. Slaves with blond hair and blue eyes were very desirous to desert chieftains.

true feelings toward the German king, one must assume that Manuel, as a good Greek, feels bound by the Hippocratic oath.

Now the French army journeys from Nicea to the city of Antalya on the Mediterranean coast. This route takes them over the rugged and snow-covered Taurus Mountains that seem to touch the sky. After much travail, they reach the southern slope where they pitch their tents for a night's rest. It is a terrible decision. The Turks have infested the mountaintops and rain arrows and spears down on the campers. Heavy stones and tree trunks follow. There is general pandemonium. Louis VII is almost killed as he single-handedly fights a group of descending Turks. According to a chronicler, the king hacks off a score of heads that bounce from the cliffs and crags to the valley below. This will become the French king's one shining moment.

At Antalya, the crusaders expect to be met by a fleet of ships from Byzantium that are supposed to transport the army to Antioch. But the fleet provided by the emperor is far smaller than expected. Instead of two hundred ships, Manuel sends five! Even worse, the ships carry few supplies. The French have received the proverbial shaft from the Eastern emperor, and they're steaming.

Crosscurrent

The crusaders accused the Byzantine Emperor Manuel Comnena of breaking promises, bad advice, and treachery. The Byzantine authorities in Asia Minor were even accused of failing to act when the Turks swept down from the hills and raided the crusaders. Most scholars now agree that the Eastern Emperor did plot the demise of the Second Crusade by failing to provide provisions and supplies.

The situation, in fact, is downright intolerable. The crusaders can't stay at Antalya and they can't sail for Antioch. The Greek shipowners demand a small fortune for each passenger. The nobles do the noble thing; they pay for passage for themselves and leave hundreds of thousands of foot soldiers and unarmed pilgrims to the mercy of the Turks. However, King Louis shows a measure of kindness by giving the governor of Antalya a small purse of 500 marks to provide some care for his abandoned army.

As soon as the ships set sail for Antioch, the good governor of Antalya locks the crusaders outside the city walls, where they have little or no chance of survival. These wretched creatures—starving, leaderless, and unprotected by knights, attempt to make their way to Antioch and safety and disappear from the pages of history.

Interlude in Antioch

King Louis, the nobles, and the ladies arrive in Antioch on March 19, 1148, where they are greeted with "the greatest magnificence." Prince Raymond, the Christian ruler of the city, is a nobleman from England. He became a prince by marrying Constance, the nine-year-old daughter of dearly deceased King Fulk and Queen

Melisende, the daughter of Baldwin II. Sources say that he was not pleased to spend his spare time with his wife in a sandbox.

Christian Chronicles

The governor of Antalya closed the city gates to the French because the citizens were running low in provisions. The surrounding countryside was occupied by the Turks and the sole source of supplies came from the sea. With the Eastern Emperor's refusal to send a full fleet of ships came the specter of famine for the people of Antalya. And with the governor's refusal to open the gates came the certainty of death for the Franks.

Prince Raymond believes that the arrival of the army will permit him to curb the rising power of Nur ed-Din, the successor of Zengi, whose career ended early (see Chapter 15, "Damascus Mystery: A Crusade Disappears!"). According to William of Tyre, Raymond …

> … felt a lively hope that with the assistance of the king and his troops, he would be able to subjugate the neighboring cities of Aleppo, Shaizar, and several others. For the arrival of King Louis had brought such fear to our enemies that now they not only distrusted their own strength but even despaired of life itself.

Prince Raymond is not only the son-in-law of the late King Fulk but also the uncle of Eleanor of Aquitaine, King Louis's lovely wife, and he is truly delighted to meet her for the first time in the flesh. The new arrivals are treated to great feasts, luxurious quarters, and nightly entertainment by jugglers and musicians. It is spring. The sap is rising. The birds are singing. And love is in the air.

Soon Prince Raymond and Queen Eleanor begin to exchange glances that are neither familial nor avuncular. This is not surprising. Eleanor is a lusty 28 and Raymond a randy 49. Who can blame them for a little slap and tickle? After all, Eleanor's husband refuses to have sex for the duration of the Holy Crusade and Raymond's wife is still playing with dolls.

Uncle and niece meet in every dark corner of the Prince's palace, and sounds of laughter and lovemaking echo through the chamber rooms, the kitchen, the great hall, and even the chapel. The affair becomes the talk of the town and King Louis is seen as a silly old cuckold. When finally reproached by a count for her scandalous conduct, Eleanor quips, "I expected to marry a man, but I ended up with a monk." Everyone laughs but Louis.

The situation continues. The moans, coos, and cries of the lovers fill the corridors morning, noon, and night, and Louis remains the subject of repressed smiles and muffled laughter.

At last, Prince Raymond actually decides to address the matter of the Crusade. He says that the Christian army should set off to attack Aleppo, the headquarters of Nur ed-Din. This made sense. The army has traveled three thousand miles to suppress the Moslem menace, and Aleppo remains vulnerable to a carefully calculated attack.

Crosscurrent

Neglected or chided by Louis, Eleanor of Aquitaine opened her bedchambers to numerous lovers. Louis bore these dalliances and her sharp tongue with infinite patience (he was terrified of her), but St. Bernard condemned her as a wanton adulteress. In 1152, she sued Louis for divorce claiming they were related in the sixth degree. The Church approved her petition.

But guess what? Louis nixes the idea. He says that his first priority is to visit the holy tomb in Jerusalem and join in the celebration of a solemn Mass. "A Mass!" Raymond shrieks. "You must be mad. You're not here for a Mass but for a massacre!"

Eleanor sides with Raymond and chides Louis for his failure to take the appropriate action. The argument goes on and on. Finally, Louis says that his mind is made up and that he and his army will head off for the Holy Land in the morning. Hearing this, Eleanor tells Louis to make the trip without her because she has no intention of leaving Antioch no matter what her monk of a husband says or does!

That night, Louis and his knights storm Raymond's palace, kidnap the screaming queen, and set sail for Acre. Eleanor is irate and vows to file for divorce. The king allows her to rant and rave without comment until the happy couple finally arrives in Jerusalem.

A Preposterous Plan

King Conrad III, now in excellent health, also shows up in the Holy City, and the two Christian kings from the West attend a great council at the court of Queen Melisende and her son, the newly crowned King Baldwin III. At the council, the nobility consider how "they might endeavor to enlarge the Kingdom and add to the glory of the Christian name." What should they do? Should they attack the Saracens in Cairo? The caliph in Baghdad? The Turks at Aleppo? After several days, it is decided that they should attack the one Moslem city that is in alliance with the Christian Kingdom. They should lay siege to Damascus, the city whose friendship is necessary for their survival, and oust Unur, the one Emir with whom they were united.

The Second Crusade has gone crazy.

> ### The Least You Need to Know
>
> ➤ St. Bernard of Clairvaux was the spokesman and salesman of the Second Crusade.
>
> ➤ The Second Crusade was led by two kings: Louis VII of France and Conrad III of Germany.
>
> ➤ Almost a million Christians, including women, set out to save Edessa and to fortify the Holy Land.
>
> ➤ The German army suffered a terrible defeat at Dorylaeum.
>
> ➤ The Eastern Emperor, Manuel Comnena, failed to provide provisions, supplies, and ships for the crusaders.
>
> ➤ Hundreds of thousands of crusaders were left for dead at Antalya.
>
> ➤ The crusaders, for some unfathomable reason, made plans to attack, not the Turks at Edessa, but their own Moslem allies at Damascus.

Chapter 15

Damascus Mystery: A Crusade Disappears!

In This Chapter

➤ Zengi gets zapped and his son, Nur ed-Din, takes over

➤ The crusaders are victorious at Damascus

➤ The Christian army makes a puzzling retreat

➤ The Second Crusade self-destructs

While the crusaders plan to attack Damascus, their only friend and ally in the Middle East, major developments are occurring in the Moslem world. The Moslems are intoxicated with "jihad" and the triumphs of Zengi. They want to launch a counter-Crusade that will cast the crusaders into the garbage heap of world history.

Zengi's Son Takes Up the Banner

Zengi, a great general, has led the Turks to the glorious victory in Edessa. He has caused a panic in the Western world. He's united tribes and nations that had been divided for hundreds of years. He has been hailed as the Mahdi, or Deliverer, but he is also a hopeless alcoholic.

Zengi is a simple and austere man, but as soon as he's alone, Zengi uncorks the wine and drinks himself into a stupor.

Like most Moslem leaders, Zengi employs a good number of eunuchs. Eunuchs are a necessary appendage to every collection of wives and concubines (known as "harems"). If you want your very own eunuch, you have to purchase one at a slave market or from a friendly caliph. They come at extremely high prices.

One night, after a particularly heavy night of drinking, Zengi opens his eyes to see one of his sneaky eunuchs drinking from his wine goblet. He murmurs some threat and falls back to sleep. The eunuch is terrified. He knows that the great man would have his head for the heedless sip. And so, as Zengi starts to snore, the eunuch withdraws his dagger and stabs him repeatedly, until the hope of Islam is dead.

Crusade Aid

A wealthy Moslem often had as many as 100 wives and 200 concubines. Wives often gave their husbands concubines as presents on special occasions. Concubines were trained by slave dealers in music, song, and seduction. The average price for a good one was $500,000.

The Damascus Debacle

Zengi is succeeded by Nur ed-Din, his son, who never drinks anything stronger than herbal tea. According to the chronicler Ibn al-Athir: "Nur ed-Din was a tall, swarthy man with a beard but no moustache. He had a fine forehead and a pleasant appearance enhanced by beautiful, melting eyes."

The Moslem chronicler Kemal ad-Din writes that Nur ed-Din "abandoned luxurious garments and instead covered himself with rough cloth." The new Turkish ruler further insisted on calling himself not Nur ed-Din (Light of Religion) but plain, Mahmud. Before battle, he would pray: "O God, grant victory to Islam and not to Mahmud. Who is this dog Mahmud to merit victory?"

From the very moment that he comes to power, Nur ed-Din expresses his goals in the slogan: "Jihad and unity." He is bound and determined to bring all of the Middle East, including Egypt, under his domination. He even has a pulpit built in Aleppo, ready and waiting to be installed in the al-Aqsa Mosque when he conquers Jerusalem.

By the time the Second Crusade gets underway, most of Syria is under Nur ed-Din's control. The principal holdout remains Damascus. This is the major block to unification and the triumph of Islam over the Christian invaders. And he will stop at nothing to achieve his goal.

Unur, the governor of Damascus, doesn't want to lose control of the city. This is why he forges an alliance with the Christians. Damascus represents the one city in the Moslem world that poses no threat to the Kingdom of Jerusalem. This is why we have to scratch our heads over the decision of the crusaders to undermine the power of their one and only ally.

As the Christians march against Damascus, Nur ed-Din sits and watches from his fortress at Aleppo with a broad smile on his face. The action is so contrary to rhyme and reason that it has to be caused by the will of Allah. The crusaders have decided to defeat themselves.

The situation at Damascus now sets the stage for one of the most incomprehensible moments in the annals of mankind.

The Crusaders Take a Wrong Turn

One side of Damascus is surrounded by orchards of fruit trees that stretch out for five or six miles in the direction of Lebanon. The trees are closely planted together and the orchard appears as a dark, impenetrable forest. The other sides of the city offer no such protection. They are accessible to attack.

Guess which way the crusaders decide to launch their assault? They head straight through the dark and narrow paths of the orchards so that the defenders of the city can cause a ceaseless rain of arrows to fall upon them.

Over 10,000 crusaders—one third of the great army—wander into the orchards, and over half are slaughtered before the end of the first day of fighting. The regular militia of Damascus has been fortified by thousands of Turkish volunteers eager to fight for the faith.

Christian Chronicles

The conquest of Damascus was the secret desire of Queen Melisende, the Queen of Jerusalem. She was a close friend of Conrad III and may have forced her desire upon him. Strategically, an attack on Nur ed-Din's fortress at Aleppo (the plan advanced by Raymond of Antioch) made much more sense.

Describing the orchards surrounding Damascus, William of Tyre writes:

> To indicate the limits of each orchard and also to prevent trespassers entering at will, these groves are enclosed by walls of mud. The vast number of trees planted close together and the very narrow paths make it difficult—nay, almost impossible—for anyone to approach Damascus from that side

The next day, the crusaders again attempt to plow through the thick orchards. Again, they are met by a downfall of arrows. When they get close to the walls, the crusaders are stabbed by sharp lances that are thrust through peepholes. As they turn a corner to approach the main gate, a militia of Damascenes rushes out to greet them with swords and spears. It is another bloodbath. Conrad III, the king of Germany, becomes so frustrated that he morphs into a one-man army. He rushes at the enemy swinging his broadsword like a madman. With one blow, he not only cuts off a soldier's head, but his entire neck and left shoulder, with the arm attached. No one has ever seen such a sight. He has almost hacked a man in half with one blow—and his foe was wearing a full breastplate of heavy armor. The other Germans, inspired by the king, become killing machines, hacking the defenders to bits and pieces.

The savagery of the German attack causes panic among the Damascenes, who retreat behind the city walls with their tails between their legs. They are filled with fear. The crusading army now stands before the gates of Damascus. The people are ready to surrender. Unur declares that all is lost. They expect the appearance of catapults and battering rams. They cry out to Allah. And a remarkable thing happens: At the very moment of victory, the crusaders retreat to an uncultivated plain beneath the eastern walls of the city.

What's going on? No one seems to know. As soon as the crusaders pitch camp, the three Christian kings—Louis, Conrad, and Baldwin—have a ferocious argument. They can't decide who should be granted the honor of breaking through the gates and entering the city. Should it be Louis who led the greatest army in this Crusade and suffered the most terrible losses? Should it be Conrad who displayed such bravery in the field of battle? Should it be Baldwin, who is the king of Jerusalem and, by extension, the sovereign of Damascus? The first king to enter the city not only will achieve glory in heaven and earth but also the right to a lion's share of the booty. The argument intensifies and it goes on for hours, days, weeks.

Crosscurrent

The decision of the crusaders to abandon their hard-won position in the orchards and reestablish a position on the open plain of the city to the east shows that there was no military strategist in that Christian force. The Moslems reoccupied the orchards almost immediately, while the Christians found themselves on a site without water that faced the strongest section of the city wall.

The Christians Decline Their Victory

Then the strangest of all strange things happens. The crusaders retreat from the city and head back to Jerusalem. Why? They've achieved their objective; they have (for all intents and purposes) conquered the city. They've attained (after the agony of inglorious defeats) a moment of triumph. But they withdraw in haste as the people of Damascus gape in surprise and wonder. Allah has delivered them!

As the Christian army packed up their bags and slunk away "in miserable confusion and disorder" they were harassed every step of their way back to Jerusalem by Damascene archers. The route became littered with corpses of men and horses. "The bodies smelled so powerfully that the birds almost fell out of the sky," wrote one chronicler.

An Unsolved Mystery

As soon as the Christians leave, Unar and the people of Damascus begin negotiations with Nur ed-Din. The city falls under his rule and the Turks remain united under the rallying cry of "jihad and unity." The Christians have accomplished for the Moslems something that they could not accomplish for themselves: They have strengthened and unified the Islamic world. Incredible as it may seem, the Second Crusade has not merely failed. It has backfired.

What went horribly wrong for the crusaders at Damascus? Why did they retreat in shame at the moment of victory? No one knows. But some historians have come up with possible explanations:

➤ The tension between the three kings became so insurmountable that they could no longer remain in military alliance.

➤ King Baldwin III may have been bribed by Unur, the ruler of Damascus, to encourage the Franks to break camp with talk of the approach of a Turkish army.

➤ The kings may have thought that they lacked the manpower to hold the city after the conquest.

The chronicler William of Tyre says that he "often interviewed wise men and those whose memory of those times is still fresh" to unearth a sensible explanation. But he never obtains one.

Asked for an explanation for the retreat by Queen Melisende, Conrad III says that he "perceived the Lord had withdrawn favor from him." He boards a ship to take him and the remainder of his men back to Europe.

King Louis stays in the Holy Land for almost a year, saying that it is necessary for him to celebrate Easter at the Church of the Holy Sepulcher. He, along with his nobles and the ladies, boards a Sicilian ship and sets sail for Italy. As a final humiliation, the Sicilian ships are attacked by the Byzantine navy at Peloponnesse, and Louis's troublesome wife Eleanor is carried off to Constantinople where she is held for ransom. Louis makes another terrible mistake by coming up with the cash.

When news of the collapse of the Second Crusade reaches Europe, a German monk in Wurzburg condemns the undertaking as the work of the devil and denounces Bernard of Clairvaux and his associates as "pseudo-prophets, sons of Belial and witnesses of Anti-Christ, who by stupid words misled the Christians and by empty preaching induced all sorts of men to go."

Bernard himself is perplexed at the outcome of the righteous cause and can only complain to the pope that it seems "to point to the end of existence." Upon reflection, he later lays the blame on Emperor Manuel Comnena and the treachery of the Greeks.

Crusade Aid

Following the collapse of the Second Crusade, Nur ed-Din conquered Antioch and swept into the hinterland to the sea. In sight of his soldiers, he bathed in the Mediterranean and said that the sea also had been conquered by him.

Although the causes of the debacle remain debatable, there is no doubt about the outcome. The situation of the Moslems has been strengthened and the position of the Christian Kingdom in Jerusalem remains in greater peril than ever before. There is one further result: No one wants to go on any more Crusades. They couldn't care less about the Holy Tomb and the troubles in Palestine. William of Tyre writes:

> The nobles justly declined all plans for another Crusade as treacherous and showed indifference about the affairs of the Latin Kingdom in Jerusalem. Their influence caused others who had not been present there to slacken in love toward the kingdom. As a result, fewer people, and those less fervent in spirit, undertook the pilgrimage thereafter. Moreover, even to the present day, those who come fear lest they be caught in the same toils. From this time on, the condition of Latins in the East became visibly worse.

The Least You Need to Know

➤ Zengi, the hope of Islam, was slain while asleep by a eunuch.

➤ Nur ed-Din, Zengi's son, carried on the cause of jihad.

➤ The Christian attack on Damascus furthered the cause of Moslem unification.

➤ There is no known reason for the retreat from Damascus and the collapse of the Second Crusade.

➤ Following the retreat of the crusaders, Nur ed-Din extended his kingdom throughout Syria.

Chapter 16

The Crusader Kingdom Is Cursed

In This Chapter

➤ Nur ed-Din's dream of Moslem unity

➤ Nur ed-Din's army invades Egypt

➤ Saracens and Christians join forces against Nur ed-Din

➤ Crusaders massacre everyone in the city of Bilbeis in Egypt

➤ The Shiite and Sunni Moslems unite

➤ Saladin's star rises

➤ Jerusalem has a leper king

In the wake of the Second Crusade, Nur ed-Din achieves the dream of his father, Zengi. He now rules over Damascus. His first act is to assemble the government officials and religious leaders in order to assure them that their property and riches will be secure under his administration. Next, he provides food for the hungry populace and alms for the poor. Over the next few years, he shows himself to be a model public official.

For the first time in over 50 years, Aleppo and Damascus are joined under one ruler. Syria has been united by jihad. Now Nur ed-Din turns to accomplish something that no one has accomplished before: He sets his sights on Egypt and the Fatimid dynasty.

Nur ed-Din, a Turk and a Sunni, is attempting to subjugate the Shiites under his reign. He is seeking to unite not only all of Asia Minor but the entire Moslem world.

Nur ed-Din Eyes the Nile

Nur ed-Din has a problem: The Fatimids don't want to be subjugated. They don't want to turn over their riches and palaces to troublesome and avaricious Turks who, when you really think about it, aren't even Arabs.

Nur ed-Din, however, remains determined to fulfill his dream. He sends a military expedition to the Nile commanded by his faithful general, Shirkuh, a short, fat, one-eyed Kurd. Shirkuh takes along his twenty-seven-year-old nephew named Saladin for the excursion. (If this was a movie, the music would swell at the appearance of Saladin in our story and a special "Saladin theme" would be played to establish his importance.)

Christian Chronicles

In his journal, Saladin wrote: "My uncle Shirkuh turned to me and said: 'Yusuf, pack your things, we're going.' When I heard this order, I felt as though my heart had been pierced by a dagger, and I answered: 'In Allah's name, even if I were granted the entire kingdom of Egypt I would not go.' But, in the end, I did go with my uncle. He conquered Egypt, then died. God then placed in my hands power I had not expected."

The Saracens Seek Christian Help

The Fatimids in Egypt (the Saracens) are in a bind. The Turks are at their gates and they don't have the military might to send them back to Syria. It's a terrible dilemma. After much agonizing, Shawar, the sultan of Egypt, takes the doomsday option and calls upon the Christian king of Jerusalem.

It's very possible that the Latin kingdom in the East could be crushed by Nur ed-Din, but the Turkish ruler, fortunately for the Frankish nobles, remains focused on the conquest of Egypt.

It is 1164; the forces of the Turks (who are heretics and barbarians in the eyes of the Fatimid dynasty) are camped at Cairo, ready to conquer the jewel of the Nile. The

Fatimids ask the one-eyed general and his soldiers, quite politely, to go away and leave them alone. But Shirkuh refuses to comply with this request.

The king of Jerusalem, who has been called upon by the Saracens for military assistance, is a curious Frank named Amalric. Amalric succeeded Baldwin III. Amalric is Baldwin III's younger brother. He never speaks to anyone if he can avoid it. This is because he has a stutter like Porky Pig. King Amalric has a strange shape. "He was excessively fat," William of Tyre tells us, "with breasts like those of a woman, hanging down to his waist." He also has a strange way of laughing that causes his entire body to erupt in convulsions.

Amalric might be weird looking but he is also very ambitious. He, too, has his eye on Egypt and wants to annex it to his kingdom. In 1163, he leads a military expedition to Egypt to inaugurate the process of conquest.

A Combined Saracen and Christian Force!

In the third week of July in 1164, a combined force of Egyptian Moslems and Christian Franks under the command of King Amalric attacks Shirkuh and his Turkish (Syrian) army who are holed up in the Egyptian city of Bilbeis. "What a marvel!" wrote al-Qadi al-Faded in praise of the expedition. "We oppose one enemy with the help of another. Allah be praised! The crosses now serve to rescue Islam!"

You might be cross-eyed at reading this because it is so bizarre. So here's an outline of this development:

➤ The Turks are Sunni Moslems who are under the command of Nur ed-Din, the son of Zengi. Nur ed-Din now controls the great cities of Damascus and Aleppo in Syria.

➤ Nur ed-Din is anxious to expand his power, so he sets out to control the Shiite Moslems in Egypt in order to create one great Islamic kingdom.

➤ Nur ed-Din, to accomplish this purpose, sends out his most trusted general, the one-eyed Shirkuh, who is something of a military genius.

➤ Shirkuh sets out for Egypt with his nephew, a pious young man named Saladin.

➤ The Shiites in Egypt are horrified at the approach of the Turks, whom they view as heretics and barbarians.

Crusade Aid

In 1163, Amalric and his Christian army attacked the Egyptian army outside the walls of Bilbeis. The survivors fled behind the city walls. The Christian siege was repelled when the Egyptians opened the dikes, drowning many crusaders in the waters of the Nile.

➤ Shawar, the vizier of Cairo, realizes that the Egyptian army is no match for the forces of Nur ed-Din.

➤ Shawar calls upon Amalric, the Christian king of Jerusalem, to come to his aid.

➤ The Egyptian Moslems and the Christian Franks are now in alliance and they attack the Turks, under Shirkuh, at Bilbeis.

Nur ed-Din Captures Crusader Hierarchy

Now that you have everything straight, let's cut back to the story. Knowing that Shirkuh and his troops are in trouble, Nur ed-Din attacks a Frankish fortress near Antioch. This is a diversionary tactic to turn Christian attention from Egypt to Syria. The Frankish knights, who have remained in the kingdom, rush to Antioch, only to fall into a trap. Thousands are massacred and their leaders are carried off as captives. Among the captives are the count of Tripoli; the governor of Cilicia; the count of Edessa; and Reynald, Prince of Antioch. (The movie music now hits dark and somber notes. Reynald is introduced. He will become a major player in coming events and, single-handedly, may have caused the Third Crusade. When we see him now, he is strapped to the back of a camel and carried off to a dungeon in Nur ed-Din's fortress, where he will spend the next sixteen years of his life.)

Syrian confidence in the rule of Nur ed-Din soared when so many proud Christian princes were chained at the neck "like the lowest of slaves" and hauled off to Aleppo. "They were cast into prison," one chronicler writes, "to become the playthings of the infidels."

A Truce—And a Second Try

Nur ed-Din sent several bags of Christian scalps and banners to Shirkuh with instructions that they should be displayed on the ramparts of the fortress at Bilbeis for King Amalric and his soldiers to see. The sight of the bloody scalps of the knights and the soiled banners of captured princes weakens the Christian king's knees (and we are told also his bowels) and he immediately decides to come to terms with the Turks. The Christians and the Turks agree to leave Egypt and head home. (In Shirkuh's case, the deal is sweetened by a payment of 30,000 dinars from Shawar, the sultan.)

This doesn't put an end to Egypt's dilemma. Two years later, Shirkuh returns with his army in a second attempt to subjugate the Fatimid dynasty to the rule of Nur ed-Din. This time, the one-eyed general has no intention of leaving until he's accomplished his goal. Poor Sultan Shawar has no alternative but to push the panic button for King Amalric and the Christian army to appear.

Amalric sets his terms: the payment of an annual tribute of four thousand gold pieces. Shawar agrees, but only with the guarantee that the Franks and Amalric "shall not depart from Egypt until Shirkuh and his entire army are utterly destroyed or entirely driven from Egyptian territories."

Now we have a chase scene like something from a Joseph E. Levine epic with Steve Reeves. The Egyptian-Christian army pursues Shirkuh and the Turks across Egypt. Shirkuh finds an ideal battleground at Beben among the desert dunes. The two armies clash. There is heavy hand-to-hand combat in which the young Saladin commands the central battalion.

The Egyptian-Christian army retreats for reformation and the Turks disappear behind the dunes. Amalric and his armies march out in tight formation toward the Turkish camp that is situated between two hills. Shirkuh now can order his troops to race down the slopes and slaughter the Christians. But there is something in the tight formation and rigid discipline of the Franks that causes him to pause and reconsider his plan. The forces are moving forward in the manner of some war machine. They've created a human tank with the most heavily armed knights on the outside to protect the foot soldiers within. Shirkuh doesn't know how to attack this column. He does the unexpected. He retreats into the desert and heads for Alexandria.

A Second Truce

This time of running around the desert results in a second truce. Shirkah tells his men: "We are wasting our time here, and the days are passing without result. Many duties await us at home." The Christians come to the same conclusion. It seems as though the exhausting battle for Egypt has come to an end. The Turks cannot conquer it as long as Shawar, the Egyptian sultan, keeps calling upon the Christians for protection.

When the Turks return to Damascus, Nur ed-Din puts Shirkuh in the proverbial doghouse, saying: "You have exerted yourself twice, but have not achieved what you sought." It seems that the dream of Moslem unification under the concept of jihad will not become a reality. Saladin is also despondent and says: "I suffered such hardships in Egypt as I shall never forget."

Christian Chronicles

Before leaving Egypt, Saladin was a welcome guest at the camp of King Amalric. He stayed several days with the king and the two exchanged gifts. The Turkish emir was given a bodyguard for fear that one of the Christian soldiers might attempt to kill him. During this time, it was rumored that Saladin was knighted by King Amalric's Constable, Hugh of Toron.

Alliances Go Haywire

But this desert adventure doesn't end with the second truce and the alleged knighting of Saladin. It has a different and totally macabre ending that will change the face of the Middle East forever.

Crusaders Terrorize Egypt

Before the ink is dry on the truce, Amalric and his army return to Egypt, attack Bilbeis, and demand the immediate surrender of the strategically located city. The garrison troops refuse. Amalric drags in the siege towers and the catapults and begins the bombardment. Three days later, the Egyptian city falls into Amalric's hands.

Now things get really ugly. Every man, woman, and child within Bilbeis is hacked to pieces by the crusaders and every Christian soldier is free to take whatever loot he wants. It is a holocaust that is meant to terrify all of Egypt into submission.

After transforming Bilbeis into a desert, the Christians turn their sights to Cairo. They are intent upon crushing the very people who have called upon them for protection. This is one of the horrors of the Crusades that is difficult to watch, let alone comprehend.

Crosscurrent

The official reason for the slaughter of the innocents at Bilbeis was that Shawar was plotting with Nur ed-Din against the Franks. William of Tyre, however, refused to buy this argument and the breach of the alliance. "Many claim that the war made against Sultan Shawar and the Egyptians was unjust and contrary to divine law; that it was merely a pretext invented to defend an outrageous wrong."

The Christians capture the son and nephew of their old friend, Shawar, and demand a ransom of two million pieces of gold. Only a small part of the money is paid and the army is prevented from plundering Cairo because Shawar orders a large portion of Cairo to be set on fire. What a turn of events! The Christians who set out to save the Holy Tomb from infidels are now slaughtering civilians, violating all sacred oaths, and causing untold misery for millions of Moslems. By such barbarity, they're giving rise to the unification of Islam and the destruction of the Christian kingdom in the East. They've managed to accomplish for the Moslems what the Moslems could not have accomplished for themselves.

Saracens Ask Nur ed-Din's Help

Shawar next calls upon Nur ed-Din, his old enemy, to protect him against the Christians. The tables have turned. Friends have become enemies. And enemies have become friends. The events in Egypt are mind-boggling. Nur ed-Din can't believe his luck. After five bloody years of attempting to conquer Cairo by force, he is now being presented the keys to the city for a favor.

Moslem Unity

A few days after the Christian army withdraws from Cairo, the Turkish army once again makes an appearance. General Shirkuh meets with Sultan Shawar and Egypt becomes annexed to the Turkish Empire of Syria. The Sunnis are united with the Shiites. This means that there is no longer a distinction between Saracen and Turk. The Moslems are one people under the rule of Nur ed-Din, whose empire now stretches from Northern Iraq to the upper stretches of the Nile River.

Saladin Moves Up

As a sign of friendship, Saladin invites Shawar to accompany him on a pilgrimage to a holy shrine in Damascus. Shawar cannot refuse such an invitation, as the pilgrimage will celebrate the unification of the Arab world. He sets out with Saladin and a military escort. Almost as soon as the pilgrimage starts, Saladin orders the entourage to a halt. He pulls Shawar from his horse, orders his arrest, takes him to a makeshift camp, and, several days later, cuts off his head. This is payment for Shawar's dealings with the Christian dogs. The head is kicked among the soldiers like a soccer ball. Later it is revealed that Caliph al-Abid had approved of the assassination of his loyal, trusted, and obedient sultan.

While the Turks are kicking around the head of Shawar, the Christian king Amalric is forging a new treaty with Manuel Comnena, the Byzantine emperor. As part of the treaty, Amlaric agrees to marry the emperor's grand niece Maria Comnena, who is about as pretty as a possum. The marriage takes place in Tyre and Maria becomes Queen of Jerusalem.

Crusade Aid

The fountain of all religious truth, the ultimate judge, and the owner of all Egypt, was the Caliph. The ruler who made the day-to-day decisions was the sultan. The Caliph lived in the fortress palace of al-Kahira, which was one of the wonders of the medieval world. The Caliph at this point in history (1167) was 16-year-old al-Adid.

Christian Chronicles

Few individuals have been more trusting (and naïve) than Shawar, the sultan of Egypt. He trusted the Turks to uphold the first treaty and the Christians to uphold the second. He trusted Shirkuh, Amalric, Saladin, and the Caliph, and they would all turn against him. He represents the cardinal premise in Middle Eastern negotiations: "Trust no one."

Saladin Succeeds Shawar

The new vizier of Egypt is now Shirkuh, the Turkish general. Now jihad against the Christians will be proclaimed from minarets throughout the Moslem world and the mighty sword of Islam will be swung with full force against the Crusader Kingdom that stands in the jaws of a vise between Syria and Egypt.

But now another unexpected development occurs. In March of 1169, three months after his appointment as Sultan, Shirkuh drops dead at his palace in Cairo, a victim of either poisoning or a severe heart attack. A new vizier of Egypt must be appointed. The choice falls upon Saladin, the man responsible for killing Shawar and placing his uncle Shirkuh in power.

Salad Days for Saladin

The dice continue to roll. In 1174, within two months of each other, Nur ed-Din and King Amalric die of natural causes. The successor to Nur ed-Din's throne is Saladin by acclaim of the people of Damascus. "We dawned on the people like light in the darkness," Saladin writes in his journal. "The people rushed before us both before and after we had entered the city in joy at the coming of our rule."

Saladin claims that he has assumed power for the sole reason of the conquest of Jerusalem. Everything he will do, he says, will be done for the cause of the Holy War. The unity of Islam under him is a necessary step for the expulsion of the Franks from the Holy Land.

Who is this Saladin? His name really isn't Saladin. It is Yusuf ibn Ayyub (Joseph, son of Job). He calls himself "Salah al-Din" that means "Rectifier of the Faith." He was born in 1138 at Tekrit on the upper Tigris, of Kurdish—not Semitic—stock. His father Ayyub became governor of Baalbek under Zengi, and later Vizier of Damascus under Nur ed-Din. Saladin, who was raised in the courts and palaces of Baalbek and Damascus, is well versed in the arts of statesmanship and war. With these qualities he combines fundamentalist piety and an ascetic simplicity of life. His chief garment is a coarse woolen robe; his only drink is water; and his sexual temperance astonishes the Arab world. He is a slender man of average height, with a dark beard, dark skin, and dark eyes that reflect his dark thoughts.

After becoming Master of Syria, Saladin returns to Cairo where he takes the title of King and establishes the Ayyubid dynasty. At Cairo and Damascus, he continues to display the stern orthodoxy of his faith. He builds mosques, hospitals, monasteries, and madrasas (theological schools). He encourages architecture, has

Crusade Aid

Nur ed-Din's choice for a successor to his throne was his son al-Salih. As the boy was only 10 years old, the emirs began to fight among themselves for the position of regent. Finally, it was decided that the only one who could continue the jihad was Saladin.

little use for secular science, and shares Plato's contempt for poetry. All wrongs in his domain are quickly redressed, and taxes are lowered while public works are extended.

Upon seizing Aleppo from al-Salih and his supporters, Saladin turns his attention to Franks and vows to attack the Christians as no one has ever done before. He will keep this promise.

The Crusader Kingdom on the Ropes

The king of Jerusalem is now Amalric's 13-year-old son Baldwin IV. He is the bravest, the most intelligent, and the most compassionate of all Christian kings. He is kindly and gracious to others; he performs his duties with diligence and distinction, and he is extremely skilled in the art of war. No knight is better suited for the position. He is loved by nobles and commoners alike. He is the perfect king, except for one flaw: Baldwin IV is a leper.

William of Tyre became aware of this illness when Baldwin IV was nine. At that time, he was playing with other boys who were pinching each other with their fingernails to see who could bear the pain the longest. The other boys screamed and yelled, but Baldwin was impervious to the pinches. It was then discovered that he had no nerves in his right arm and right hand. William checked the medical books and found in Hippocrates words that indicated lack of feeling as a symptom of leprosy.

The best doctors were consulted, ointments were rubbed into his skin, medications (including poisons) were administered to him. But nothing worked. The illness continued on its terrible course, attacking the boy's limbs and his face.

By the time Baldwin IV dies at the age of twenty-four, he will be hairless, blind, without a nose and ears, without hands and feet, and with skeletal limbs that have become limp and gangrenous.

He is truly the embodiment of the cursed Crusader Kingdom.

Christian Chronicles

Baldwin IV, the Leper King, possessed inner strength that permitted him to endure his affliction without complaint. William of Tyre tells us that he had very bright eyes, an aquiline nose, blond hair drawn back from his forehead and reaching his shoulders, and an infectious laugh. He measured his words because he disliked attracting attention to himself without reason.

The Least You Need to Know

➤ Nur ed-Din, the son of Zengi, planned to unify Sunni and Shiite Moslems in the cause of the jihad against the crusader states.

➤ Nur ed-Din sent a large Turkish army to undertake the conquest of Egypt.

➤ Egypt formed an alliance with Amalric, the Christian king of Jerusalem, to ward off the Turkish invasion.

➤ When the Turks withdrew, the Christians decided to conquer Egypt, and massacred every man, woman, and child within the city of Bilbeis to spread terror.

➤ The Egyptians united with the Turks to prevent a Christian invasion.

➤ Saladin, the nephew of Shirkuh, became the ruler of Syria and the king of Egypt.

➤ Baldwin IV, Amalric's successor, was afflicted with leprosy.

Chapter 17

Saladin Triumphant: The Crusader Kingdom Collapses

In This Chapter

➤ Reynald of Chatillon on a collision course

➤ Reynald's raiders capture Saladin's sister

➤ Saladin assembles the Moslem army

➤ The Christian army is destroyed

➤ Jerusalem falls to Saladin

➤ The Crusader Kingdom is no more

At the close of this chapter, we will cut away to the third and the most glorious Crusade. It will center on two of history's most compelling heroes: King Saladin, the Moslem ruler of Asia Minor, and King Richard the Lion Heart of England. But now it's time that you meet one of the great villains of the Middle Ages: a Christian knight named Reynald of Chatillon. This guy almost single-handedly causes one of the greatest wars since the dawn of creation. He is charming, bold, daring, and a perfect case study of a manic aggressive. In fact, he appears to possess every mental disorder known to man, from paranoia to schizophrenia. Reynald endangers everyone and everything he encounters without the slightest care for the chaos and misery he creates. He can be counted on to do crazy, absurd, and terrible things any time he pops up in the pages of this book.

Reynald of Chatillon

Reynald first appears in history when he arrives in Jerusalem with King Louis VII in 1148. He comes from a very wealthy and prominent family. His father is the count of Gien, but being the second son, Reynald does not inherit title or property. And so, he sets out for fame and fortune in the East. He obtains both. Being rakishly handsome, he catches the eye of the pretty and pleasure-loving Constance. Princess Constance is twenty-something and a widow. Her late husband was Prince Raymond of Antioch, the very same Raymond who seduced Queen Eleanor of Aquitaine.

Raymond of Antioch, you may recall, married Constance when she was nine years old. Now, in 1153, she is fully developed, headstrong, sexy, and available. King Baldwin III gives her a list of suitable husbands, but she chooses the foxy and fascinating Reynald. Knowing that the king will scream bloody murder at the prospect of such a union, she secretly weds the knight in the dead of night without obtaining her father's permission. Concerning this marriage, William of Tyre, the tireless chronicler, writes: "Many there were who marveled that a woman so eminent, so distinguished and powerful, who had been the wife of a very illustrious man, should stoop to marry an ordinary knight."

Crusade Aid

Constance, the wife of Reynald, was the daughter of Prince Bohemond II and Princess Alice of Antioch. Bohemond II was killed by Turks when he was 23. Princess Alice then ruled Antioch. When Constance was two years old, her mother tried to marry her off to Zengi, the Moslem prince, on the condition that she remain ruler of Antioch. To sweeten the offer, Princess Alice sent Zengi a gift of a snow-white palfrey with silver horseshoes, a silver bridle, and a saddle covered with silver brocade.

Raid on Cyprus

Reynald is now Prince of Antioch, the second most important city in the Holy Land. He is one of the most powerful men in the Middle East and he is as nutty as a jaybird. When he comes to believe that the Patriarch Aimery of Antioch (the head of the Orthodox Church) might have criticized his actions in private, Reynald has the old bishop stripped and scourged until Aimery is a bloody mess. Then he orders his soldiers to tie the Patriarch to the roof of the palace and to smear his body with honey so that he'll be covered with flies as he slowly roasts in the desert sun.

By some miracle, Patriarch Aimery survives this punishment, and Reynald next orders him to come up with the necessary cash for a raid on Cyprus! This is a bizarre request: Cyprus is prosperous, peaceful, and supportive of the Crusader Kingdom. Moreover, the island is not Moslem, but Christian—Orthodox Christian, and the crazy Reynald is demanding that Aimery sponsor a raid on his own subjects. Recalling his days and nights on the roof as human flypaper, however, Aimery dips into the Church's coffers and gives Reynald the money.

Of course, the people of Cyprus are not expecting an attack—especially not from the Latin Christians whom they saved from starvation during the First Crusade. But Reynald possesses the sense and sensibility of a pirate and he seeks simply to plunder everything in sight. When he arrives in Cyprus, Reynald creates havoc and disaster to his dark heart's content.

Christian Chronicles

William of Tyre, speaking of this adventure, writes: "Reynald completely overran the island of Cyprus without meeting any opposition, destroyed cities and wrecked fortresses. He broke into monasteries of men and women and shamelessly raped nuns and young virgins. Although the precious vestments and the amount of gold and silver that he carried off were great, yet the loss of these counted as nothing in comparison with the violence done to chastity."

Reynald Does Time

Cyprus belongs to Manuel Comnena, the Byzantine emperor. In recognition of Manuel's sovereignty, Reynald sends the emperor the noses that he has cut from the faces of the Byzantine priests. This is the prince of Antioch's idea of a great joke. Manuel is not amused.

King Baldwin III is desperate to placate the Eastern Emperor for Reynald's outrageous escapade in Cyprus. To reestablish good relations, Baldwin III agrees to marry the Princess Theodora, the daughter of Isaac Comnena, Manuel's older brother. At the time of her marriage, Theodora is 13, radiantly beautiful, very tall, with thick, full hair. Baldwin III is 27.

Emperor Manuel is pleased to have Baldwin in the family but he remains ready to feed Reynald to the jackals. Three years later, he leads his mighty army to Antioch to teach the psychopathic prince a lesson. Reynald behaves in a completely unexpected manner. He appears before the Byzantine emperor on his hands and knees in a woolen tunic with short sleeves and a noose around his neck. William of Tyre, observing this, writes: "Reynald threw himself on the ground at the emperor's feet, where he lay prostrate until all were disgusted and the glory of the Latins was turned to shame, for he was a man of violent impulses, both in sinning and repenting."

The emperor thinks that the prince of Antioch has learned his lesson, and forgives him. A celebration is held in Antioch. The emperor rides stiffly through the streets with Reynald walking by his side and holding the bridle in token of complete submission.

Of course, it's all an act. Reynald is submissive to neither God nor man. A few weeks later, he's out stealing herds of sheep and goats from Moslem and Christian farmers. The Turks catch him by the tail and carry him off to a dungeon in Aleppo. Nur ed-Din, the ruler of Aleppo, thinks that King Baldwin III or Emperor Manuel might pay a ransom for the Christian prince. They won't cough up a dime. And so, Reynald stays in the slammer for 16 years.

Christian Chronicles

The Lady Stephanie was previously married to the proud and haughty Miles of Plancy, who was the guardian of King Baldwin IV. In 1174, Miles of Plancy was stabbed in a public street in Acre. The murder took place at sunset and the assailants got away, but not before the body of the nobleman was subjected to terrible indignities, including castration.

Back in the Saddle

Released in 1176, Reynald finds that his wife Constance is long dead and that he is no longer Prince of Antioch. Still and all, he cuts a dashing figure and has a natural way with the ladies. He comes to woo and wed Lady Stephanie, who is the heiress of the Transjordan with the great desert castle of Kerak, about 10 miles southeast of the Dead Sea.

In 1180, King Baldwin IV negotiates a peace treaty with Saladin that guarantees free movement of goods between Moslem and Christian territories. A season of goodwill permeates the war-plagued Middle East.

Trade flourishes. Moslem merchants freely enter Christian settlements and sell their wares. Moslem physicians attend Christian patients. Moslem worship is permitted in Jerusalem, and the Koran is taught in Moslem schools in Antioch and Tripoli. Traveling through Christian Syria in 1181, ibn-Jubayr describes his fellow Moslems as prosperous and "well-treated by the Franks." He visits Acre only to find the port city "swarming with pigs and crosses" and rancid with the smell of cheesy Christians, but he believes that the infidels soon will be civilized by the powerful civilization to which they have come.

It starts to look like the story of the Crusades might have a happy ending after all. At least, there's the possibility, a sense of hope. But let's not forget that Reynald is on the loose with a new wife, a new position, and a new army that remains at his bidding.

Seeing the caravans travel past his castle, Reynald cannot contain himself. He must capture one, truce or no truce. The caravan he raids is on its way to Mecca. Reynald carries off all the possessions of the pilgrims: their provisions, personal belongings, goods, and animals. They are left destitute by the Dead Sea. Saladin demands restitution under the terms of the treaty. Reynald tells the great Moslem ruler to get lost and pound sand.

Saladin practices patience. He is not eager to disrupt this period of prosperity, but Reynald cannot be controlled, not even by King Baldwin. In fact, Reynald now says that he is the king of the Transjordan and not bound by treaty or truce. He continues to raid caravans.

Reynald the Raider

Reynald is not content with simple theft. He concocts another scheme: a raid against Mecca. His army collects timber from the forest of Moab, builds a squadron of galleys, and puts them on trial by raiding ships on the Dead Sea. The raids are successful, so Reynald and his men transport the galleys through the desert to the Gulf of Aqaba. There, the boats are launched and Reynald's pirate crew wreaks havoc on the rich merchant ships on the Red Sea.

Strange as it may seem, Reynald's war galleys raid all the way down the African coast to the Nubian port of Aidhab, opposite Mecca. He and three hundred knights disembark with the aim of marching on the Holy City of Islam. Crazier than ever before, Reynald vows to destroy the tomb of Mohammed—"the accursed camel driver"—at Medina and to smash the Kaaba at Mecca into tiny fragments. His small force is surprised by an Egyptian detachment. Over two hundred are cut down; a few escape with Reynald, and the rest are carted to Mecca where they are slaughtered instead of goats at the annual pilgrimage sacrifice.

Saladin is beside himself with rage. He swears that he will put Reynald to death with his own hands for the attempted outrage. Reynald returns home to Kerak, delighting in his reputation as the man the Moslems most love to hate.

Crusade Aid

Reynald built his ships in standard sections so they could be transported across the desert by camel and assembled with little difficulty on the shores of the Red Sea. Each ship was built to the exact specifications of the other ships, making them the first naval modular units in history.

From his castle by the Dead Sea, Reynald continues to capture caravans that pass through his territory even though they are now heavily armed for protection. When he captures a caravan traveling from Damascus to Mecca that carries Saladin's sister as a passenger, Saladin is furious. Reynald's capture of this caravan of pilgrims is almost as great an outrage as his attempted desecration of the tomb of the Prophet.

Crusade Aid

On June 13, 1183, Saladin took control of Aleppo from Nur ed-Din's son. Saladin now ruled from the Tigris to the Nile, from the frontiers of Ethiopia to the far reaches of Persia. He now called himself King of All the Kingdoms of the Orient.

Christian Chronicles

The wedding between Humphrey of Toron and Princess Isabelle is important for future developments in the Crusades. Six years after this blessed event, Holy Mother Church will annul the marriage in order for Isabelle to marry Conrad of Montferrat, the defender of Tyre, who held off Saladin's forces after the fall of Jerusalem.

Baldwin IV attempts to intervene. He orders Reynald to restore all the prisoners, Saladin's sister in particular, and booty. Hearing this, Reynald laughs like a hyena. In his rejection of the king's authority, the insane prince is digging a grave for the Crusader States.

Saladin Goes on the Attack

Saladin can take no more. He attacks Reynald's castle at Kerak, the launching ground of his madcap adventures. Saladin wants to conquer this castle even more than the city of Jerusalem because he knows that the crazy fox remains safely sequestered behind its walls.

For two months, Saladin attacks the castle with seven powerful catapults day and night without let-up. But it is all to no avail. The castle is well provisioned and the walls are impregnable.

The Moslem king leaves, only to return in the summer with a larger army and nine massive catapults, known as mangonels. Saladin vows to break down the walls and choke the life out of the troublesome infidel once and for all.

As it happens, Reynald is hosting a wedding party for his wife's son, Humphrey of Toron, and Princess Isabelle, King Baldwin's half-sister, who is eleven years old. In the midst of the celebration, the walls of the castle tremble as the siege begins. The pounding continues incessantly, but the guests have traveled from all over the Latin East for this party and they're not about to put an end to the festivities over a mere Moslem attack. Finally, at the onset of evening, Lady Stephanie, Reynald's wife, has her servants take some dishes from the wedding feast to Saladin's tent.

Saladin is delighted to receive the gifts and offers profuse thanks to Lady Stephanie. He then asks where the newlyweds will be spending the night. When the servants point out the location, Saladin orders his army not to bombard that tower until morning.

The attack continues, with the mangonels hurling huge boulders against the massive walls without let-up. William of Tyre records that "even those who had fled to the innermost apartments, the most retired seclusion, shrank with terror before the crash and roar of the incoming missiles."

The nightmarish wedding reception continues for a month, until King Baldwin IV arrives with a relief column from Jerusalem. The leper king is now a living corpse. He has to be transported to the site of the siege on a litter. Baldwin is greeted by everyone within the castle as though he had been sent by God.

Several months later, Baldwin IV dies at the age of 24. He is buried in the Church of the Holy Sepulcher and will be remembered as the greatest of the Christian kings. His passing is mourned by Christian and Moslem alike. Imad ed-Din of Isfahan writes of him: "The leper child knew how to make his authority respected."

The choice of a successor is obvious. The crown must pass to the young son of Princess Sibylla, Baldwin IV's eldest sister. Baldwin V is only five years old and in very delicate health when he is crowned in March 1185. Raymond of Tripoli is named regent. The new regent, who will act as king until the boy comes of age, is a man of many talents. He is a skilled diplomat who negotiates a new truce with Saladin that is supposed to last for four years. When a famine strikes Jerusalem in 1186, Raymond even arranges for Saladin to supply the city with corn and grain.

But disaster happens. Baldwin V dies in August 1186. Some say the boy died of natural causes; others suspect poison. Who should serve as king? The nobles quarrel among themselves. In a move so fast that it takes everyone by surprise, Princess Sibylla—sister of Baldwin IV and mother of Baldwin V—has herself crowned as Queen of Jerusalem. She then turns to her husband, Guy of Lusignan, places a crown on his head, and proclaims him to be King. Everyone is dumbfounded. Guy of Lusignan has proven himself to be a wimp. When Saladin confronted the Frankish army at the Pool of Goliath in 1183, Guy refused to advance and engage the Moslem army in battle. He just waited for Saladin to go home. The other knights looked upon him as a powder puff, and now he was King, crowned not by popular acclamation, not by lawful succession, not by the authority of Holy Mother Church, but by his wife!

Crowning her husband as king of Jerusalem, Queen Sibylla says: "I choose as King, Guy of Lusignan, who is my husband. I know him to be a man of prowess and honor, someone who is well able with God's aid to rule His people. I know too that while he is alive, I can have no other husband, for scripture says: 'Those whom God has joined together let no man put asunder.'"

Many nobles refuse to bend a knee before the new monarch and threaten to elect their own king. The country is on the edge of a civil war. Baldwin of Ramleh, one of the great barons of the Crusader States, says: "The new king will not last a year! The Kingdom will not last a year!"

Reynald Raids Again!

It is at this precise moment—the most precarious of all moments—that Reynald manages to ignite utter calamity. The crazy old fox swoops out of his castle to raid another rich caravan on its way to Cairo. He throws the Moslems in a dungeon and places their goods and possessions in his storehouse.

Saladin exerts incredible restraint. He sends a peremptory letter to Reynald demanding the release of the prisoners and their goods. Reynald responds by saying: "Since they trusted in Mohammed, let Mohammed save them now."

Crosscurrent

When Reynald attacked this last caravan in 1187, he violated the truce that Raymond of Tripoli had effected with Saladin. Under its terms, Reynald was to collect customs dues from the travelers and pilgrims rather than order outright confiscation of their goods and the ransom of prisoners.

Saladin, in a last ditch effort, appeals to King Guy for a return of the captured caravan. King Guy goes to Reynald and appeals to him for the love of God and the sake of the kingdom to comply with Saladin's demand. But Reynald says it is not King Guy's business to give him orders. As the ruler of the Transjordan, he is beyond the law of Jerusalem and has no intention of apologizing or giving back the booty.

The Great Moslem Army Assembles

It is Reynald's arrogant response that breaks the camel's back. Saladin sounds the call for jihad with the pledge before Allah that he will kill Reynald "with his own hand." The call is issued from minarets throughout the Arab world and a great Moslem army gathers.

It consists of over a hundred thousand soldiers and volunteers. In a letter to the Caliph in Baghdad, Saladin boasts that the widest plain in the world is too narrow for his army and that the dust the army raises on the move through the desert darkens the eye of the sun.

On Wednesday, July 1, 1187, Saladin leads his army across the Jordan Valley and to Tiberius. Tiberius falls to his forces within an hour. King Guy is in a panic. He calls a council at Acre. Most nobles, including Raymond of Tripoli, encourage the king to do nothing, as the battle against Saladin must be conducted on grounds that are conducive to victory. Nothing can be gained by marching to the Sea of Galilee to save Tiberius. It's the hottest month of the year, when the light army of Saladin will have a distinct advantage over the armored knights of the kingdom. Finally, Raymond lays down the trump card against an encounter at Tiberius, by saying, "Between here and Tiberius there is no water except a small spring called the Spring of Cresson, which cannot water an entire army. You and your men will die of thirst before the multitudes of Moslems hem you in for slaughter."

Christian Chronicles

Raymond of Tripoli advised King Guy that no purpose would be served by an attempt to recapture Tiberius from Saladin's army. He maintained this position, even though his wife, his children, and all his possessions were in the city. He said that he would rather lose everything than lose the kingdom. Raymond, the wisest of the nobles, believed that Saladin, after taking Tiberius, would be tempted to march across Palestine and could only be defeated if the crusaders stayed where they were—at Suffuriyah, a fortress north of Nazareth.

Of course, Raymond's argument makes perfect sense. The distance between Acre and Tiberius is not great—about 25 miles as the crow flies—but the crow must fly over a parched desert where the temperature soars to 110 degrees in the shade! This would be bad enough for a crow, but imagine how it will be for a knight in a full suit of armor. He could melt into a puddle of human soup in the blazing desert sun!

Yes, the king agrees, the Christians will have to wait until Saladin moves from Tiberius so they can meet him on their own turf and on their own terms. The council is concluded. Common sense has won the day—or so it seems.

Hell on the Horns of Hattin

After the council concludes, Reynald, with Gerard of Ridfort, corner King Guy and accuse Raymond of being a coward and a Saracen sympathizer. "Sire," they say, "you should sound the alarm. Let everyone take his place in battle formation and follow the banner of the Holy Cross."

The advice is sheer lunacy, but King Guy, who's tired of being called a wimp and a powder puff, takes it as inspired guidance. At the crack of dawn, the trumpeters sound the call to arms. The sleeping camp awakes. The nobles rush to the king's tent and ask why the sudden change in plans. The king responds that his task is to command and their

Crosscurrent

Guy of Lusignan had accepted Raymond of Tripoli's advice at the Pool of Goliath and had held his army back from attacking the forces of Saladin. That decision had been sound and led to the Moslem retreat. But strategic inaction seemed unchivalrous to the other Franks and gave Guy the reputation of a milquetoast.

duty is to obey. This must be the same advice Custer gave members of the Seventh Calvary before the Battle of Little Big Horn.

Off they go with their banners limp in the oppressive heat. Raymond of Tripoli is at the vanguard, King Guy leads the center, and Gerard of Ridfort (the Grand Master) takes up the rear. They march across the plains of Sephoria toward the Sea of Galilee. The heat is unbearable. You could fry an egg on the chain mail of any given soldier. The columns move along in a cloud of dust that is kicked up by thousands of horse hooves. Within a few hours, the army is choking mad with thirst.

Adding to the discomfort, Moslem raiding parties keep attacking the rear guard. They descend from the dunes, shower arrows at the flanks of the slow moving army, and gallop off in clouds of dust.

By the time they reach the Horns of Hattin, a hill with twin peaks several miles from the Sea of Galilee, King Guy calls a halt so that the rear guard, still busy fighting off Moslem skirmishers, can catch up with the rest of the army. Everyone is utterly exhausted and ready to surrender their swords and spears for a few drops of water.

But the one source of water, the Spring of Cresson, has been drained and poisoned by Saladin's soldiers. The place where the crusaders are camped is the dry crater of an extinct volcano. The ground is strewn with black basalt that's treacherous to men and horses. It is a perfectly wretched place to camp and everyone is exhausted, parched, and utterly miserable.

Saladin's army, meanwhile, has moved to a well-watered valley less than a mile from the Christian camp. Toward dawn, while an easterly wind is blowing, the Moslems set fire to the dry grass and scrub around the Horns of Hattin, sending clouds of suffocating smoke into the Christian camp.

Christian Chronicles

As the crusaders pitched camp on the Horns of Hattin, Raymond of Tripoli was heard to say: "Alas, Lord God, the battle is over. We have been betrayed unto death. The Kingdom is finished." The Bishop of Acre, who had been carrying the jeweled True Cross, was killed in battle. The Cross was picked up by the Bishop of St. George of Lydda, who was so foolish that he wandered right into the hands of the Moslems and was captured. He thought the Cross would repel them just as it repels vampires. The holy relic was conveyed to the Great Mosque in Damascus where it was buried under the threshold so that every Moslem who entered the mosque would step on it.

At dawn the Moslem archers unleash tens of thousands of arrows. The Christians are in a frenzy. They cannot breathe or see because of the smoke, and they're being picked off like flies. It's a scene of sheer pandemonium.

Hundreds of Christian infantrymen, uncontrollable in their desire for water, race toward the Sea of Galilee for a drink and are hacked to pieces. The knights, however, fight bravely and attempt to hammer through the encircling ranks of Saladin's army by a series of head-on charges.

Saladin Destroys the Christian Army

The battle continues for a day and a half. By the time it's over, the entire Christian army has been destroyed. The scene, as described by Imad ed-Din, is one of complete carnage:

> I rode across the battlefield and learned many lessons. I saw heads lying far from their bodies, eyes gouged out, bodies covered with powdery ashes, their beauty marred by the claw marks of birds of prey, limbs mangled in battle and scattered about, stumps of flesh, crushed skulls, cloven necks, sliced heads, feet cut off, noses cut off, extremities hacked away, open bellies, shriveled mouths and gaping foreheads out of which eyeballs dangled from sockets …

The Crusader Kingdom Falls

After the battle, Saladin has King Guy and Reynald brought to his tent. King Guy is suffering terribly from thirst, and Saladin gives him a goblet of water cooled by the snows of Mount Hermon. The King takes a drink and passes the goblet to Reynald. Saladin breaks out in an uproarious laugh and dances around his prisoners, saying: "You gave him the drink, King Guy, not I."

Saladin Beheads Reynald

King Guy and Reynald are dumbfounded. They do not know the rule of Moslem hospitality that says a stranger who has received drink or food is under the protection of the host: He cannot be killed or maimed in any way. Saladin runs out of the tent, kicking his heels in merriment. He returns with a saber and stabs Reynald in the throat.

As Reynald is gagging for air, Saladin cuts his enemy's head off with an axe and holds it high in

Crusade Aid

On July 5, 1187, the day after the battle, Saladin sent a courteous note to the wife of Raymond of Tripoli, who remained in the heavily fortified city of Tiberius. In the note, he offered the countess safe passage through Galilee to rejoin her husband. Her children, her servants, her soldiers, and her possessions were allowed free passage through the country.

the air. The eyes of Reynald appear to blink at the king and his mouth opens to emit a voiceless scream. King Guy shudders in horror, thinking he will be the next victim. Saladin, still in a state of giddiness, says: "This man was guilty of unimaginable crimes. His perfidy and insolence brought about his death. You should have no fear, for a king does not kill a king."

King Guy Held Captive

Saladin lives up to his word. He does not kill King Guy. He rather opts to keep the king at Damascus like an exotic animal for chosen guests to view. But he orders the execution of his other captives, including the Knights Templar and the Hospitallers, by mullahs. The mullahs are religious teachers who accompany the army. They are Sufi holy men who have never raised a sword or wielded a battle-axe. It is most amusing for the Moslems to watch the mullahs attempt to hack off the heads of the Christians. Most of the executions are botched, and the heads are left hanging from severed necks. Other captives are struck in the arms, shoulders, and chest before the blade strikes the jugular vein. The great Saladin and his soldiers laugh uncontrollably at the funny *Sufis*.

After his victory at Hattin, Saladin sweeps over the Christian Kingdom. Within a week, he conquers the city of Acre, frees four thousand Moslem captives, and acquires the wealth of the richest city on the Palestinian coast.

By the end of August, only two Christian cities remain in the Middle East: Tyre and Jerusalem. Saladin is not concerned about Tyre. His mind is focused on the Holy City.

Warrior Words

Moslem mystics were called **Sufis** because of the simple robe of wool that they wore (*suf*). Like the Hindus, the Sufis believed that a mystical revelation of God could only be received through a course of discipline. This course consisted of purifying exercises of devotion, meditation, obedience to a Sufi master (a mullah), and a complete abandonment of personal desire.

Jerusalem Falls

The attack on Jerusalem begins on September 20, 1187. One of the defenders of the city later writes that the Moslems came down upon it from the Mount of Olives screaming war cries and blowing trumpets. "Arrows fell like raindrops, so that one could not show a finger above the ramparts without being hit. There were so many wounded that all the hospitals and physicians in the city were hard pressed just to extract missiles from their body."

Within two weeks the Christians surrender and Saladin with his great army enters the city. In sharp contrast to the way the crusaders conquered Jerusalem 88 years before, not a building is looted and not a person is harmed.

In accordance with the terms of surrender, five dinars must be paid for each man, five for each woman, and one for each child. The poorest 7,000 are released for the payment of 30,000 dinars (the sum provided by Henry II of England as penance for the assassination of Thomas Becket). Al-Adil, Saladin's brother, asks for a gift of 1,000 of the unransomed slaves. His request is granted and he frees them as an offering to Allah. Balian, the leader of the Christian garrison in Jerusalem, asks a like boon and receives it. He frees another thousand. Bishop Heraclitus, the Christian primate, asks, receives, and does the same. Now Saladin says, "My brother has made his alms, and the bishop and Balian have made theirs, now I will make mine." He frees all the old who cannot pay the ransom.

Crusade Aid

Saladin agreed to the terms of surrender because Balian of Iberlin, in command of the Christian forces, threatened to set Jerusalem on fire, destroy all the holy places including the Dome of the Rock and the al-Aqsa Mosque, and massacre the 5,000 Moslems who remained in the city. He painted a picture of Doomsday, and Saladin was convinced that Balian meant every word he said.

Coda

Despite these displays of generosity, 15,000 of the captured Christians remain unransomed. They are marched off to Damascus where they're sold to the highest bidder. So many Christians are sold that the price for slaves plummets to a bargain basement low. Abu Shama, the Moslem chronicler, records that one prisoner is sold for a well-worn shoe.

Saladin now sets about to cleanse the city. The Dome of the Rock, which had been converted into a church, is purified of Christian polytheism by being sprinkled with rose water, and the golden cross that had surmounted the cupola is cast down, to the cheers of the Moslems. Saladin's advisors urge him to destroy the Church of the Holy Sepulcher, but he simply closes it for three days, only to open it to pilgrims again—for a fee.

Latin Christianity has suffered the greatest calamity since it became the official religion of the Roman Empire. The Crusader Kingdom is gone—save for the cities of Tripoli, Antioch, and Tyre.

Hearing the news of the Moslem conquest of Jerusalem, Pope Urban III falls in a swoon and collapses in the Lateran Palace. The Holy Father never recovers. Within a week, he is dead. It is apparent to everyone that he died of grief.

The Least You Need to Know

➤ Reynald of Chatillon was the loose cannon of the Second Crusade.

➤ Reynald became the ruler of the Transjordan and attacked Moslem caravans in violation of a treaty with Saladin.

➤ Reynald incurred the wrath of all Moslems by an attempted raid on Mecca and the capture of Saladin's sister.

➤ Saladin retaliated for his offenses by wiping out the Christian army and beheading Reynald.

➤ After the deaths of Kings Baldwin IV and V, Queen Sibylla—their sister—crowned her husband, Guy of Luisignan, King of the Crusader Kingdom.

➤ Saladin's forces swept over the Crusader Kingdom and conquered Jerusalem.

Part 5

The Third Crusade: The Rage of a Lion

The preceding chapters set the stage for the main event. Saladin has demonstrated the power of Islam to overcome all obstacles. Sitting in his unadorned tent, Saladin possesses the power of the Caesars. The East is in the hollow of his hand and the West trembles at the mention of his name. He is the master of the Arabic world, and greater than any king. He is an emperor who reigns over many countries and diverse peoples. He has conquered the Christian Kingdom and the Holy City of Jerusalem. A lost city is even more compelling than a lost tomb, and a great king will come to reclaim it. He is young, brave, handsome, chivalrous, and cunning. The great Saladin will meet his match—Richard the Lion Heart—and the entire world will quake on a field of battle.

CALLING ALL KNIGHTS!!

Chapter 18

After the Fall: The Call for a Third Crusade

In This Chapter

➤ The fall of Jerusalem is followed by dissolution

➤ The Church blames the sinful for Jerusalem's plight

➤ Pope Gregory VII calls for a Third Crusade

➤ "Saladin's Tithe" builds a war chest

➤ Frederick Barbarossa leads the charge

➤ The German Crusade is a debacle

The Holy Mother Church knows the reason for the fall of Jerusalem. It is God's punishment on the sins of His people. "Boys are taught evil as soon as they can babble," one churchman said, "and as they grow up they become steadily worse until they are Christians only in name." Redemption lies in the launching of a Third Crusade.

A Moral Morass

By 1187, illegitimate children litter Europe. Knights and nobles exchange their concubines with one another, rape is common despite the severest penalties. Even knights who uphold the ideals of courtly love and languish for the mere touch of a highborn lady's hand are not above consoling themselves with one of the lady's maids. Drugs are peddled that produce abortion and increase wantonness. A penitential formula decrees three years' penance for any woman who mixes the sperm of her husband with her food to better receive his love.

Surely, the promiscuity of the age is related to its prosperity. With the reappearance of a money economy, towns and villages bustle. A hundred and fifty years ago, ninety percent of the people were serfs who scratched the soil for a living. Now only ten percent are *villains*, or farm workers. The vast majority live in towns producing goods and services that people can buy because they have money. This is evident in William Fitz-Stephen's account of London in 1173:

> Those engaged in the several kinds of business, sellers of several things, contractors for every kind of work, are distributed every morning into their various localities or shops. There is in London on the river bank, among the wines in ships sold by the vintners, a public cook shop; there eatables are to be found every day, according to the season, dishes of meat, roast, fried and boiled, great and small fish, coarser meats for the poor, more delicious for the rich, of game, fowls and small birds.

Warrior Words

A **villain** during the Middle Ages meant a serf or a peasant. Villain comes from the Latin *villanus*, meaning a farm servant.

Crusade Aid

Drunkenness was a favorite vice during the Middle Ages for all classes and sexes. Cider and perry (made from apples and pears) provided cheap intoxicants for the poor. Taverns were numerous, and ale was plentiful. Beer was the regular drink for the peasants, even at breakfast.

"Anything for a buck" is the motto of the day. Mercenaries, fugitive criminals, and ruined knights make the roads unsafe by robbing every pilgrim and traveler. Thieves break into manors, residences, and cathedrals in search of cash. In England, murders are twice as numerous as deaths by accident. "The lust for money," complains Berthold of Regensburg, "has become stronger than the lust for sex." Cheap cloth is substituted for fine cloth after a purchase is made; stones are concealed in sacks of hay and wool that are sold by weight; meatpackers catch stray dogs and cats and convert them into sausages and puddings unfit for human consumption. Even menial workers and peasants walk about with signet rings to make a mark that serves as a signature. The rich are dressed in fur, silk, satin, and velvet and "sweep the dusty ground with their prodigal trains of mantles and robes." No age, the moralists say, has manifested more malice and more iniquity.

God's Judgment Launches the Crusade

The justice of God will not be mocked; the scales of His justice must be balanced; all transgressions require punishment. And God's judgment on the avarice, the greed, the corruption of the age is crystallized by the plight of Jerusalem. Saladin, the son of the devil, has snatched the Holy Land from Christian hands.

"The loss of the Crusader Kingdom," Pope Gregory VIII proclaims, "is punishment for our sins." We can make amends only by taking up the Holy Cross and marching as a Holy Army once more to Jerusalem. "Let Christians now forget earthly riches and lay up treasure in heaven. Let them turn from the allures of this dying world to the glory of eternal life in heaven."

Gregory VIII circulates a letter throughout Christendom calling for the Third Crusade. This appeal is intensified by letters from Hospitallers and Knights Templar to the nobles of Europe. In one letter, Terence, the Grand Master of the Templars, writes:

> The wrath of God has lately permitted us to be scourged by innumerable calamities which our sins have brought down to us. Know that the Turks assembled an immense multitude of their people and with bitter hostility they invaded the territories of the Christians. Since nearly all the inhabitants of these territories have been slain, we shall not be able to hold them unless we speedily receive divine assistance and the aid you can bring to us.

Finding Followers and Funds

Refugees from the Holy Land such as Joscelin, Archbishop of Tyre; and Heraclitus, Archbishop of Jerusalem; travel throughout Europe with the pope's blessing to drum up support for the new Crusade. The response is overwhelming. King Henry II of England and King Philip of France, moved to tears of repentance by Joscelin's words, agree to stop waging war on one another, to sign a truce, and to take up the cross. The English, it is agreed, are to wear white crosses; the French red; and the Flemish green.

The two kings agree that the call is so urgent that a special tax must be levied on every individual in both countries. This heavy tax, called *Saladin's Tithe,* must be paid in the presence of a local committee that consists of a priest, a Hospitaller, and a Templar. If you attempt to cheat on your statements, you will be excommunicated from the Church and cast into exile from the Christian Kingdom.

Warrior Words

Saladin's Tithe was a tax that took a tenth of everyone's income. "Moveable goods," with the exception of precious stones, were also to be taxed. A knight's arms and horses were exempted, as well as a cleric's horses, books, and vestments.

A huge war chest is accumulated to equip the new army. This is only proper and fitting. It's not cheap to supply a knight with a suit of armor and battle weapons. The cost in today's currency would easily exceed $180,000 per soldier.

Emperor Frederick Feels His Oats

While Henry II and Philip are busy collecting taxes and recruiting soldiers, the Holy Roman Emperor, Frederick Barbarossa, sets out from Regensburg without delay in May 1189. He is seventy years old and looks upon the Crusade as the crowning act of his illustrious career. The army he leads is one of the largest ever to leave Europe. Some estimate that it comprises over 100,000 men-in-arms. Another writes: "No one in all Germany was considered to be of any manly steadfastness at all, who was seen without the saving sign and who would not join the comradeship of the Crusaders."

Why the enormous support for this undertaking? The answer lies in the fact that it is not only a matter of God, but of Mammon. The situation in the Holy Land jeopardizes trade and the stability of the Western world. The great Italian cities of Venice, Pisa, and Genoa depend on trade with the Middle Eastern port cities of Jaffa, Tyre, Acre, Beirut, and Ascalon. If these cities are unable to obtain goods from the East, they will be unable to purchase goods from the West. Commerce will come to a screeching halt. The fairs will close. The marketplaces will vanish. The towns will disappear. And the Dark Ages will return with a vengeance. It doesn't take a Peter Abelard to understand the economic urgency of the political situation.

Crusade Aid

The trade caravans from the East made Italian merchants incredibly wealthy. To such port cities as Tyre, Acre, and Jaffa, the Genovese and Pisan merchants brought goods such as wool and wood from the West to be traded for silks, sugar, spices, and exotic perfumes. The Moslem occupation of the coastal cities of Palestine threatened a billion dollar business.

Frederick's army was so vast that there were not enough ships to transport it across the Mediterranean Sea to the seaport in Palestine. It had to march overland through Asia Minor—a route that no Christian army had successfully negotiated since the First Crusade.

The German crusaders travel without serious incident through Hungary, but trouble breaks out when they arrive in Byzantium. Isaac Angelus Comnena, the new Eastern Emperor, has entered into a secret alliance with Saladin to safeguard his empire. He's agreed to impede Frederick's progress by neglecting to provide food and supplies for the crusaders in exchange for Saladin's pledge not to invade his kingdom. This forces Frederick to occupy Philippopolis and provision the army in Thrace. Isaac gets irked and seizes two German envoys as hostages. Frederick responds by pillaging a large area around Thrace and issuing threats to capture Constantinople. By the end of March 1189, Isaac decides that Frederick is not kidding. He releases the hostages and agrees to transport the Germans across the Dardanelles.

For a while, all goes well. Frederick's soldiers inflict a series of defeats on the Turks on the plains of Anatolia. But as they move across the remorseless desert, the great German army, no less than in the First and Second Crusaders, experiences incredible hardship and suffering. They fall prey to constant ambushes from the Turks and experience such terrible thirst that they chew horse manure for moisture.

Frederick and His Army Fall

On May 18, 1190, the German army conquers the Turkish stronghold of Konya and enjoys several weeks of rest and recuperation in the orchards and gardens outside the walls before setting out for the mountain passes of the Taurus and the coastal plains of the Mediterranean.

They reach the banks of the little river of Salef in Cilica after a grueling march "through the glare of the sun and the burning heat of summer along a tortuous road that led across rocky cliffs accessible only to birds and mountain goats." Frederick, looking at the river now swollen by melting snow from the high peaks of the Taurus Mountains, decides to go for a refreshing swim. He jumps into the river, gets sucked into a whirlpool, and drowns.

The sudden death of the Holy Roman Emperor shatters his army. The Duke of Swabia, Frederick's son, attempts to pick up the pieces and continue the march to Palestine, but thousands of soldiers cast down their spears and head for home. Food runs out along with water. The Turks follow the troops and slaughter all stragglers.

Christian Chronicles

The Duke of Swabia, Frederick's son, had his father's body pickled in vinegar and carried in a barrel so that the old man could fulfill his vow by reaching Jerusalem. At Antioch, the rotting body was blamed for causing the plague, and it was quickly and rather unceremoniously buried.

The Black Death Returns

Reaching Antioch, the crusaders bury (or pour) what is left of Frederick Barbarossa, their great king, in St. Peter's Cathedral. They are only able to salvage two bones of the old warrior as relics.

In Antioch, another disaster awaits. The crusaders experience strange swellings in their armpits and groins. The swellings ooze blood and pus and give rise to huge boils that appear all over their bodies. They suffer incredible pain, cough blood, and die within a week. It is the return of the Black Death. Of Frederick's great army, few survive to set off south to Acre.

The Moslems heave a sigh of relief. "Thus did God spare us from the evil power of the Germans," one Arab chronicler writes.

But the Third Crusade is far from over. In fact, it is just about to really begin.

The Least You Need to Know

➤ The Church blamed the fall of Jerusalem on the sins of the Christian people.

➤ Pope Gregory II called for a Third Crusade to redeem Christendom.

➤ To raise money for the Third Crusade, nobles in France and England imposed a Saladin Tithe.

➤ The reconquest of the port cities of Palestine was crucial for trade.

➤ Holy Roman Emperor Frederick Barbarossa set off with a huge German army to rescue the Holy Land from Saladin.

➤ Frederick drowned in Asia Minor and the German Crusade collapsed into shambles.

Chapter 19

Richard: The Real Lion King

In This Chapter

➤ King Richard takes up the cross

➤ Richard and Philip of France get a legendary send-off

➤ Richard sets things right in Sicily

➤ Cyprus falls to Richard's army

➤ The legend of Richard Lion Heart begins to take shape

Henry II, King of England, is dead. His successor is Richard, who will be called *Coeur de Lion,* that is, "the Lion Heart." He'll be remembered as one of the greatest of England's monarchs and a major hero of history. He will pass into folklore, legend, and literature. He will be the sovereign lord of Robin Hood and Ivanhoe. The English will call him "good King Richard" throughout the ages. But, in truth, Richard is not English; he's a Norman who was born and bred in France. He has French tastes and a French temperament. He doesn't speak a word of English and has complete contempt for Englishmen. He finds the country wet and boring. He says he would like to sell the city of London to anyone who can come up with a few shillings.

King Richard

By his appearance, Richard commands respect. He is tall, square-shouldered, and athletic, with flaming red hair and gracious manners. He inherited his good looks and easy charm from his mother, Eleanor of Aquitaine, and his boundless energy from his father, Henry II. He is a superb musician and an excellent poet, but his major talents rest with military architecture and operations.

When he hears about Saladin's destruction of the Christian army at the battle of Hattin, he vows to take up the cross and to reconquer Jerusalem. This is more than a vow. It is a fixation that will consume his every waking moment, as well as his dreams.

Crusade Aid

For sailors guilty of such crimes as theft, boiling pitch was to be poured over their shaven bodies. They were then to be covered with chicken feathers and cast ashore at the next port so that all would know them as miscreants.

Christian Chronicles

King Richard and King Philip agreed to depart for the Crusade from the town of Vezelay. Vezelay had special significance to the kings. It was the place where St. Bernard delivered the sermon that initiated the Second Crusade. The fourth of July also had special significance for them; it was the day of the Battle of Hattin.

Richard Prepares to Go East

As soon as he acquires England, Richard puts everything up for sale to raise money for the Holy War: castles, titles, official offices, even towns. He removes all sheriffs from their positions and orders them, under threat of imprisonment, to buy back their sheriff-hoods. He combs the countryside for every penny and pound until England is on the verge of financial ruin. Then, before leaving his sacked kingdom, he proclaims a general amnesty, opening wide the gates to every prison and sending out to every town and village thieves, rapists, and murderers.

With the loot, Richard orders the building of a large fleet of 250 ships to transport crusaders to the Holy Land. He sets rules for sailors that display his no-nonsense approach to the process of crusading: Whoever kills a fellow sailor shall be bound to his dead shipmate and cast in the ocean. Thieves are to be tarred and feathered and put ashore. Those who engage in fisticuffs "will be plunged into the sea three times." What's more, there will be heavy fines for anyone who curses or uses bad language.

Two Kings Get a Great Parade

Before setting off for the Holy Land, Richard meets King Philip of France to join him on the sacred mission. He wants to take Philip along, but not because he likes him; on the contrary, Richard dislikes and distrusts Philip, who is austere, poorly educated, one-eyed, and clumsy. But if Philip goes along, Richard can be sure that there's no way he can attack and seize Richard's territories. King Philip, on his part, is being pressured to join the holy war, by popular opinion and by the French clergy.

The two kings meet at Vezelay and head out for the Holy Land on July 4, 1190. This is the grandest procession in medieval history. Hundreds of thousands of knights and foot soldiers take part in it. Englishmen, Frenchmen, Angevins, and Normans march side by side singing crusader songs and shouting Christian cheers. The procession continues through towns and villages until the crusaders reach Lyons. Villagers come out to give them bread, wine, and cold water from their wells. Women hold up their babies for the knights to touch with the belief that these lords are in a state of special grace. The procession includes thousands of black-robed priests who chant Latin hymns and mumble prayers as they pass through France.

At Lyons, the two kings part company. King Philip heads for Genoa and Richard for Marseilles, where the great English fleet awaits to take him and his force to Sicily.

Christian Chronicles

In Sicily, Norman rulers issued orders in Latin, Greek, and Arabic. A Moslem traveler to the island in 1186 was surprised by the pervasive Orientalism. The king kept black slaves, and his chamberlains were eunuchs. The crusaders found the inhabitants loathsome. One chronicler, Ambroise, wrote this rhyming account of his time on the island:

> For townsfolk rabble and the scum
> of the city, bastard Greek were some,
> and some of them Saracen born
> did heap upon our pilgrims scorn.
> Fingers to eyes they mocked at us
> Calling us dogs malodorous.
> They did us foulness every day;
> Sometimes our pilgrims they did slay.
> And the corpses in the privies threw
> And this were proven to be true.

Richard's Sicilian Sojourn

Richard has business in Sicily, serious business. William II, his brother-in-law, had been king of this island and agreed to serve in the campaign. Unfortunately, he died, and an illegitimate cousin by the name of Tancred of Lecce seized the throne. This would be all well and good as far as Richard is concerned, if Tancred had not cast Richard's beautiful sister Joan in prison, confiscated her dowry, and seized for himself all of the dead king's possessions.

The Messina Mission

No one messes with Richard's loved ones or steals his possessions. Richard captures Joan's castle at La Bagnara and returns it to her. He seizes a monastery on an island in the Faro River, expels the monks, and transforms it into his military headquarters. Next, he sets out to capture the capital city of Messina. While the English army storms the main entrance, Richard strolls around the walls of the city. He spots an unguarded posterial gate, smashes the hatch with a hatchet, and enters the city with two soldiers. It is dark now and they are unnoticed as they creep along the curtain wall. They quickly reach the unattended main gate. Richard opens the gate and his soldiers pour in. He has conquered an entire city almost single-handedly.

Tancred now must come to terms with Richard. He restores Joan's dowry and Richard's inheritance, and gives them 40,000 gold ounces as a peace offering.

The Bride Imbroglio

The crusader army gathers to winter in Sicily. This gives Richard and Philip time to quarrel about everything under the sun, but, most especially, Richard's long-standing engagement to Philip's sister Alice. Richard announces that he has no intention of marrying Alice because she is "damaged goods." Philip becomes enraged. "How can you make such a statement about my beautiful and chaste sister?" Philip yells. Richard replies, "I can make the statement because Alice acted like a little tart when she was sent to England as a teenager. As a matter of fact, every night, she climbed into bed with my father!" "Your father! This is outrageous!" Philip says. "Yes, it is outrageous, and, if I marry her, I'll be committing incest by proxy," Richard answers.

The argument intensifies when Richard says that he intends to marry, not Alice, but a big-breasted blond named Berengaria, the daughter of the king of Navarre. Such a marriage, Richard says, will help to stabilize the relationship between Spain and the Aquitaine. He doesn't seem to realize that by this statement he is ruining the relationship between England and France.

Civility is only restored between the two kings when Richard agrees to pay Philip 10,000 silver marks to be released from his betrothal oath to Alice.

Crusade Aid

Richard managed to produce "documentary proof" that his father had bedded his fiancée Alice in England. When Philip was shown the evidence, he accepted the 10,000 silver marks from Richard and issued a proclamation, in the name of the Blessed Trinity, that he no longer had a quarrel with Richard over Alice's fate, and that the two kings had established peace and friendship.

The "Laws of the Crusade"

At the end of the long winter, Richard has a series of meetings with the great Christian mystic Joachim of Flora and undergoes a conversion experience. He decides to perform penance for the sins of his flesh in a chapel at Messina. The archbishops, bishops, priests, and soldiers gather as Richard, barefoot and wearing a simple shirt, walks toward the altar. He strips off the shift, kneels before the altar, and pleads for God's mercy in his nakedness. It is a remarkable sight. "From that hour on," says the chronicler Roger of Hoveden, "he became a man and feared God and abandoned what was evil and did good."

Newly chastened, Richard and Philip draw up the "laws of the Crusade" that had never before been drafted. The laws stipulate the following:

➤ There will be no gambling except by knights and clergy.

➤ No knight or clerk will be allowed to lose more than 20 shillings.

➤ Soldiers found gambling will be whipped naked by the army for three days and thrown into the sea for three consecutive mornings.

➤ No crusader will be permitted to hoard goods.

➤ No one in the army will be permitted to buy bread and sell it for a profit.

➤ The price of bread is fixed at a penny a loaf.

➤ No women except washerwomen shall be permitted to commiserate with the crusaders.

The Crusaders Set Sail

King Philip with his army sets sail for Acre on March 30, 1191. A few days later, Queen Eleanor, Richard's mother, arrives in Messina with Berengaria, Richard's new fiancée. A few days of festivities follow. Eleanor departs for England, and Richard with his great army set sail with the blushing Berengaria and Richard's sister Joan for the Holy Land in an armada of 200 ships.

Two days out at sea, a violent storm erupts and the ships are shattered. Twenty-five are lost without a trace. Richard prays fervently through the night until the storm abates.

A week after leaving Messina, Richard arrives at the island of Crete, in search of lost ships from his fleet. He is grief-stricken because one of the lost ships bore his princess and his sister. But this is not all. The ship containing the ladies also contains the treasure he had amassed for the Holy War.

Richard's Cyprus Rout

God is with Richard; he is soon delighted to discover that his sister and his princess are safe. But Richard is infuriated to learn that Isaac Ducas Comnena, who has a forged document stating that he is emperor of Cyprus, has seized his treasure and imprisoned many of his shipwrecked sailors. Richard wants them back. But the emperor remains heedless. To make matters worse, the emperor sets up defenses on the shore to prevent an English landing. Behind the makeshift barricade, according to a chronicler, are the emperor's men "ever so nicely decked out in expensive multicolored costumes with war steeds and precious golden banners waving." To the Normans, the soldiers of Cyprus look like Greek cross-dressers.

Richard's men—"baying like dogs"—row their skiffs toward the shore in a hail of arrows and crossbow bolts. When the offensive seems to falter, Richard jumps from his barge "like a raging lion and to set out upon the Cypriots." The other soldiers follow. In no time at all, the king and his soldiers are off pursuing the fancy-pants Byzantines and their idiotic ruler.

As dusk is falling, Richard and his troops enter the city of Limassol in triumph. He finds ample supplies of oil, wine, corn, and meat. He flies his flag from the city walls and sets out to encounter Isaac Comnena and his men, who are holed up in a thickly forested valley. There is a short, bloody battle. All of Isaac's horses, weapons, and treasures are captured, together with his splendid tents and gold-embroidered battle standard. The terrified ruler leaps naked from his bed and runs off into the woods.

Christian Chronicles

The day after Isaac fled naked into the woods, Berengaria was crowned Queen of England in the chapel of the castle of Limassol. Following the coronation was the wedding service, then followed the inevitable feast. Instead of bedding his new bride, Richard set off in search of Isaac and the remnants of Isaac's army.

Three days later, Isaac, under safe conduct, meets with Richard on a field near Limassol and agrees to release the shipwrecked prisoners, to make restitution for the confiscated goods, to send 500 of his men to the Holy Land, and to pay a penalty fee. Isaac bows and scrapes before Richard and gives him the kiss of peace.

"Once an idiot …." When Isaac returns to his fortress at Famagusta, he assumes he's safe from the crusaders' clutches. He places the crown back on his head and issues orders for Richard to leave the island.

This is the last straw. Richard conquers the island within a matter of days, places Isaac in chains, confiscates all his possessions, appoints one of his officers to serve as Governor of Cyprus, and sets sail for Palestine.

After falling on his knees and begging Richard for his life, Isaac's only request is that he should not be placed in iron chains. Richard agrees to this request and orders that Isaac be bound in chains of silver.

When Richard arrives in Acre, he leads Isaac to the battlefield like a chained monkey. He later sends him to Tripoli, where the "emperor of Cyprus" is cast into a dungeon in the fortress of Margat, which belongs to the Templars.

The Legend Is Born

Richard has not yet reached the Holy Land but he already has made the king of Sicily his vassal, added the kingdom of Cyprus to his kingdom, married a Spanish princess, and secured an offshore base for the kingdom of Jerusalem.

After setting sail from Cyprus, his ship encounters a ship flying French colors. Richard thinks she looks suspicious and sends envoys to board her. The captain of the ship says that his crew is traveling from Antioch to assist in the siege of Acre, but Richard is still suspicious. He questions the captain and his crew about France, only to discover that they are Saracens in disguise. Richard orders an attack. The Englishmen crawl over the Saracen ship like military ants and find treasure chests of gold and precious jewels. More than 1,400 Moslems throw themselves into the raging sea.

Richard has established himself as a formidable crusader, and he has yet to arrive in the Holy Land.

The Least You Need to Know

➤ Richard I succeeded Henry I as King of England and was, with Philip of France, co-ruler of the Third Crusade.

➤ Richard raised funds for the Crusade by selling castles, titles, offices, and even towns.

➤ Richard conquered Sicily and made the Sicilian king his vassal.

➤ Richard conquered Cyprus, which would serve as an offshore base for the Third Crusade.

Chapter 20

The Battle at Acre

In This Chapter

➤ Guy of Lusignan is released from captivity by Saladin

➤ King Richard helps Guy conquer Acre

➤ Guy is restored as Jerusalem's king

➤ Richard attempts to collect what's due from Saladin in their treaty

➤ Richard's army slaughters the innocents of Acre

King Richard, in Cyprus, is informed of the arrival of honored guests from the Holy Land who have just arrived from Acre with a small fleet of well-armed vessels. Richard summons them to his court at Limassol. In strolls the least likely person to pop up in the pages of the Third Crusade. It is none other than King Guy of Lusignan, the king of Jerusalem!

Guy's Quandary

The last time we saw King Guy, he was hauled off to Damascus as Saladin's prisoner. In 1189, the Moslem ruler had freed the captive king upon Guy's promise that he would return to France and never take up arms against the people of Islam. But a promise to a Moslem doesn't mean a thing. As soon as Guy gets sprung, he has his vow annulled by a priest. Then he sets out to take command of the Christian forces at Tyre.

The people of Tyre don't want Guy to become their king. They remember his incompetence at Hattin, and tell him to go away. They're very happy under the command of Conrad of Montferrat, who's kept the Moslem forces outside the walls of the city for four years.

But Guy is the king and Conrad is merely a Flemish knight. Unfortunately, Guy doesn't have enough of an army to lay siege to Tyre and feed Conrad to the Moslems, so he's forced to set off along the coast to Acre, which is occupied by Moslem forces. Guy may be a wimp, but he's not an idiot. He knows that Acre is a pivotal city for Mediterranean trade and that the wealthy merchants of Pisa will be willing to fund his siege of the port city.

Crosscurrent

Saladin wisely released King Guy of Lusignan from prison knowing the crusaders' innate gift for infighting. To help things along, he released a host of other Franks to accompany Guy to Tyre. At Tyre, the squabbling got underway as soon as King Guy made an appearance.

Crusade Aid

King Guy and his soldiers had laid siege to the city of Acre for two years before they enlisted Richard. They were able to inflict damage on the city because of the development of new and improved siege engines, or catapults. These siege engines contained counterbalances that enabled them to hurl heavier and more damaging ammunition than the human-powered artillery of the First Crusade.

Guy Eyes Acre

The Pisans send supplies, equipment, money, and a small force of soldiers to join Guy's troops. They dig massive ditches around the city in an effort to cut off the people of Acre from the hinterland. It is grueling work that goes on for months. Eventually, more Christian troops come to Guy's aid, including survivors from Hattin, the remnants of Frederick Barbarossa's army, and military groups from Europe. Guy feels confident that he will conquer the city in a matter of months.

But Guy hasn't learned much from his military encounters. As soon as the king is finished digging his ditch, Saladin assembles a powerful army around the Christian camp so that Guy's army is caught in a deadly vise. It's a horrible predicament. King Philip arrives just at the right time to alleviate the pressure with his massive French army. The Christians now have enough manpower to overwhelm the garrison troops. But as soon as they launch an attack, the defenders begin banging drums and making smoke signals so that Saladin's outer army will come to the rescue. It is utterly frustrating.

What to do? Philip decides to send Guy and some nobles to fetch Richard from his honeymoon in Cyprus. And so, King Guy appears in all his glory before Richard and begs him to set sail with his soldiers to Acre.

Richard Joins the Cause

Richard arrives at Acre on June 8 with 25 war galleys and Isaac Ducas Comnena, the former emperor of Cyprus, in chains and shackles. Cheers resound throughout the Christian camp. The soldier-chronicler Ambroise writes: "No pen can sufficiently describe the joy of the people on the night of great King Richard's arrival." Everyone is in high spirits and an all-night party takes place. The only one who is not as pleased as punch is King Philip. Philip is sick with a terrible disease called arnaldia, which has caused his hair and fingernails to fall out. The French King, with his one eye, now looks like a Cyclops from hell.

Richard immediately supervises the construction of huge catapults that are christened with such names as "Bad Neighbor" and "God's Own Sling." There is also a huge grabbling ladder called "The Cat." The last details of the assault are being planned when Richard comes down with a case of arnaldia even worse than Philip's. Not only does Richard lose his flaming red hair and fingernails but his skin falls from his face, making him look like the living dead.

Though weak and listless, Richard is carried on a stretcher to the front lines of the assault troops. He props himself up to a sitting position and shoots arrows at the watchmen on the towers. Even the Moslems are amazed at Richard's resolve. As a gesture of respect, Saladin sends the sick king fruit and snow. It is just what a good doctor would order, as arnaldia, as it turns out, is a form of scurvy.

Acre Surrenders

King Philip, who has now recuperated from the terrible disease, launches a series of assaults against the Accursed Tower of Acre. On June 17, the French army storms the gates and the Moslems begin banging their kettledrums for Saladin's counterattack. There is fierce fighting on two fronts. Geoffrey of Lusignan, Guy's brother, distinguishes himself by rushing against the enemy with a battle-axe, slaughtering 20 Moslem soldiers and taking 50 prisoners. The day is without victory for either side. There are mountains of dead to be thrown into ditches.

On July 2, there is another massive attack by the French. By this time, Richard and his soldiers succeed in digging a massive tunnel under the Accursed Tower. All the soil is removed and timbers are used to shore up the tunnel. The Tower is now standing on stilts. The French set the timbers on fire, and the Tower starts to totter. The Moslems scramble to fortify it with boulders.

In the midst of this, Alberic Clemens, the military commander, and a large number of French soldiers begin to scale the walls of Acre with their new scaling ladder, the "Cat." Alberic vows that he will enter Acre that day or perish. As they scramble toward the ramparts, the Moslems let down a gigantic grappling hook and pull Alberic up for the sheer pleasure of killing him. At the same time, they throw down a multitude of heavy rocks that kill the French soldiers scaling the wall. To annoy the attackers even more, a Moslem wearing the armor of Alberic Clemens parades along the wall and makes mocking gestures at the crusaders. Richard, though still sick and lying on a silken mattress, aims his crossbow and shoots the taunting Moslem soldier through the heart.

Crosscurrent

At Acre, King Philip demanded that Richard grant to him half of Cyprus as they had taken an oath to split all booty. Richard told him to get lost. The rift between the two kings widened. When Richard heard that Philip was paying his men three gold coins a month, he offered four to any knight who entered his service. When the Pisans and Genoese flocked to Richard's colors, he refused the services of the Genoese because they had pledged themselves to the French king.

Now Saladin's forces launch the counterattack. It is pure pandemonium and an orgy of bloodletting. By the end of the day, the crusaders are too exhausted to bury the dead or to come to the aid of the wounded.

The heat is scorching and relentless. An outbreak of a strange disease called "leonardie" now erupts in the Christian camp. It reduces the soldiers to a state of helpless lethargy. At the same time, typhus takes its toll. Food is so scarce that horse entrails cost 10 copper pennies, and strips of leather are shredded and boiled to make soup. Soldiers eat insects and earth. Misery is all around. Thousands of putrid corpses remain unburied. They are covered with black clouds of flies; rats crawl among them; vultures and packs of wild dogs find an endless feast.

Inside Acre, conditions are even worse. Saladin can no longer send supplies to the beleaguered city because Richard's fleet has managed to completely block the harbor. There are reports of cannibalism, and the garrison troops no longer have munitions.

To alleviate the situation at Acre, Saladin raids and burns Haifa, uproots all nearby vineyards, and cuts down all the groves of fruit trees around Acre in an attempt to draw the Christians from the siege. But it doesn't work. The Christian army under Richard's command holds firm.

On July 12, Saracens come out of Acre to bargain for a truce. Richard sets the terms. The True Cross must be returned to the Christians; 1,500 prisoners in Saladin's hands must be released; and Richard and Philip must receive a payment of 200,000 gold coins. The Saracens have no option except to agree.

The Christians make a triumphant entrance into the city. Richard takes up residence in the palace with his wife and his favorite sister Joan. Philip and his nobles move into the Templar stronghold. Richard and Philip both raise their standards in recognition of their agreement to share the spoils. Leopold of Austria, who commands the pathetic remnant of the German Crusade, raises his standard next to Richard's in an effort to show that he deserves a part of the take. Richard tears down Leopold's standard and throws it in the moat. It's an act that he will come to regret.

Christian Chronicles

The real issue after the conquest of Acre was not which noble got what building but rather which city got what rights of commerce. For Pisa and Genoa, the struggle for the supremacy of Acre was a struggle for economic life and death, particularly as the Church now forbade any trade with Egypt. The Pisans were supporters of Guy; the Genoese of Conrad. Guy's family, the Lusignans, were Richard's vassals from his county of Poitou; Conrad was King Philip's first cousin.

Post-Battle Business

Guy's right to the crown of Jerusalem is in question; Philip leaves for home, jeopardizing Richard's lands; Richard is having a hard time getting Saladin to honor the truce agreement; and the Pisans see an opportunity to cash in on the confusion.

Guy Runs for King

Who will be recognized as the real king of Jerusalem? Guy wears the crown only because of his marriage to Queen Sibylla, now deceased along with her two daughters. Will he continue to wear the crown? Many believe that he forfeited his claim to power because of his ineptitude and stupidity at Hattin. Nevertheless, he fought bravely at Acre and has the support of the rich merchants of Pisa, not to mention that of King Richard. King Philip, however, believes that Conrad of Montferrat deserves the throne, not only because of his command of Tyre, but also because he is married to Princess Isabelle, the half-sister of Baldwin IV and the former wife of Humphrey of Toron. Conrad is also well connected with moneymen; he has close ties with the rich merchants of Genoa. When Richard and Philip are finally done squabbling over the crown, it's decided that Guy of Lusignan will remain King during his lifetime. When he dies, the crown will pass on to Conrad.

The French and Germans Go Home

Crusade Aid

King Richard wrote a letter to his subjects informing them of King Philip's sudden departure from the Crusade. He wrote: "Know that after the taking of Acre, the king of France ... abandoned the purpose of his pilgrimage and broke the will of God to his eternal shame and the shame of his realm."

On July 31, Philip departs from Acre and makes his way to Tyre. He is now suffering from a severe case of dysentery and spends all day on a chamber pot. He is bone tired, fed up with Richard, and convinced that the armies of Islam cannot be destroyed. Besides, he has an excuse to leave. Wars are raging in France and he needs to suppress them. Philip packs up his bags and boards one of the Genoese galleys that will take his army back to Europe. Before he leaves, he promises not to attack any of Richard's lands until Richard returns home.

The French are not the only soldiers calling it quits. Leopold and his German army also leave the Holy Land. The proud Duke of Austria feels that he was cheated out of the loot and disgraced by the English King.

Richard Runs Amok

Richard alone remains in Acre. He has more than 3,000 captured Moslems on his hands and seeks a meeting with Saladin so that he can receive full payment of the terms of the treaty in exchange for the prisoners. But Saladin is not anxious to meet with Richard. He doesn't want to comply with the outrageous terms of a treaty that was signed without his permission. He is not willing to part with the True Cross (that has no more significance for him than a piece of firewood), let alone 200,000 gold coins and 1,500 Frankish prisoners. He decides to buy some time until fresh troops arrive from Damascus and Egypt so he can renew his attack on the Christian forces. He sends Richard costly presents, along with a Negro slave. The ploy doesn't work. Richard wants neither the slave nor the gifts. He tells Saladin that the terms of the treaty must be met within 30 days.

A month passes, but no payment has been made. Saladin doesn't even promise that the check is in someone's chain mail. Richard is boiling with rage. On August 20, he hauls the Moslem prisoners of Acre to a hill of Ayyadieh in full view of Saladin's field headquarters. He orders the killing of all prisoners: men, women, and children. The prisoners are dragged before the executioners. Their heads are lowered and the axes fall. Soldiers slice open their bodies and remove their bowels in search of gold and silver. It is a scene of incredible savagery. In the afternoon, Richard abandons the hill and the dead and returns to Acre. The screams from Saladin's camp can be heard throughout the night.

Christian Chronicles

Of all Richard's actions, the massacre at Ayyadieh of 3,000 Moslem men, women, and children certainly is the most horrifying. But Richard, for all his courage, cunning, and chivalry, was a creature of his age. Massacre was the order of the day. When Moslems captured a fortress, they inevitably massacred the captives, except for leading knights, whose lives were worth a ransom. An unwritten code of medieval warfare stipulated that officers on both sides were treated with courtesy and kindness, while the ordinary foot soldiers were hauled off like sheep for slaughter.

The Pisans Procure

The Pisan merchants, knowing that Richard has captured the city, immediately decide to profit from the event. They send to Acre what is needed most by the Christian soldiers, a boatload of salacious prostitutes. Saladin's secretary records their arrival as follows:

> Tinted and painted, desirable and appetizing, bold and ardent, with nasal voices and fleshy thighs, they offered their wares for enjoyment, brought their silver anklets up to touch their golden ear-rings, made themselves targets for men's darts, offered themselves to the lance's blows, made javelins rise toward shields. They interwove leg with leg, caught lizard after lizard in their holes, guided pens to inkwells, torrents to the valley bottom, swords to scabbards, firewood to stoves, and they maintained this was an act of piety without equal, especially to those who were far from home and wives.

Overnight, Acre becomes the liveliest nightspot in the desert. Richard has no stomach for decadence. He is a man with a mission. He collects his army for a march to Jaffa through enemy territory in the heat of full summer with little food and less water. The order testifies to Richard's moral resolve and ironclad will. The soldiers dutifully obey.

The Least You Need to Know

➤ Guy of Lusignan was released by Saladin and attempted to wrest control of Tyre from Conrad of Montferrat and reclaim his throne.

➤ Conrad, the commander at Tyre, also laid claim to the Christian crown.

➤ King Philip of France and the merchants of Genoa supported the claims of Conrad, and King Richard of England and the merchants of Pisa supported the claims of Guy.

➤ King Richard joined forces with Guy to conquer Acre.

➤ When Saladin refused to honor the terms of the truce agreement, Richard massacred 3,000 Moslem prisoners.

➤ Guy was appointed King of Jerusalem by a council of nobles, and Conrad was named heir to the throne.

➤ King Philip and many French crusaders left the Holy Land after the victory at Acre.

Chapter 21

Richard vs. Saladin: The Clash of Titans

In This Chapter

➤ Saladin's army is defeated at Arsuf

➤ Richard's truce proposal goes nowhere

➤ Richard's army stops short of Jerusalem

➤ Count Conrad is assassinated

➤ Richard's daring rout of Jaffa becomes legend

➤ The titans negotiate a delicate truce

The Third Crusade is marching to Jerusalem, and Richard has rescued his soldiers from the arms of the shameless whores. No hanky panky for these guys! They are soldiers in the Lord's army. As they march from Acre in the blazing hot sun, Richard is happy the crusaders will have the opportunity to regain their moral bearings and concentrate on the sacred mission of purging the Holy Land of all infidels. Richard knows that fornication is a mortal sin, and adultery even worse. How can God bless the army if it is made up of rank and randy sinners? Now the only women Richard will allow among the ranks are washerwomen, who are old women known for their piety. The task of the washerwomen is to keep the crusaders' linen clean, to wash their hair, and to delouse them, at which task they are "as adroit as monkeys." The Moslems are amazed at the sight of the frumpy fraus in the midst of the Christian army. One later writes:

"The army was full of old women. They exhorted and incited men to summon their pride, saying that the cross imposed on them an obligation to resist to the bitter end."

Richard's March to Jerusalem

Marching to Jaffa, the vast Christian army of more than 85,000 men is ordered by Richard to stay in very tight formation. Richard wants his army to remain intact with no part weaker than any other. The army is divided into twelve brigades and grouped in five divisions; each brigade includes a cavalry and an infantry. They march in three columns. The column on the right, near the seashore, includes the soldiers who are carrying supplies, along with the pack animals. In the center rides the cavalry and on the left the infantry. The Templars form the advance guard, and the Hospitallers the rear. Richard rides up and down the lines to make sure there isn't a break between the guards. Even the slightest break could cause a portion of the army to be cut off from the rest. This would mean they could be surrounded and cut down.

Saladin and his great army follow the crusaders on the landward side like a menacing shadow. They take every opportunity to pick off stragglers—the lame, the weak, and the wounded—and to ambush parties foraging the countryside for food; intermittently, Saladin's light cavalry makes hit-and-run attacks.

Christian Chronicles

Baha ad-Din, Saladin's chronicler, watches Richard's army from the high ground and can't conceal his admiration for its order and discipline:

> The Moslems sent in volleys of arrows from all sides, deliberately trying to irritate the knights and force them to come out from behind the wall of infantry. But it was all in vain. The knights kept their temper admirably and went on their way without the least hurry.

> They never marched a long stage, for they had to spare the foot-soldiers. Half of the infantry carried the baggage and the tents, for there was a lack of beasts of burden. It was impossible not to admire the patience shown by these people. They bore crushing fatigue without a whimper.

It's slow going. Marching only in the morning, Richard's army covers six or seven miles a day at best. They encounter no fortresses, for Saladin has destroyed every town and castle in sight.

The real problem comes at night. Saladin sends Nubian slaves armed with only scimitars and shields into the Christian camp under the cover of night. Screams punctuate the darkness, and the bodies of dead soldiers are discovered every morning.

And there is the tarantula problem. They bite the crusaders as they sleep and leave painful, bulbous swellings. The knights can go to the doctors, who apply oils and balms to their bites, but the foot soldiers cannot afford such luxuries. At last, they discover a simple way to deal with the spiders. They discover that tarantulas are repelled by loud noise. All night long, you can hear the banging of drums, the clashing of helmets, and the beating of pots and pans. No one sleeps, but fewer tarantulas are crawling around the campgrounds.

Also, during the night King Richard's heralds call the men to prayer with the cry, *Sanctum Sepulchrum adjuva!* ("Free the Holy Sepulcher!") "On hearing these words," a chronicler writes, "the whole multitude of crusaders would take up the cry, stretching forth their hands to heaven and with copious tears, praying to God for aid and mercy."

On any given night, the heralds would call the crusaders to prayer three or four times. During times of grave danger, prayers would be raised from the Christian camp all night long. The tireless Richard was known to keep prayer vigils until the crack of dawn.

The Battle at Arsuf

The decisive battle takes place on September 7, 1191, at Arsuf, 30 miles from Jaffa. The Saracens emerge from the woods shortly before 9 A.M. like screaming banshees. At first come the foot soldiers—Negroes, Nubians, and Bedouins—shooting arrows and throwing javelins. Next comes the Moslem cavalry with axes, swords, and lances. Wave after wave appears until a cloud of dust conceals the sun and the sky. "For the space of two miles," writes one chronicler, "you could not see as much earth as could be taken up in one's hand, so numerous were the Turks."

If a gap appears in the Christian formation, the process of cutting up the crusaders could go on indefinitely. There is danger that the rear guard, moving at alarmingly slow speed, could open up a hole that would be filled by the enemy. The

Christian Chronicles

At the battle of Arsuf, Henry of Champagne rides into the pages of history. He is the son of Richard's half-sister and the grandson of Queen Eleanor of Aquitaine. It is his duty to ride out from the formation and keep watch on the hills. When the Saracens emerge, Henry signals the rest of the army.

Crusade Aid

The battle of Arsuf was won when the Saracens fled back into the woods. Some of them hid in the branches of trees, and Christian crossbowmen amused themselves by engaging in target practice. After the battle, Saladin's army continued to harass the Christian army by sporadic attacks on its flanks. But the decisive battle had been won.

Hospitallers cry out for Richard to unleash the cavalry. But Richard wants his army intact, knowing that the separation of one column will cause certain calamity.

The Saracens dismount so they can aim more accurately at the infantry with their arrows and lances. Suddenly, the trumpeters sound the alarm and the mounted knights plow through the first column toward the startled Saracens with swords and lances. Behind the knights come the infantry with fixed bayonets. At the head of the charge, of course, is Richard, as reckless and bold as ever. He joins the Hospitallers at the rear guard. "Then the king, the fierce, the extraordinary king, cut down the Turks in every direction, and none could escape the force of his arm."

In the wake of the battle, 1,000 Christians and 10,000 Saracens lay dead. Richard has clashed with the great Saladin in a field of battle—and won.

Saladin is deeply disturbed by the defeat. He withdraws into himself, keeps strangely silent, and refuses food and drink. He doesn't even seem to hear his emirs as they attempt to console him. The great Moslem leader has lost his aura of invincibility.

Impasse at Jaffa

The Christians reach Jaffa after traveling 29 days to cover 80 miles. Here, at last, they can finally rest. They make camp in an olive garden just outside the city walls because nothing is left of Jaffa. The city has been destroyed by Saladin. The rebuilding takes months. But such work is necessary, as Jaffa is supposed to serve as a center of support for the attack on Jerusalem.

During this time, Richard sends a letter to Saladin with an offer to begin negotiations. "The Moslems and Franks are bleeding to death," he writes, "the country is utterly ruined and goods and lives have been lost on both sides. The time has come to stop this. The points of issue are Jerusalem, the Cross, and the land."

Saladin does not meet with Richard because he knows that he's in a weak position. Still, he doesn't want to offend the king, so he sends his brother Saphadin to meet with Richard and attempt to establish an agreement.

The negotiations between Richard and Saphadin are conducted in the presence of Humphrey of Toron. Remember him? He was the first husband of Princess Isabella, who is now the wife of Conrad of Montferrat, the man who would be king. Humphrey is an Arabic scholar and a practiced negotiator. Richard's terms are simple: the payment of 200,000 gold pieces (as per the agreement at Acre), the return of the

True Cross, and the surrender of Jerusalem and all territory west of the Jordan. Saphadin smiles. "Sure," he says, "you can have the True Cross, but the other matters merit discussion."

During the meetings, something strange happens. Richard and Saphadin become good friends. They dine together, watch Syrian dancing girls perform, and exchange gifts. After several weeks, Richard makes a truly bizarre offer: that Saladin should give up all the disputed lands, and immediately afterward, Saphadin should marry Richard's sister Joan, the Dowager Queen of Sicily. As a dowry, Joan would receive all the coastal cities that are now in the hands of the crusaders. You might shake your head at this outrageous solution to the dilemma, but think about it! It will make everyone happy: Joan will become Queen of Jerusalem and Saladin's brother will become King! Everybody wins—Christian and Moslem alike.

There's only one problem. When Joan hears about this scheme, she's transformed into a screaming shrew. She will not become the wife of any Moslem for any reason. How could Richard even think of such a thing? The very idea of "a Bedouin in her bed" makes her cringe in horror!

Crosscurrent

Richard was willing to make a deal with Saladin at Jaffa because so many problems were cropping up in the Christian camp. Many soldiers and knights were slipping away by sea to Acre with hopes of heading home. At Acre, Conrad of Montferrat, now husband of Queen Isabelle, was conspiring with the Genoese to become master of the kingdom. To make matters worse, at Cyprus, a group of men still loyal to Isaac Ducas Comnena were starting a rebellion.

Richard's Strategic Retreat

So much for negotiations! Richard now plans to conquer Jerusalem. He leads his army to Beit Nuba, only 12 miles from Jerusalem. The prize is within his grasp, and it is Christmas Day. There is wild enthusiasm among the crusaders. The sick and wounded are carried from Jaffa to the camp, hoping that by the end of the week they'll be taken to the Holy Sepulcher where their sickness will be healed and their wounds cured. The Christians sing hymns, pray, and prepare themselves for the assault on the Holy City. But Richard studies plans, listens to spies, and speaks to his soldiers.

Christian Chronicles

The French, in fact, have established a very fashionable camp at Tyre. They dress in smooth, tight clothes with embroidered belts, jeweled collars, and flowers in their hair. While Richard and his men have been off fighting battles, they've been turning into effete dandies. You can always count on the French for a descent into decadence in the middle of a military campaign.

Crusade Aid

When Conrad set sail for Acre, the Pisans got word of it and planned an attack. As Conrad's ship approached the seawalls of the city, the Pisans let fly the boulders from the siege engines. Richard was in Caesarea when he heard of the bombardment of Conrad's ship. He jumped on his horse, set out for Acre, and immediately called for a ceasefire.

Finally, he comes to the conclusion that, if they took Jerusalem, they could not hold it after Richard and his army left for home. There are not enough Christian knights willing to stay on in the Holy Land.

Richard is compelled to retreat to Ascalon. A terrible storm ensues. Baggage carts get stuck in the mud; men sink in marshes; horses drown. This is a perfect touch for this moment in the Crusade. Thunder rumbles. Lightning cracks through the air. (Cecil B. DeMille would approve.)

When the dispirited army arrives at the coastal city of Ascalon, they find it in ruins, and begin the task of reconstructing it into a fortress. Richard summons Conrad of Montferrat to come and help, but he refuses; the French forces that King Philip had stationed at Tyre also refuse to come to Richard's aid.

Richard and his army have to climb over heaps of stones to enter Ascalon. Richard then set everyone to labor in the rebuilding of the city. Knights and clerics find new occupations as masons and bricklayers. Richard himself carries stones to the walls. He is determined to make Ascalon a Christian fortress in the south.

But something nefarious is afoot. Conrad wants to be king of Jerusalem, and he wants Richard, who supports Guy of Lusignan, to go home. Behind Richard's back, Conrad has been conducting secret meetings with Saladin to plot Richard's demise. Now open warfare is taking place between the Pisans (the merchants and mercenaries of Pisa), who support King Guy, and the Genoese (the merchants and mercenaries of Genoa), who support Count Conrad.

Richard travels to Tyre to settle things between Acre and Tyre, the English and the French, and the merchants of Pisa and the merchants of Genoa. He calls for a meeting of all Christian nobles to decide the political issue. The nobles decide that Conrad should be King, as he has the makings of a war leader, as evidenced by his defense of Tyre. Guy, on the other hand, remains permanently disgraced by his failure at the battle of Hattin.

What should Richard do? He is aware of the following:

➤ He knows from his good friend Saphadin that Conrad has entered into secret talks with Saladin.

➤ He knows that his conquests will be in vain if Conrad should become King.

➤ He knows that he cannot oppose Conrad's coronation without causing an irreparable rift between the French and English crusaders.

➤ He knows that he can't spend much more time in the Holy Land as his brother John is creating trouble in England and Philip is threatening Normandy.

➤ He knows that he owes a debt to the Pisans who provided his army with supplies and equipment during the siege at Acre.

Surely, Richard has to do something. He cannot permit Conrad to assume the throne, or all will be lost.

Monarchy, Murder, and Matrimony

Now we have another incredible scene in medieval history that never fails to stun students and scholars alike. On April 28, 1192, Conrad is struck down and killed in the streets of Tyre. The culprits are captured, and confess that they're Hashish Drinkers, a.k.a. Assassins, who were ordered to murder Conrad by the "Old Man of the Mountain," Sheik Rashid al-Din Sinan. They further say that King Richard the Lion Heart paid for the hit. Richard, of course, denies this allegation and professes to have no knowledge of the Old Man of the Mountain or the Assassins. But his problems have been most conveniently solved.

Crosscurrent

When Count Henry of Champagne arrived in Tyre to attend the funeral of Conrad of Montferrat, the people lined the streets to see the young and handsome feudal lord of the wealthiest and most civilized province of France. They shouted that he should marry Isabella. He had never met the queen and was startled by the wild enthusiasm. He was also less than eager to marry the new widow who was bearing Conrad's child. By the next day, the fourth day after Conrad's death, the engagement of Henry and Isabella was announced in the Cathedral of Tyre.

Richard arranges for King Guy to be crowned king of Cyprus and Henry of Champagne to ascend to the throne of Jerusalem by popular acclamation. Henry is wealthy, talented, brave, and handsome. He is also, by chance, Richard's nephew. Five days after the assassination of Conrad, Henry is not only crowned, but also married to Conrad's widow, Princess Isabella. Princess Isabella, we are told, is not only not lamenting the loss of her dearly beloved husband, she is head over heels in love with her new mate.

Henry's Strange End

There is an interesting footnote to this episode of murder and matrimony. Two years after the assassination, the Old Man of the Mountain dies and his successor invites Henry of Champagne to pay him a visit at his stronghold near the Caspian Sea. He apologizes for the killing of Conrad and admits that murder-for-hire always leaves someone upset. He then asks Henry to witness a demonstration. Pairs of men in white robes emerge from the pleasure garden, as high as kites on hash. The Assassin Chief orders them to form a line, march to the edge of the ramparts, and jump to their deaths without making a sound. Henry watches as hundreds of young men with blissful smiles on their faces jump from the high ramparts and splat on the stones below. It goes on for an hour. Then the Assassin Chief asks if Henry would like to see the demonstration repeated. Henry, badly shaken by the spectacle, says no. Then the Assassin Chief politely asks if there is someone the Assassins can kill for him.

Crusade Aid

Aimery of Lusignan became Queen Isabella's fourth and final husband. Aimery was the brother of the former King Guy of Lusignan. In this way, the rift between the supporters of Guy and the supporters of Conrad was finally mended. Aimery also suffered an untimely demise while eating "a surfeit of fish."

This story has a strange twist. Not long after this riveting demonstration, Henry slips on something like a banana peel, tumbles out of the window of his castle, and falls to his death. Queen Isabella sheds a few tears, and goes in search of husband number four.

Richard Drops In at Jaffa

Richard has sworn that he will only set eyes on Jerusalem at the time when he can deliver it from Moslem hands. On June 12, while out on patrol, he catches sight of the Holy City in the distance. He sadly covers his face with his shield and asks God's forgiveness. He knows that Saladin has fortified the city and laid waste to the countryside by cutting down trees and poisoning wells to prevent the Christians from gaining any advantage from the terrain.

Negotiations with the Moslems seem to be coming to an end and Richard moves to Acre, preparing for his departure to England. But Saladin suddenly swoops out of Jerusalem and attacks Jaffa with a massive army in three divisions. By the second day, the wall of the city near the Eastern Gate falls. The Moslems pour into Jaffa and the garrison troops take shelter in a citadel. They fight bravely, but they can't hold out against such overwhelming odds without immediate help from Richard.

Richard immediately sets sail for Jaffa with a small force of soldiers. Seeing the flag of Saladin's standards flying from the battlements of the besieged city, he is overcome with rage, and impetuously unstraps his leg armor, jumps overboard, and wades toward the shore with his shield above his head and his Danish battle-axe in his hand. The other soldiers follow his lead.

They quickly capture the seawall and fight their way through the city. The Moslems are caught completely off guard. They think that the garrison troops within the citadel have capitulated and that the city is safely in their hands. They're in the process of looting everything in sight when they look up and see Richard with his soldiers and marines slashing through the huge Moslem army. In true swashbuckling style, with no more than 50 knights and a hundred marines, Richard recaptures the city and saves the garrison troops.

Crusade Aid

Richard was a brilliant commander but a reckless warrior. Once, he pursued a retreating force in France with such abandon that he forgot to put on his armor and take along his sword. When William the Marshall, the celebrated knight, turned to engage Richard in combat, he realized that the king was completely unarmed. Knowing that he could not kill Richard, he satisfied his blood-thirst by killing Richard's horse.

Richard the Lion Heart

Saladin does not retreat to Jerusalem. He remains on the outskirts of Jaffa waiting for the right time to catch Richard and his men sleeping. On August 5, 1192, in the dead of the night, the Saracens sneak into the Christian camp. A soldier wandering on the plain sees a glint of armor and sounds the alarm. Richard immediately mounts his horse, gives orders to the crossbowmen and archers to be posted between the spearmen, and waits for the Moslems to advance.

The Saracen army charges but they can't break through the crusader lines. Richard and 10 mounted knights counterattack with such violence that the Moslems reel back. The battle lasts all day. The Moslems retreat to a hillside.

One of Richard's chroniclers recorded this picture of Richard, the perfect knight, fighting the Moslems on the plains of Jaffa:

> The King was a very giant in the battle—now here, now there, wherever the attacks of the Turks raged the hottest. He slew numbers with his sword, which shone like lightning; some of them were cloven in two from their helmets to their teeth, while others lost heads, arms, and other members, which were lopped off at a single blow.

Now comes the greatest moment in medieval history. Richard rides his war-horse before the great army of Saladin, lance at rest, and no one dares to attack him. He is unlike any other knight, any other warrior, any other crusader. He is the greatest of all heroes, a king with a heart of a lion.

The Titans Talk Truce

A few days later, Richard falls seriously ill. He is delirious with fever and cries out for fruit. Hearing of Richard's condition, Saladin graciously sends him peaches and sherbet cooled with the snows of Mount Hermon. Richard accepts the gifts in the spirit of chivalry and a peace treaty is finally signed between the Moslem and Christian kings.

The treaty is simple. It stipulates that the Christians will retain the coastal area from Jaffa to Tyre; the Saracens will keep the rest. The treaty further gives Christians permission to make pilgrimages to Jerusalem any time they please. Richard makes one further addition. The agreement will hold only for a period of three years. By that time, Richard believes he will amass the money and men needed to wrest Jerusalem from Saladin's grasp. When Saladin hears this codicil to the agreement, he smiles, and says that if he must lose his land, he would rather lose it to Richard than any man alive.

Richard sees Palestine for the last time from the deck of the France-Nef on October 9, 1192. His passage home is almost as eventful as his Crusade. On his way through Austria, he's captured by Duke Leopold, the arrogant noble who placed his standard next to Richard's only to see Richard rip it down and cast it in the garbage heap. Leopold accuses Richard of the assassination of Conrad of Montferrat, and he's kept in prison until his subjects pay 150,000 marks as ransom.

Christian Chronicles

In September 1193, the Old Man of the Mountain, the ruler of the Assassins, wrote a letter to Duke Leopold pleading for Richard's release. In the letter, the Chief Assassin said: "We declare to you that the lord Richard, King of England, had nothing whatsoever to do with the killing of Count Conrad of Montferrat." The letter was delivered by envoys from the castle of Masyaf. When the envoys were tortured, they confessed that Richard had instigated the murder.

Glory Goes to the Grave

For the next five years, Richard wages war continuously in France and England. He dies at the age of 42 in 1199 from a gangrenous arrow-wound he received while inspecting the defenses of a tiny castle he was planning to attack. He leaves no children, but for centuries, Arab children will be warned when they get naughty: "You better behave or Richard will come and get you!"

Five months later, Saladin dies at the age of 54. His death causes convulsions of grief throughout the Moslem countries. He leaves behind seventeen sons who fight among themselves for his throne. In Saladin's possession at the time of his death are 1 piece of gold and 47 pieces of silver. He had given away his great wealth to his poor subjects.

The Least You Need to Know

➤ Richard defeated Saladin's forces at Arsuf.

➤ Richard attempted to arrange a wedding between his sister Queen Joan of Sicily and Saladin's brother.

➤ Due to time and circumstance, Richard was unable to lay siege to Jerusalem.

➤ Conrad of Montferrat, the Christian ruler of Tyre, entered into secret negotiations with Saladin in an attempt to capture the throne of Jerusalem.

➤ Conrad was killed by Assassins through a hit arranged by Richard.

➤ Richard routed the Moslem forces at Jaffa.

➤ The terms of the final truce between Richard and Saladin stipulated that Christians retain control of coastal areas from Jaffa to Tyre, while the Saracens keep the rest of the Holy Land.

Part 6
The Fourth Crusade

Vainglorious young knights. A blind villain. A deal that leads to damnation. A lust for gold. The rape of Constantinople. The Children's Crusades. Barbarism on an epic scale that will change the course of world history. You're about to embark on the fourth and most fiendish crusade, and you'll never reach the Holy Land.

Chapter 22

Naïve Nobles Court the Doge to Fund the Fourth Crusade

Pope Innocent III claims to have authority not only over spiritual matters but also temporal issues. "The Lord left to Peter," he says, "the government not only of all the Church, but of all the world." He says he has the right to take away the sovereign right of any monarch. Kings are afraid of him, and obey his commands. When they fail to obey them, he takes out a bell, book, and candle, and pronounces them anathema to the Christian people.

He attempts to get the Fourth Crusade underway by the simple art of persuasion; it doesn't work. He pleads. He begs. He cajoles. And finally, he threatens the Christian rulers not only with excommunication but with interdict. Interdict means that all religious services will be suspended in their realm. This means that no one can receive the sacraments. Without the sacraments, no one can receive sanctifying grace. And, without sanctifying grace, no one can escape the eternal fires of hell.

Enlist or Be Damned

Wielding the threat of interdict, along with the Crusade Encyclical of 1198, Innocent III attempts to have Richard the Lion Heart and Philip II lay aside their differences, come to a five-year truce, and return to the Holy Land. But before the truce can be signed, Richard dies besieging the castle of Chalus.

Crusade Aid

Pope Innocent III was the third pope to be called "the Great." He ascended to the papal throne at the age of 37 and claimed that he, as the successor of St. Peter, was the "Vicar of Christ"—the vicarious representation of Christ on earth. He established his authority in Rome by laying claim to the Papal States; he crowned Otto IV King of Germany but excommunicated him when Otto invaded southern Italy; he insisted that bishops visit Rome every four years to pay obeisance to him; he defined the Eucharist in terms of transubstantiation, and he decreed that all Christians must confess their sins once a year.

Despite the fact that no one can fill the leather boots of Richard, Innocent still insists that the Crusade must get underway by the spring of 1199. He speaks of the fire-and-brimstone future all those who refuse to engage in the Holy War against Saladin can expect. In a sermon in which he makes himself part of the Godhead, Innocent says: "We firmly believe on behalf of the Apostle Peter that all those who refuse to join the Crusade will have to answer to us on this matter in the presence of the dreadful judge on the last day of severe judgment."

The pope tells husbands to leave home and hearth and to journey to the Holy Land without the permission of their wives. He orders clerics to leave their monasteries and parishes and to take up the sword and the cross. He commands bishops to send knights, or substantial cash contributions.

But the cost of a Crusade keeps coming up. The siege engines with the counterbalances are much more sophisticated and much more expensive. The chain mail for knights consists of minutely interlocked links of steel that fall from the shoulders to the knees. It takes metal workers weeks to equip one knight, let alone a vast Christian army. And ships are needed to transport soldiers, artillery, and horses from Italy to Palestine.

Desperate for funds, the pope announces a tax on every Christian in Christendom that amounts to a rate of one-fortieth of all revenue per year. It is to be collected until the Holy Land is back in Christian hands.

Money comes pouring in but it isn't enough, especially with the massive bureaucracy of cardinals, archbishops, bishops, clerks, and scribes that is forming around the pope in the Lateran Palace.

Christian Chronicles

By levying a tax for the Crusade, the pope placed the burden of financing a holy war on the people. Prior to this, the great lords had to pay for their own troops, equipment, provisions, and transportation. From now on, it would be less of a financial burden for nobles and knights to go on a Crusade. In fact, Crusade leaders could be reimbursed by the Church from the crusader tax, and even make a profit.

The Boy Nobles Take Up the Cross

In November 1199, something significant happens at a tournament of knights in France. Thibault, the count of Champagne, hosts the fun and games, and guests have arrived from far and wide. At a feast following an afternoon of jousting and mock battles, Thibault stands and asks all the nobles and knights present to join him in taking up the cross. Count Louis of Blois, Thibault's cousin, immediately rises to his feet and pledges his sword to the cause. Count Baldwin of Flanders is also on his feet swearing his allegiance to the holy cause. Now hundreds of knights are standing and swearing to kill every Saracen in the Holy Land.

Thibault is 23 years old. He is handsome, rich, and indolent. He spends his time hunting, jousting, and entertaining snobby post-adolescents like himself. The Crusade will give meaning and purpose to his life. It will fulfill his sense of destiny. Thibault, after all, is the grandson of Queen Eleanor of Aquitaine. His mother was the half-sister of King Richard and King Philip II.

His brother, Henry, had journeyed to the Holy Land, married Queen Isabella, and become King of Jerusalem. After ruling the kingdom rather well for five years, Henry fell out a window and broke his neck. Now Thibault wants the crown. He believes it is his by the simple process of default. And he is well aware that it's better to rule in Palestine than to serve in France.

The young crusaders meet with Church officials and receive the blessing of Pope Innocent. Innocent, however, tells them that they still must raise millions in cash to get the undertaking off the ground.

Throughout Europe, enthusiasm for the Crusades is rising again when Thibault and the other Franks vow to take up the cross. A hundred years has passed since Godfrey of Bouillon, Tancred, and Count Raymond scaled the walls of Jerusalem. Now the Christian Kingdom of Jerusalem is in the hands of the Moslems, and the surviving crusaders are clinging to a few coastal towns on the Mediterranean Sea, like men clinging to the edge of a precipice. Saladin is now dead, and there is hope that the kingdom can be restored.

Envoys Tap the Doge

Where should they go for cash? The people in England, Spain, and France aren't exactly flush, and the Germans are notoriously cheap. That leaves the Italians. The Italians are the ones who most benefit from trade with the Middle East and, by freeing Jerusalem, commerce will flow like never before.

Warrior Words

The chief magistrate of Venice was called a **Doge**. The word comes from the Latin *dux*, meaning "ruler."

Where should they go in Italy? Genoa and Pisa have been tapped out by longstanding trade wars. That leaves Venice, the richest of all the cities in Italy. Thibault and his friends decide to tap the ruler of Venice, an old blind guy called the *Doge*.

Naturally, being blue-blooded, Thibault and the boys think it's beneath their dignity to seek a loan. So they decide to send six envoys, granting them the right to make a binding business deal on their behalf.

The envoys arrive in Venice in February of 1201 and are politely received by the Doge, Enrico Dandolo, a most astute businessman, who hails from the most illustrious family in the city. He has lost all his sight due to an accident that occurred in Constantinople. He hates the Byzantine city with all his heart.

The envoys of the French lords are well intentioned but not well informed. They don't question what their noble bosses told them to do: make preparations for the transport of 4,500 horses, 9,000 squires, 4,500 hundred knights, and 20,000 foot soldiers; together with fodder, food, and provisions for nine months. Now this is a tall order. The figures are seven times those of the French army under King Philip II in 1190. How Thibault and his noble pals came up with these numbers remains a mystery; they have no basis in reality. The only explanation is that the French lords wanted to impress the old Doge and the Venetians with the scale of their Crusade.

Hearing the number of soldiers, 33,500, makes the old Doge scratch the hairs on his chin. He knows it's a preposterous figure, as many of the great lords from England,

Spain, and Italy will be chartering their own fleets. But these simpletons appear to be sincere; they actually believe that a force of this magnitude will arrive. And they bear official papers from the French nobles, asking that they be treated as "plenipotentiaries," fully empowered to make a binding financial arrangement.

Crusade Aid

Venice was the right place for the crusaders to turn for a huge maritime contract. In 1187, Venice had executed a contract to build and man the entire Byzantine navy. Its primary business concern in the East was Constantinople. The specialists in maritime commerce in the Holy Land were Genoa and Pisa, but the two cities were at war with one another. This meant that any fleet hired by one stood a good chance of being attacked by the other.

The Doge and the Grand Council of Venice say they'll need eight days to come up with a figure. During this time, they make inquiries about the envoys to make sure these goofy guys have the backing, not only of the great Frankish lords, but also of Pope Innocent III. They find everything in order.

The cost, the Doge tells the six envoys, will be 85,000 marks. To sweeten the deal, the Doge tells them, he's decided, out of his commitment to the cause, to provide 50 armed galleys at no charge—but only on the condition that the Doge and the Grand Council receive 50 percent of the booty, including all captured territory.

The offer, of course, is an outrageous rip-off. The Doge and the Grand Council are charging fifteen times the amount they'd extracted from King Philip! In modern dollars and cents, it's a deal that costs anywhere from $5 to $10 billion. They expect the envoys to tell them to shove the offer, and storm out of the Doge's palace. But the envoys simply turn their eyes to the blind Doge, and ask: "Where should we sign?" A member of the Council points to the dotted line.

High Drama at High Mass

A High Mass is held at St. Mark's, with thousands of Venetians in attendance. The Doge tells the envoys that they must win the consent of the people for their endeavor. Of course, this is not true. The people have no more say in this deal than the pigeons in the square, but the envoys believe him. One envoy, a straw-haired chap with buckteeth and the unwieldy name of Villehardouin, is invited to speak from the pulpit. Villehardouin tells the congregation that he and the other envoys have been commanded to fall at the feet of the noble people of Venice, and not to rise until the Venetians agree "to take pity on the Holy Land over the sea." The other envoys join Villehardouin in kneeling before the congregation with tears streaming down their cheeks and their hands lifted to heaven in the manner of humble supplicants. It is pure and unadulterated hokum.

The Doge now lifts the envoys to their feet one by one and embraces them in Christian charity. He is weeping genuine crocodile tears. Soon all the people are overcome with emotion. They're weeping uncontrollably as they cry out: "We consent! We consent!" There is such tumult and uproar that it seems as if the earth is being torn asunder.

Christian Chronicles

The Doge's offer to provide 50 armed galleys at no charge was a great incentive for the envoys to sign the contract. They realized that it would require 7,000 crewmen to man these additional vessels. What they didn't realize was that the crafty old Doge was offering him 50 vessels from the Byzantine fleet that already had been purchased by the Byzantine emperor. The Venetians were unhappy with the emperor, as he had fallen into arrears in paying off his debt.

The Dubious Deal

Following the service, the envoys meet again with the Doge and the Grand Council to discuss payment terms. The entire sum of 85,000 marks is to be paid by a series of simple payments. The first payment of 15,000 marks is due August 1, 1201; the second payment of 10,000 marks on November 1 (All Saints' Day); the third, of 10,000, on February 20, 1202 (the Day of the Purification of the Virgin); and the final payment of 50,000 marks is due at the end of April 1202, a year after the signing of the covenant.

It is further agreed that the crusaders will set sail for the Holy Land on the Feast of Sts. Peter and Paul, June 29, 1202, unless the date is changed by common consent.

The envoys, believing that the Venetians are manifesting the meaning of Christian charity, consent to their terms without the slightest objection. Indeed, the deal seems too good to be true. They break out in tears again. The Doge also weeps for joy, along with the members of the Council. Someone brings holy relics into the council chamber and everyone swears upon the blessed bones to honor the terms of the covenant. The envoys don't seem to realize that nothing will be delivered to the crusaders until the Council receives full payment.

The envoys are elated. They rush back to France to report the good news, but they are horrified to discover that Thibault, their forthright leader, cannot lead the Crusade. He's a young man of 24, but he's wasting away of some dreadful disease. Still, Thibault is so overjoyed at the arrangements and the terms of the deal that he rises from his deathbed and mounts his horse. He dies a few days later, leaving in his will a large sum of money to be divided among his noble friends who have promised to undertake the Crusade.

Villehardouin later expresses surprise at the great number of Thibault's good friends who had accepted his money and refuse to take up the Holy Cross. The envoy weeps again. Such blatant betrayal of a good lord's trust is a crying shame.

The Least You Need to Know

➤ Pope Innocent III said that eligible men who failed to enlist in the Holy War would suffer eternal damnation.

➤ Innocent III imposed a Crusade tax on every Christian in Christendom.

➤ The Fourth Crusade was organized by a group of Frankish nobles and knights under the leadership of Thibault, the brother of the late King Henry of Jerusalem.

➤ The Frankish lords sent six envoys to negotiate a deal for transportation with the Doge and Grand Council of Venice.

➤ The Christians agreed to pay the Grand Council 85,000 marks up front and half of all the booty.

➤ Thibault, the leader of the Fourth Crusade, died before the gathering of the great army in Venice.

The Crusaders in Venice: Deals and Detours

The Fourth Crusade needs a new leader. The nobles turn to Boniface of Montferrat, the brother of the late Conrad of Montferrat, the man who would be King of Jerusalem only to end up the target of Moslem Assassins. This choice of a leader seems a bit incestuous, as the brothers of Boniface and Thibault were both married to the voluptuous Queen Isabella.

Boniface's ties to the Holy Land are strengthened by the fact that his brother William married the Princess Sibylla, the daughter of King Amalric of Jerusalem. William and Sibylla were the parents of King Baldwin V, who died of mysterious causes at the tender age of five.

Boniface also has ties with Constantinople: His brother Renier was unhappily married to the daughter of the Eastern Emperor, Manuel Comnena, before someone, for some silly reason, mixed poison in his wine.

Boniface is fifty-something, given to easy living, and a lover of poetry, music, dance, and fancy clothing. In other words, he's something of a fop, with absolutely no military training or experience. In August of 1201, he attends a council of nobles of Soissons where he is invested with the command of the Fourth Crusade by the bishop.

The Christian Army Gathers in Venice

At this time, the crusading armies are gathering in Venice to board ships for the Holy Land. An enormous number show up—more than 11,000, but that is merely a third of the projected 33,500. The crusaders are expected to pay their own way for their horses and themselves. Now they find that they owe the Doge and the Grand Council three times more than they'd expected: three kilos of silver per man, and a half-kilo per horse. Many can't afford it; they pack up their bags and return home. Others scramble to come up with the cash. They sell their table services of gold and silver plates, along with their precious jewels and ornamental weapons. Still, when all the money is collected, the crusaders are 34,000 marks short of the 85,000 they owe the Doge (the financial agreement is covered in Chapter 22, "Naïve Nobles Court the Doge to Fund the Fourth Crusade").

Things are getting hairy. Winter is nearly upon them and there is no way they can afford to quarter their forces until the next sailing season. To make matters worse, they must rely on the Doge and the Grand Council for food and supplies.

The crusaders are camped on the Lido, the long, thin island at the tail end of the Venetian lagoon. The Venetians are charging exorbitant prices, and the army is going deep in debt. More and more disillusioned knights are calling it quits, and now the Venetians are threatening to cut off the supplies unless they are paid in full.

The Doge's New Deal

The situation is desperate and the old Doge has the crusaders exactly where he wants them: in the palm of his hand. He proposes a way that they can satisfy their debt, and commence with the Crusade. The following is what he presents as the deal to his fellow Venetians:

> The King of Hungary has taken from us our city of Zara in Slavonia, one of the strongest places in the world; and we shall never recover it, even with all the forces at our disposal, without the help of the French. So let us ask them to help us to recover it, and we will allow them to postpone payment of the 34,000 silver marks they owe us until such time as God shall permit our combined forces to win the money by conquest.

That's the deal. The crusaders will help the Venetians recapture the Hungarian city of Zara, and their share of the plunder will permit them to meet the financial obligation of their contract so the Crusade to the East can continue as planned.

It sounds almost acceptable if you can overlook a few glaring problems:

➤ Zara is a Christian city under the protection of the pope. The crusaders are being asked to turn their weapons on their own people to come up with the cash for the Doge and the Grand Council. Surely, the Franks did not embark on this mission to kill Latin Christians! This is utter madness.

➤ King Emeric of Hungary is not only a sincere and loyal supporter of Pope Innocent III, who had called this Fourth Crusade into being, but also a distinguished knight who had taken up the cross to fight the Moslems during the Second and Third Crusades.

In other words, they are being asked by an old, blind Venetian who has never served any holy cause to take up arms against a fellow crusader.

But the Doge knows the importance of Zara. It's the most important Adriatic port after Venice itself. It had been conquered by Venice in 998, but through a series of upheavals and revolts, it had come under the care and protection of Hungary; it represents that country's only outlet to the sea. The wealth and power of Zara is now growing to such an extent that it threatens Venice's control of the Adriatic trade.

Hearing of this outrageous plan, Pope Innocent actually foams at the mouth with rage. He sends legates to Venice with bulls prohibiting the Doge from engaging in this venture and leading crusaders to attack fellow Christians.

Christian Chronicles

Zara was located 200 miles southeast of Venice on the Adriatic coast. It had previously served as a supply base for the Venetian fleet. As Zara was rich, the contents of its treasury could be used to pay off the crusaders' debt, with a good deal left over for the Venetians.

The Doge Takes Charge

For the sake of public relations, the blind Doge climbs the steps of the lectern before a High Mass in the Church of St. Mark and addresses a large crowd of Venetians and crusaders. "Sirs," he says, "I am an old man, weak and in need of rest, and my health is failing. At the same time, I realize that no man can control and direct you like myself, your lord. If you will it, I will take up the cross so that I can protect and guide you. I shall go to live or die with the pilgrims." Hearing these heart-wrenching words, the Venetians cry out in one voice: "We beg you in God's name to take the cross and go with us." The Doge kneels before the altar and priests sew a cross to the front of his cotton cap for all to see.

By one strategic move, the crafty old Doge takes control of a Crusade that was started by young, idealistic knights. *He* commands the great Christian army—not Boniface and not the pope. And the crusaders are setting off, not for the shattered Kingdom of Jerusalem, but for a Christian kingdom that has no idea that the wrath of the Roman Church's holy warriors has been unleashed against it.

Boniface, by the way, likes having the Doge as the boss. This will keep the holy fire from the pope's mouth away from his tail and will still permit him to take a princely share of the profits.

The Zara Imbroglio

On November 10, when the fleet arrives at Zara, the Abbot of Vaux rows out to present the Doge and the leaders of this crazy Crusade with a letter from the pope. The pope writes: "My lords, in the name of the Blessed Peter and his apostles, I forbid you to attack this city; for the people in it are Christians and you wear the sign of the cross."

An argument breaks out between the Doge and some of the Frankish lords. Simon of Montfort orders his ship to withdraw from the siege and he pleads with the other lords to follow his example. The Doge responds by turning to the nobles and saying: "You have given me your promise to assist me in conquering this city, and I now summon you to keep your word."

Crusade Aid

Long before the crusaders dropped anchor in Zara's harbor, the people had been warned of the Doge's plans. They'd taken the necessary precautions; the walled city had crosses painted on its walls to remind the invaders that Zara was a Christian city. In addition, they acquired from Pope Innocent III a formal statement that anyone who attacked the city would be excommunicated.

Crusade Aid

The inhabitants of Zara who criticized the Doge for his attack on a Christian city were decapitated. Some managed to flee and take refuge in Arbe or Belgrade. A few managed to seek sanctuary in a nearby monastery, St. Damien of the Mountain.

The Crusaders Conquer Zara

The crusaders, of course, do the wrong thing and stick with the diabolical Doge. The siege begins in earnest. The siege towers and massive catapults are brought from the war galleys to attack the walled city landward. The fleet surrounds the rest of the city and ladders are fixed from the top of the walls to the masts of the ships. For five days, the crusaders batter and pound the city into submission. The city fathers of Zara, realizing that the body of St. Chrysogonos buried beneath the walls will not save them, wave the white flag and surrender.

When the gates are opened, the crusaders enter the city and ransack everything in sight. The Venetians keep the lion's share: the port, the warehouses, the shipyards, and the ships. The Franks get the rest of the city, and lodge in the dwelling places of the citizens, who are now reduced to slaves.

The Pope Excommunicates the Crusaders!

Three days later, the crusaders, fearing they might be the next victims of the Venetians, begin to attack and kill every Venetian sailor and soldier they can find. There is not a street in Zara where there is not fierce fighting with swords, lances, crossbows, javelins, and battle-axes. All hell is let loose. The fighting continues throughout the night. Finally, fearing the outbreak of civil war and the total collapse of the crusading army, the Doge, with the help of French knights, restores order.

But the victory at Zara is bitter. More and more crusaders abandon the cause and sail for home. The Franks and Venetians at last settle in for a long winter with a growing sense of despair and dread. To make matters worse, the pope excommunicates the entire crusading army—Venetians and Franks alike! They are not allowed to attend Mass and receive Holy Communion or the Sacrament of Penance. They are bound over to the Devil and his dominion for all eternity.

Alexis vs. Alexis

Now something extraordinary takes place. In April, Boniface of Montferrat, who has decided to visit Rome instead of attacking Zara, arrives with news of an important development. The crusaders are urgently needed in Constantinople. The Eastern Emperor Isaac Comnena has been ousted, blinded, and cast into prison by his brother Alexis Comnena, who now rules the empire.

The son of the ousted emperor, Alexis Angelus, has escaped from the clutches of the usurper and managed to make his way to Rome, where he sought the help of the pope and the crusaders. You're not reading double; there are two guys named Alexis who have crashed into our story. One is the evil Emperor Alexis, who has snatched the crown from Emperor Isaac, his brother. The other is Prince Alexis Angelus, the son of the blind and imprisoned Isaac, who seeks help in overthrowing his nasty uncle. One more thing about Alexis Angelus: He is barely 13 years old, and rather immature even for 13.

Christian Chronicles

Alexis Angelus, the teenage fugitive from Byzantium, made his way to Germany, to the court of Philip of Swabia, his sister's husband. He then settled in Verona, proclaiming himself to be the rightful emperor of Byzantium. He sent messages to Boniface of Montferrat, begging his help in regaining his father's throne and promising incredible rewards from his father's treasury.

Alexis Angelus's Tempting Deal

If the pope and the crusaders are willing to come to his aid, Prince Alexis Angelus is willing to give them the riches of Byzantium on a gold platter. This is the deal: When the Crown Prince is restored to power, he will …

➤ Pay off the debt that the crusaders owe the Venetians.

➤ Give 200,000 silver marks to the Venetians and to the Franks.

➤ Assume the entire cost of the conquest of Egypt from Moslem hands.

➤ Provide an army of 10,000 Byzantine knights to aid in the reclamation of Jerusalem.

➤ Place his entire empire under the authority of the Roman Church.

Now let's face it. You can't get a better offer than that. The pope gets to double his kingdom; the crusaders get enough recruits to drive the Saracens to China; and the Franks walk away, free and clear, with a profit of 200,000 marks on an investment of 85,000. No deal could be more tantalizing to the Doge, who wants, more than anything else, complete control of the trade concessions in Constantinople. It satisfies everyone—almost.

The Pope and Count Walter Object

The pope, even though his tongue was hanging out at the prospect of gaining control over the Byzantine Church, expresses his reservations about this plan. He's met with Prince Alexis Comnena and found the kid to be a bit of an idiot. The pope also dislikes the idea of Christians killing Christians. The Crusade, he still believes, should be directed against Moslem infidels, not separated brethren. Yet despite his objections, he rescinds the ban of excommunication on the crusaders.

A group of crusaders under Count Walter of Brienna also protest the plan to visit Constantinople with the cry: *Ire Accaron* ("Go to Acre"). Walter feels the Doge is leading them once again in the wrong direction. He also dislikes the fact that the Venetians are now charging them a small fortune for a crust of bread in Zara. More and more French knights and soldiers fall under Walter's persuasion and make plans to separate themselves from the Doge and his army.

Crosscurrent

In an act of rebellion, the crusaders under Walter of Brienna struck their tents and marched inland into a valley some distance from Zara to demonstrate their opposition to the Doge and involvement in Byzantine politics. The French crusaders hoped that ships from Brindisi would rescue them from the Doge and Boniface.

Boniface Plays to the Crowd

Boniface takes decisive action to hold the Christian army together: He appears in the camp of Walter of Brienna's army and throws himself to the ground. Those who accompany him do likewise. Boniface says that he'll remain with his nose to the ground until Walter and the soldiers hear his plea. Everyone in camp is stunned at Boniface's act of humility. This guy is normally as proud as a French hen in a Saxon barnyard.

Boniface rises to his feet and explains why it is fitting and right for the Christian army to restore the young Alexis Angelus to the throne of his father: The usurper to the throne, the phony Emperor Alexis, is in league with Saladin's brother to prevent the Holy Sepulcher from being rescued by righteous Christians. Once the Crown Prince is established in office, his treasury will be placed at the service of the crusaders, and the good people of Constantinople will come under the care of the Holy Father in Rome. What's more, Boniface says, the diversion will require little or no fighting and no plundering of Christian households.

Christian Chronicles

The argument that Boniface raised to Walter of Brienna and the disgruntled crusaders was pragmatic, rather than theological. "What shall we do in Babylon or Alexandria," he asked, "when we have neither provisions nor money to enable us to go there? Better for us before we go there to secure provisions and money by some good excuse than to go there and die of hunger. Moreover, the emperor offers to come with us and maintain our navy and our fleet a year longer at his own cost."

The Crusaders Take Constantinople

The deal with Crown Prince Alexis Angelus is signed and sealed, and the reunited French and Venetian forces sail off for the fabled capital of Byzantium. In April, the crusaders catch sight of the towering churches and palaces above the massive honey-colored walls of Constantinople. One chronicler writes:

> You should know that people who had never before set eyes on Constantinople were astonished, for never had they imagined that so rich a city could exist in

the world, and as they gazed at the high walls and noble towers that ringed it around, and the splendid palaces and the towering churches—there were so many of them that no one could possibly believe it until they saw it with their own eyes—they were amazed by it, and especially by the height and breadth of the city, which was sovereign above all other cities. You should know, too, that there was not a single man among us whose flesh did not tremble at the sight of it.

Seeing the great fleet arrive, Alexis III, the usurper, tries to pay off the invaders. If they want supplies, he's willing to provide them. If they need soldiers, he's ready to release them. If they want gold, he'll pay them what they want as long as they go away. But the crusaders won't go away. They don't want supplies or soldiers or money. They want the empire.

For days, a galley sails close to the walls of Constantinople with the Crown Prince on deck grinning like a Cheshire cat while the captain cries out to the Greeks on the ramparts: "Here is your natural lord. The man you now obey as your lord rules over you without just or fair claim to be your emperor, in defiance of God and the right." The Greeks stare at the geeky teenager. They really don't want him as their emperor.

On the appointed day of the attack, the Doge reveals new, mind-boggling naval weapons. They are flying bridges that sailors attach to the high masts of the galleys. The flying bridges are built by a system of tackles and counterbalance weights so that they can stretch out from the vessels to the parapets of the high walls. They're over 100 feet long and 20 feet wide. The tops of the bridges are covered with hides and tarps to protect soldiers from projectiles and Greek fire.

Christian Chronicles

A Byzantine chronicler describes Alexis III as soft, devoid of pride, fearful, and anxious since he'd plucked out his brother's eyes after seizing his throne. He further says that Alexis III exuded poison, so that animals could smell it, noting also that his horse reared frantically on the day he was crowned, almost unseating him, and casting his crown into a gutter.

The garrison forces pay little attention to the Venetian fleet sailing around the city. They're getting quite accustomed to this sight. They don't even notice the flying bridge as it's attached to a watchtower.

In a matter of minutes, a scouting party of crusaders is in the city. They know they are too few in number to do any damage to the Greek army and so they run about setting fires before anyone can capture them. Almost instantly, the city is ablaze. The flames reach St. Sophia (destroying the mosaics of the patriarchs), leap along the Hippodrome, and down the sea walk. All through the night, high winds fan the flames until a quarter of the beautiful city is in ashes.

As the fire rages, Emperor Alexis III, the usurper, makes a smart move. He packs up his imperial diadems and the treasures of the court, including 1,000 pounds of gold, and with a few of his cronies, slips away in the dead of the night to a faraway place on the Black Sea.

Constantinople continues to burn, and is now without a leader.

The Least You Need to Know

➤ Boniface of Montferrat, upon the death of Thibault, was named "ruler" of the Fourth Crusade.

➤ The crusaders failed to come up with enough money to pay the Venetians for transport to the Holy Land.

➤ The Venetians persuaded the crusaders to join in an attack on the Christian seaport of Zara in order to obtain the necessary funds for their journey.

➤ The crusaders attacked and sacked Zara, thereby earning a sentence of excommunication from Pope Innocent III.

➤ Alexis Angelus, a deposed Prince of Byzantium, gained the help of the crusaders in regaining his throne by promises of incredible riches.

➤ The crusaders laid siege to Constantinople, the heart of Byzantium, and it fell on July 7, 1203.

Chapter 24

The Fall of Constantinople Ends the Crusade That Never Began

> ### In This Chapter
>
> ➤ The crusaders secure the throne for Alexis Angelus
>
> ➤ Alexis IV is assassinated by the madman Mourtzouphlus
>
> ➤ Mourtzouphlus refuses to honor Alexis IV's unpaid debt
>
> ➤ The crusaders savage Constantinople
>
> ➤ Byzantium is no more

When the crusaders enter the Blachernae Palace in Constantinople, they find Isaac, the father of Alexis Angelus, sitting on the throne in a luxurious fur gown next to his empress (whom the Franks later describe as "the most beautiful woman in the world"). Isaac, as you may remember, was blinded and cast into prison by his wicked brother, Alexis, who has now headed for the hills with chests of precious jewels and 1,000 pounds of gold. Now Isaac acts as though nothing much has happened or is happening, despite the fact that the city is burning to the ground.

The Doge and Boniface meet with Isaac to present the terms of their agreement with his son. Emperor Isaac must accept the supremacy of the pope; provide 200,000 marks to both the Venetians and the Franks; send 1,000 troops to the Holy Land; and maintain 500 knights in the reconquered territories.

The Empire Changes Hands

Isaac, who has been tortured beyond human endurance, is now as nutty as a squirrel. As the leaders of the Crusade are speaking to him, he's mumbling prayers and talking jibberish. But when he comes to understand the terms of the agreement, he's sane enough to remove the crown from his head and to hand it to his son.

At 14, Alexis Angelus is crowned Emperor Alexis IV of Byzantium on August 1, 1203. For a while, all goes well. He provides the first of four payments to the Venetians and the Franks and writes a letter to the pope in which he submits to the authority of Rome.

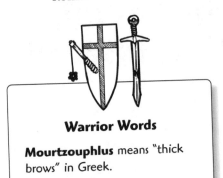

Warrior Words

Mourtzouphlus means "thick brows" in Greek.

Crosscurrent

The Greek clergy and people greatly resented Alexis IV, who toured his empire exacting submission and cash from his subjects to pay his debt to the crusaders. They further abhorred the idea of submitting to the spiritual authority of the pope. Open rebellion occurred in some places.

The crusaders decide to camp across the harbor at Estanor for the winter, while the people of Constantinople attempt to rebuild their city from the ashes. The new emperor spends most of his time at the camp of the crusaders playing cards and dice with the knights and joking with the foot soldiers.

Alexis then makes a bad mistake; he releases one of his troublesome relatives from prison. This guy, you guessed it, is yet another Alexis, Alexis Ducas. The Greeks call him *Mourtzouphlus* because his heavy eyebrows form a straight line across his brow. He becomes the new court steward.

Mourtzouphlus is a malcontent. He hates the Franks and the Venetians, and he despises the pope. He thinks that the agreement the teenage emperor has made with the crusaders is ridiculous, and he resents the payment of large sums of cash to the Westerners camped outside the city gates.

Emperor Alexis IV doesn't pay much heed to the complaints of Mourtzouphlus. He only expects his chief steward to keep liquidating assets so he can come up with the cash for his Latin friends.

One day in January 1204, the teenage emperor is seen by Mourtzouphlus walking around the palace wearing the cloth cap of a crusader; it seems he's loaned his imperial tiara to the Christian soldier. In a fit of rage, Mourtzouphlus storms into the court with an armed guard, strangles Alexis Angelus with a bowstring, and proclaims himself emperor.

Christian Chronicles

While Alexis IV sat on the throne, the crusaders strutted around Constantinople doing nothing to endear themselves to the Greek populace. Every night, the Franks and Venetians engaged in drunken brawls. During the course of one of them, a Frank set fire—again—to the city, destroying many residences. In January, an anti-crusader riot erupted in which the statue of Athena that Phidias the Athenian had made 1,500 years before was destroyed because it appeared to be beckoning the Latins to enter the city.

The Crusaders Sack Constantinople

With Mourtzouphlus in power, the crusaders have no hope of holding the Byzantines to the terms of the agreement, and no desire to turn their back on the deal and head home. They only have one alternative: to take the city, and with it the empire.

The Franks and Venetians come up with an agreement about the booty:

➤ The Venetians will receive three quarters of the loot up to the amount the Franks owe them.

➤ The surplus will be divided equally between the two armies.

➤ A new Latin emperor will rule over the Byzantine Empire.

➤ The emperor will be chosen by twelve electors—six from each side.

Having come to this understanding, the crusaders begin the final siege of Constantinople.

It doesn't begin well. On April 5, the Venetians attempt to enter the city from the flying bridges while the Franks attempt to mine beneath the walls. The Venetians are hacked to pieces as they emerge from the bridges, and the Franks are splattered like spiders by boulders that the Greeks push over the walls.

Crusade Aid

After seizing power, Mourtzouphlus sent a letter to the crusaders' camp informing them that he could no longer tolerate their presence, and ordering them to exit Byzantium. The Latin barons answered by saying they intended to punish him for murdering Alexis and that they would not rest until they had received all that was owed to them.

At the end of the day, Mourtzouphlus orders his generals to appear before him. His trumpeters blare a triumphant flourish, and he says to them: "See, my lords, am I not a good emperor? Did you ever have so good an emperor? Have I not done well? We need fear them no longer. I will have them all hanged and dishonored." It seems that everyone who gets crowned in Constantinople immediately goes crazy.

Christian Chronicles

Mourtzouphlus ordered the construction of "fire ships," small boats filled with fats, oils, and dry kindling that were let loose against the Venetian fleet. It was a great idea, but the fire ships did little damage because of unfavorable winds. Under the right conditions, the entire fleet would have been destroyed.

The City Falls Overnight

The next day is Sunday and the crusaders attend Mass, receive Holy Communion, and listen to the priests' sermons. The priests tell them that the Greeks have committed a mortal sin by supporting the murder of the young emperor, and that the soldiers who die in the siege will "benefit from the indulgence granted by the pope, as though you had completed the whole Crusade."

On Monday, the Doge has a brainstorm. He decides to tie two of the ships with the highest masts (the *Pilgrim* and the *Paradise*) together and to extend two flying bridges to a watchtower on the great wall. The plan is executed with precision. The troops swarm into the tower and on to the ramparts to attack the Greek garrison troops. Meanwhile, ladders are extended to the other towers, and more and more crusaders climb to the parapets. In no time at all, the entire crusader army is within the walls of the city.

The Franks Behave Like Barbarians

The crusaders camp for the night at the monastery of the Pantepoptos (the "All-Seeing Christ") with their weapons ready for a final attack by the Greek army. But no attack comes. In the morning, there is only silence. At last, some priests arrive to tell them that Mourtzouphlus and all the rich people of the city have fled, leaving only the poor and the desolate behind.

By consent of Boniface and the Doge, the victorious soldiers are granted three days and nights to loot and pillage Constantinople to their hearts' content. Constantinople is now subjected to a level of plunder that Rome had not suffered at the hands of the Goths and Vandals:

➤ The nobles divide the palaces among them and lay claim to all the treasures they find.

➤ The soldiers enter homes, shops, and public buildings and take whatever they can carry.

➤ Churches are stripped of gold, silver, and jewels that have accumulated over eight centuries.

➤ The high altar at St. Sophia is stripped of the sheet of gold that covers it, and the jewels are removed with daggers.

➤ Bronze statues dating back to ancient Greece are carried away and cast in a huge melting pot.

Three churches are set aside to serve as storehouses for the loot of the barons.

Most of the pillaging by the Franks is senseless. They set fire to the great libraries of Constantinople that contain collections of the golden age of Greece. The works of Sophocles, Euripedes, Aeschylus, and Sappho go up in flames. They will be lost forever. But this is to be expected; as few Franks can read, they have no use for books.

Christian Chronicles

The Venetian and Frankish soldiers acquired booty on an unimaginable scale in Constantinople. One chronicler wrote: "No one could estimate its amount of value. It included gold and silver, table service and precious stones, samite and silk, mantles of squirrel fur, ermine and miniver. So much booty had never been gained in any city since the creation of the world." The Frankish lords paid 50,000 marks to the Venetians from their share and distributed 100,000 marks among the foot soldiers, who had already helped themselves to the city's riches.

The real barbarism of the Franks is now on complete display. They capture Mourtzouphlus and members of his court and force them to jump from towers that loom 120 feet above the ground. When their bodies splatter against the stones, the Franks laugh uncontrollably.

They find even funnier the prostitute who sings, dances, and performs various sex acts on the throne of the Byzantine Patriarch in the Church of St. Sophia.

Throughout the city, women and prepubescent girls are raped and defiled; Greek nuns are forced to bear the embraces of unwashed French peasants and grooms. Few seem to be aware that it is the Holy Season of Lent.

Anarchy reigns. Children and women are left to die in the streets. The bloodshed flows unabated until the third day comes to an end.

The sack of Constantinople did nothing for the kingdom of Jerusalem. The Crusade produced a feeling of revulsion among Greeks and Moslems—and even among Latin Christians. Pope Innocent III wrote:

> How is the Greek Church to be brought back into ecclesiastical church union and a devotion to the Apostolic See when it sees in the Latins only an example of perdition and works of darkness so that now the Greek Church, with good reason, detests Latins more than dogs.

The Venetians Steal Selectively

The Venetians, as they're familiar with the city that has welcomed them as merchants, know where to find the greatest treasures; they steal with discretion and intelligence. They remove the four bronze horses from the imperial box in the Hippodrome. Known as the "Quadriga," the horses will later stand over the Piazza of St. Mark in the heart of Venice. They take other statuary, including the "Tetrarchs," four Roman emperors of the fourth century, carved in porphyry.

Literally tons of precious things are stripped from the churches and palaces so that the Basilica of St. Mark's will become transformed into a trophy house, brimming with the spoils of war: beautiful chalices in alabaster, onyx, gold, and silver and decorated with precious stones; ancient icons; gold crucifixes housed in silver cupolas; censers of pure gold—all once venerated by Greek Christians.

Of course, most of the precious religious items cannot be removed intact. The twelve gold crosses in the shapes of trees, the largest taller than a man, must be broken into pieces and tossed into sacks; and hundreds of chandeliers must be smashed and dismantled, as they're made of pure silver.

Crosscurrent

The Eastern Orthodox Church never forgave the Roman Catholic Church for the sack of Constantinople, and because of the Crusades, the schism between East and West became infinitely wider than it was when the Emperor Alexis I first called out to the West for help.

A big problem comes with the bronze statues from Greek and Roman antiquity. There is the famous bronze statue of Hercules made by Lysuppus that is so large that the waist of the stoutest Frank is smaller than its thumb, and the statue of Bellerophon astride Pegasus that is of such size, herons have built a nest in the animal's croup. They have to be cast into the melting pot, along with the massive statue of Juno that stands in the forum of Constantine and the famous bronze ass with its driver, cast by Caesar Augustus after the battle of Actium.

Holy Relics Are the Loot Most Prized

As everyone knows, the real treasures of Constantinople are the relics. There are more remains of the saints there than in any other city. Abbot Martin of Paris threatens to kill an old Greek priest unless he reveals the whereabouts of the most precious remains. The old priest takes him to an iron chest in the Church of the Pantocrator where the Abbot finds a tooth of St. Lawrence, a foot of St. Cosmas, an arm of St. James, a fragment of St. Cyprian's skull, and a splinter of the Holy Cross enshrined in gold.

Other knights and prelates remove other relics: the lance that had pierced Christ, still red with His blood; the rod that had scourged Him; the sop of bread given to Judas at the Last Supper; some hairs from the Lord's beard; the left arm of John the Baptist; the skull of St. Stephen; the finger that St. Thomas thrust into the Lord's side; the water jug used at the wedding of Cana, and much more.

All these relics are credited with supernatural powers and many reports tell of miraculous cures worked by them. The nobles of Europe eagerly seek even the slightest relic to wear as a talisman. Monasteries compete with one another for the possession of even a relic of a relic, for such relics attract pilgrims, and with pilgrims come contributions. There is nothing in medieval Christendom more precious than a relic: not silver, not gold, not the rarest of rubies. The relics of Constantinople will make rich men of all the crusaders who possess them.

Crusade Aid

Many of the soldiers who had been excommunicated by the pope because of their participation in the Fourth Crusade managed to purchase pardons by surrendering relics they'd removed from the churches of Constantinople to priests, bishops, and cardinals.

Byzantium Becomes Romania!

The crusaders celebrate Palm Sunday with hearts full of joy and thanksgiving. No mention is made of saving the Holy Land from the Saracens. The Franks and the Venetians are eager to return home with their newfound wealth. It has been a most successful Crusade. After Mass, they elect Baldwin of Flanders to serve as the Latin emperor of the Byzantine empire. No one seems to be aware that the title is an oxymoron. The empire is renamed Romania, and is divided between Boniface and the Doge.

Pope Innocent III, a true innocent, is horrified at what happened. He sends out letter after letter with cries of helpless rage. How could the crusaders be so perverse as to sack Constantinople? How could they rape nuns and murder children? How could they strip consecrated churches for private gain? It is unfathomable. They profess to be crusaders who would save the Holy Land but they are no more than thieves and mercenaries whose god is their belly.

The Crusades began with an Eastern emperor's call for help from the West. The call was answered by a barbarian horde of Christians who would come to destroy the entire empire. The Fourth Crusade never got to the Holy Land. It is an ending that could only be imagined by a complete cynic.

The Least You Need to Know

➤ The crusaders placed Alexis IV on the throne of Byzantium, but the new emperor discovered that he could not fulfill the terms of his agreement with the Venetians and Franks.

➤ Alexis IV was assassinated by his chief steward, Mourtzouphlus, who then claimed the crown and refused to recognize the agreement with the crusaders.

➤ The crusaders launched an assault on Constantinople, and the city fell overnight into their hands.

➤ The crusaders were permitted to loot and pillage at will for three days and three nights.

➤ Great works of ancient Greek literature were burned and forever lost, many art treasures of antiquity were cast into melting pots, and other art treasures—including the Quadriga—were transported to St. Mark's Basilica in Venice.

➤ The most valuable items in the eyes of the crusaders were the holy relics that could be sold in Europe for a fortune.

➤ The new Latin kingdom of Byzantium was called Romania.

➤ The Fourth Crusade never arrived in Palestine and did nothing to free the City of Jerusalem from Moslem control.

Chapter 25

The Children's Crusade: The Final March of Folly

In This Chapter

➤ German children get no farther than Rome

➤ Pope Innocent tells the young crusaders to go home

➤ French children are lost at sea and sold into slavery

➤ The spirit of the crusades fragments feudalism

The Holy War has ended as a fiasco. Its original purpose was to uphold the honor of God by saving the Holy Land from the clutches of Moslem infidels. The first three Crusades began with pleas from popes, bishops, and prelates; they offered a way of serving the Lord and obtaining forgiveness of sin and justification for earthly existence. The crusaders fasted, abstained, and suffered incredible hardships for a higher cause. Every morning began with the celebration of Mass and the distribution of Holy Communion. Throughout the night, the soldiers were summoned to prayer, like monks in a monastery. The great military orders, the Templars and the Hospitallers, were religious orders whose members were bound by oaths of poverty, chastity, and obedience.

The Crusades were a crystallization of medieval faith just as surely as are the great cathedrals of Chartres and Notre Dame. It was idealism, nothing less, that inspired this monumental attempt to change the world for the good and for God. Things became convoluted when the knights and nobles sought to take possession of new principalities and when merchants sought new sources of profit. But the ideal of the

Crusades remained untarnished, and the flame of faith, despite the catastrophic Fourth Crusade, burned as brightly as before.

Crusade Aid

The children set out under Nicholas about the time of Pentecost. They were joined by many peasants who left behind plows and carts and abandoned the animals they pastured. Many were dressed in the costumes of pilgrims, with wide-brimmed hats, palmer staffs, and gray coats with crosses sewn to the breast.

Crosscurrent

When the citizens of Cologne heard what had happened to their children, they sought out Nicholas's father and hanged him in the marketplace. Concerning Nicholas, one document reports that he came to serve in the ranks of the Fifth Crusade and fought bravely at Acre, and later at Damietta. The chronicler adds that he returned to Germany unharmed and lived to a ripe age.

Only by comprehending the depth of idealistic commitment that engendered the Crusades can we come to terms with the Children's Crusade. It arose out of the belief that goodness can conquer evil and innocence can obliterate iniquity.

German Children March to Disaster

In 1212, a German youth named Nicholas announces that God has called him to lead a Crusade of children to the Holy Land. He says that the Saracens will be overcome by the devotion of boys and girls to the Holy Cause; that they will cast away their swords and scimitars; that they will fall on their knees before the Cross of Jesus and convert to the true faith. To us, this idea seems crazy, but to medieval folk—superstitious, illiterate, and unwashed—it seems perfectly sensible.

Thousands of boys (and some girls in their brothers' clothing); young women with babes at their breasts; and illiterate priests, nuns, and monks take up the Cross and follow Nicholas. They are mostly peasant kids who are glad to get away from the crowded and squalid huts on the medieval manors and the drudgery of farm work. Many, no doubt, think they are off to an enchanted kingdom across the sea, a feudal version of the Land of Oz.

The swarm of 30,000 dirty kids, holding make-shift crosses and singing simple songs, leaves from Cologne, passes through the Rhine Valley, and even manages to cross the Alps—at a terrible cost. Many die of hunger; hundreds of stragglers are devoured by packs of wolves; and thieves regularly descend upon the marchers to steal their food and supplies.

The survivors reach Genoa where they expect to be transported to the Holy Land free of charge by the city's good Christian merchants. The merchants, of course, laugh hysterically at this request.

In despair, the children's army proceeds to Rome to petition the help of the Holy Father. Innocent III weeps when he sees them and says: "These children put us to shame, they rush to recover the Holy Land while we sleep." The pope then gently tells the "infinite multitude" to go back to their humble homes, while he retreats into the Lateran Palace. Some of the children march disconsolately back over the Alps to the arms of their mothers and fathers. Others drift to Genoa, where they come under the care of a certain Friso the Norwegian, who takes charge of them. He sells the girls into brothels and the boys into slave markets.

French Children Drown or Are Enslaved

The Children's Crusade that Nicholas starts in Germany sparks a similar Crusade in France. A 12-year-old shepherd named Stephen appears before King Philip II (the same Philip who accompanied King Richard on the Third Crusade) and announces that Christ keeps appearing to him while he is tending his flock, and bidding him to lead an army of children to Palestine. Philip advises him that he is suffering from delusions, and asks the court physician to administer a physic with the hope of purging holy hallucinations from the silly shepherd's head. The physic doesn't work. As soon as Stephen returns to his sheep, the Lord again appears to him and tells him to summon as many kids as he can and set off for Palestine.

Stephen goes from village to village recruiting as many kids as he can for the pilgrimage. He is more persuasive than Soupy Sales or Pee Wee Herman. He becomes known as "the Prophet," and those who join him are called "little prophets." He likens Jesus to a banished king and Jerusalem to a captive queen. He speaks of the sacred shrine of St. Dionysius crowded with pilgrims and compares it to the tomb of Christ vilified by Saracens and infidels. In no time at all, he has amassed a following of 20,000 youngsters who are eager for adventure.

Christian Chronicles

Chroniclers say that Stephen was very upset when he witnessed the Feast of Asses at a marketplace in Paris. This popular peasant feast made fun of the cult of the saints and the practices of the Church. The feast was structured as a Mass. Following the Introit, the Gloria, and the Consecration, the song of the ass was sung. The sermon, devoted to praise of the ass, was preached in Latin and French. At the conclusion of this mock liturgy, the priest brayed three times to the people as they brayed back.

The children make their way across France to Marseille where, Stephen promises them, the ocean will divide so that they can walk to Palestine without getting wet. The shepherd holds out his staff and commands the sea to part …

You know what happens. Stephen tries day after day to part the sea, as the seagulls caw at him with amusement. Finally, Hugh Ferreus, who owns a trading post in Acre, and William of Posqueres, his business partner, offer to take Stephen and his motley crew of kids to their destination without charge. Hugh and William own their own ships; they are well known in Marseille, and they appear to be trustworthy. At last, the prayers of the children have been answered—or so it seems.

Crusade Aid

Twelve-year-old Stephen surrounded himself with an honor guard of 12 youths from noble families, each handsomely mounted and each holding a lance. Thousands of people were attracted to him. On several occasions, the crowd pressed forth with such eagerness to touch him that many were trampled to death. The common people, believing him to be a saint, sought a thread from his coat, a splinter from his cart, or a hair from the mane of his horse, much as they sought such relics from Little Peter.

Thousands of children crowd into seven vessels and sail forth in high spirits, making merry on the decks and singing hymns of glory. Two of the ships are wrecked off the coast of the Island of St. Peter, with the loss of all on board. Pope Gregory IX, according to a chronicler named Aubrey, builds a church on the island where pilgrims come to see the bodies of the children, which miraculously never decompose.

The remaining five ships make their way to Bourgie, on the African coast directly across from Marseille, where the good Christian children are placed in chains and sold as slaves. There are so many children to sell that the slave market soon becomes saturated with tender young boys and girls, screaming for their parents; the French merchants are forced to sell the remainder of the kids in Alexandria in order to realize a good profit. When news of the outcome of this venture reaches Europe, Frederick II orders the hanging of Hugh of Ferreus and his unscrupulous partner.

The Crusade Spirit Penetrates Feudal Life

The Children's Crusades are not legendary. They are recorded by more than 30 chroniclers. They arise quickly—all in the same year of 1212—and vanish as quickly, almost before the Christian world becomes aware of what has taken place.

Eighteen years later, one of the clergy who has traveled with the children escapes from the household of his mean Moslem master and makes his way back to Rome, where he reports to the Holy Father that 700 of the unfortunate boys and girls are still living as slaves in Alexandria.

Following the Children's Crusades, monthly processions are held throughout Europe in which the faithful cry out to God for deliverance of the Holy Land. Preachers distribute the crusading cross, not just to able-bodied men, but to the old, the infirm, the blind, children, and even lepers. The Papal Curia set up a Ministry of Information to distribute Crusade propaganda. Innocent III and his successor Gregory IX proclaim, not only that men did not need to consult their wives before taking up the Cross, but that peasants do not need permission from their overlords. The Crusades, in this way, come to undermine the bonds of medieval feudalism.

The Least You Need to Know

➤ A German youth named Nicholas led 30,000 on the First Children's Crusade.

➤ The First Children's Crusade arrived in Rome where it was disbanded by Pope Innocent III.

➤ Many of the German children ended up in brothels and slave markets.

➤ A French shepherd named Stephen amassed 20,000 crusaders for the Second Children's Crusade.

➤ The French children were sold as slaves in North Africa.

➤ The Crusades served to undermine medieval feudalism.

Part 7

The Collapse of the Crusades

A great sinner will lead one crusade; a great saint another. Mamelukes will vanquish the Mongols. The crusaders will try one last roll of the dice only to come up with snake eyes. The Crusades might have been bizarre, but the most mystifying events of all have yet to unfold.

Chapter 26

The Fifth Crusade: Washout on the Nile

In This Chapter

➤ The Fourth Lateran Council imposes a new Crusade tax

➤ The crusaders reach the walls of Damietta

➤ Sultan al-Kamul makes a stunning truce offer

➤ A strange plague kills 80,000 in Damietta

➤ Frederick II, the Holy Roman emperor, is a no-show

➤ The crusaders drown in the Nile

In 1215, at the Fourth Lateran Council (the first "ecumenical" or "universal" council of the Roman Catholic Church), a new Crusade tax is imposed on all Christians. They must now cough up one twentieth of all income and revenues toward the Crusades. Another ruling says that any merchant or noble who equips a crusader (average cost of $200,000 for armor and weapons) will receive a plenary indulgence, the same indulgence he would receive if he took up the cross himself. It's a good deal if you have the dough. You won't have to serve any hard time in purgatory when you die. The punishment for your sins will be erased from the divine debit books and your soul will fly directly to the pearly gates of heaven.

The Fifth Crusade Gears Up

A new system for collecting taxes is established by the Church, and Europe is divided into 26 districts. Each district is staffed by collectors and sub-collectors, who comb every town, village, and farm for pennies, nickels, and dimes.

Crusade Aid

The pope taxed not only the people but also the clergy. All churches, monasteries, convents, and bishoprics had to pay one fortieth of their annual income to Rome. An *annate* (half of the income of a diocese) was required as a fee for confirming a new bishop. The total income of the Papal See was greater than the combined revenues of all the countries in Europe.

Money and Men

The money doesn't come fast enough to free the Holy Land, so another tax is levied. This one, called "Peter's Pence," demands that all Christians who have not enlisted in the Holy Army must pay a penny a week. Each payment will entitle them to a two-week stay from purgatory. The tax is unreasonably high, as many families exist on less than five pence a week. When they can't come up with the cash, the papal tax collector beats on their door and threatens to confiscate their goods and possessions.

In addition to a system for tax collection, the Church institutes a plan for systematic recruitment. Preachers are trained by the Vatican and sent to every district in Christendom to drum up troops. One such preacher, Oliver of Paderborn, encounters spectacular success. At times, when he preaches, supernatural events take place: Blind men see, the lame walk, the dumb speak. In the Low Countries, he's preaching to a crowd of several thousand when the only clouds in the sky come together to form a huge white cross. The same thing happens in Holland, only this time the huge cross moves in the air toward the Holy Land.

The Massive Army Shrinks

In 1217, the Fifth Crusade leaves Germany, Austria, and Hungary under the Hungarian King, Andrew. They gather in Venice to set off for Acre, the center of the remaining Christian enclave in Palestine. But problems again arise in Venice.

Based on their experience with the Fourth Crusade, this time the Venetians are savvy enough to expect far fewer crusaders than are projected by planners. But a massive army of over 30,000 arrives, and there are not enough galleys to transport them. More than half the crusaders are forced to go home with their lances between their legs.

The crusaders who get to Acre spend several months languishing in the sun, attacking and pillaging outlying towns and villages, and engaging in minor military campaigns. During this vacation time, King Andrew comes upon a relic reputed to be the head of St. Stephen. The king is so excited with his find that he decides to go back to Hungary to display the holy head to his wife and friends. Thousands depart with the gleeful king.

The Egyptian Misadventure

King John of Jerusalem now commands the Fifth Crusade. He and other Christian knights make plans to attack Damietta on the eastern side of the Nile, take control of Alexandria, and proceed to Jerusalem. This, in effect, is the same plan dreamed up by the masterminds of the Fourth Crusade.

The Damietta Siege

For three months, the crusaders lay siege to Damietta without success. Finally, Oliver of Paderborn, the great preacher who called thousands to take up the cross, takes command of the situation. He builds a massive floating siege tower by lashing two transport ships together. The tower permits the Christians to capture Damietta's chain tower and gain a firm footing to advance the siege.

News of the victory so stuns the Arab world that Saladin's brother, Saphadin (the very same Saphadin who was supposed to marry the sister of King Richard the Lion Heart) suffers a massive stroke and drops dead. Saphadin is succeeded by his son al-Kamul, who becomes overall Sultan of the Arab world.

Under al-Kamul, the Moslems counter this setback by blocking the Nile with sunken ships, so the crusaders can't launch another assault on Damietta with vessels.

Throughout the winter, attacks and counterattacks continue. At one point, the Nile floods and engulfs the Christian camp on its bank. Thousands of soldiers and horses are washed away.

To make matters worse, a virulent and contagious disease breaks out that appears to have no natural causes. The chronicler James of Vitry writes that it is "divinely sent on a great part of our army either to cleanse us from our sins or so that we should be more deserving of the crown." Boils first appear on the thighs and legs. They fester until they erupt, spewing black and foul-smelling blood. At the same time, terrible sores grow in the mouth, making it impossible for victims to speak or swallow. Between one fifth and one sixth of the soldiers die from this epidemic. During the final stage, their eyes literally pop from their sockets.

At last, the disease disappears into the desert and the crusaders cross the Nile and land unopposed beneath the walls of Damietta.

The Sultan's Great Deal

The Egyptians sue for peace. The sultan offers a thirty-year truce with the surrender of all the territories of the kingdom of Jerusalem that were conquered by Saladin. What a deal! The crusaders, by signing this agreement, will achieve what the Second, Third, and Fourth Crusades failed to: The kingdom will be restored and the Holy Tomb will return to Christian hands.

King John of Jerusalem wants to sign. But he is overruled by the papal legate, Cardinal Pelagius, who wants the surrender, not only of the Holy Land, but of all of Egypt. The sultan refuses, and the siege continues. Pelagius is confident that all of the Middle East, including Egypt, soon will fall into Christian hands, as the Holy Roman Emperor, Frederick II, is on the way with his grand army.

Hearing of the imminent arrival of the German emperor, Sultan al-Kamul becomes truly terrified. He offers a better deal. Not only will he surrender all the Christian lands conquered by Saladin, but he'll also toss in the cost of rebuilding the walls of Jerusalem (that were dismantled in expectation of a Christian victory), and the return of the relic of the True Cross that had last been seen at the Battle of Hattin.

Now this is a great deal. The Christians will get back everything that was lost—even the True Cross that everyone longs to see and touch. But Cardinal Pelagius again shakes his head. The siege goes on.

Christian Chronicles

Oliver of Paderborn writes: "As we entered the city, we encountered an intolerable stench and an appalling sight. The dead had killed the living. Husbands and wives, fathers and sons, masters and slaves had killed each other with the odor of corruption. Not only were the streets full of the dead, but corpses lay in the houses, in the bedrooms and on the beds."

Waiting for Frederick

By now, the crusaders have been at Damietta for two years, long enough to give any Frank a dose of dementia. Frederick II still fails to appear, but every day he's expected to sail into the harbor.

In November, a Christian sentry spots an empty tower. A group of crusaders bring up scaling ladders and climb to the ramparts. They look into the town and see mountains of dead bodies. Eighty thousand Moslems within Damietta have either died of famine or fallen victim to the strange disease. Only 3,000 survive. The stench of decay is overwhelming.

It is so frustrating; at this point, the Christians could win the long Holy War against the Moslems simply by pushing on to Cairo. But instead, they decide to wait at the ruined city for Frederick, who still fails to make an appearance. They wait and they wait, day after day, week after week, month after month, but the emperor never comes.

It's a Washout

Finally, a battalion of the German army arrives, but without Frederick. On July 17, 1221, Cardinal Pelagius finally decides to march into Egypt and capture Cairo. They pitch camp in a place called Sharimshah on a narrow neck of land at the confluence of two branches of the Nile. Nobody seems to realize it's a flood plain; the sultan destroys the flood barriers, and the Christian army is washed away. It's almost enough to make even the stupidest foot soldier scream.

Cardinal Pelagius finds a boat and escapes from the waters and the crocodiles that engulf the crusaders, carrying with him most of the food and water supplies. When he lands on dry shore with the wreckage of the Fifth Crusade, the cardinal is offered yet another truce by the sultan. He is told that he can take the remains of his army and even the True Cross, as long as he gets out of Egypt immediately and swears never to return.

The cardinal swallows what's left of his pride, and accepts. The crusaders exit Egypt having accomplished absolutely nothing. Later, Cardinal Pelagius sends an envoy to the sultan to obtain the True Cross. Sorry, the sultan says, we seem to have lost it.

One nagging question remains about this wretched crusade. Where was Frederick II? Why did he fail to show up when his very appearance would have ensured the Christians complete and utter victory over all of Islam?

The Least You Need to Know

➤ The pope demanded that all peasants pay a penny a week ("Peter's Pence") to save the Holy Land, more than one fifth of what most families lived on.

➤ The Christian army arrived at the port city of Damietta to commence the conquest of Egypt.

➤ Sultan al-Kamul of Egypt offered as terms of a truce all the Christian territories conquered by Saladin.

➤ The crusaders declined to sign any truce because they believed the Holy Roman Emperor Frederick II would arrive with a great German army.

➤ More than 80,000 Moslems died of a mysterious pestilence at Damietta.

➤ Frederick never arrived, prompting the crusaders to march upon Cairo.

➤ The crusading army, camped on the Nile's flood plain, drowned when the Moslems opened the flood barriers.

Chapter 27

An Excommunicated Emperor Leads the Sixth Crusade

In This Chapter

➤ Emperor Frederick II is called "the stupor of the world"

➤ A marriage is arranged to separate Frederick from his harem

➤ The massive army waits while Frederick wanders

➤ The pope excommunicates the emperor

➤ Frederick joins forces with the Moslems against the Mongols

➤ Frederick gains Jerusalem, but the pope closes its churches

At the close of the last chapter, we were waiting for the Holy Roman Emperor Frederick II to show up and save the Fifth Crusade. If Frederick had arrived, all would have been won, but as he fails to show up, all is lost. This has to strike you as stupefying. It should. Frederick is called *stupor mundi* (the "stupor of the world"). He is a powerful ruler, a first-rate intellectual, and he will confuse, confound, and frustrate everyone he encounters. Eight hundred years from now, he'll still be exasperating people with his bizarre behavior.

The Enigmatic Emperor Frederick II

Frederick is short, nearsighted, beardless, with unruly red hair and a lack of natural grace except when he's mounted on horseback. He seems to be completely lacking in faith and piety and has no regard for the pope. In fact, Frederick has no regard for any Christian prince or ruler. He believes that he is a superman, who is beyond all human boundaries of good and evil.

Crusade Aid

Frederick II was fluent in Latin, Greek, French, Italian, and Arabic. He was knowledgeable in medical arts, philosophy, theology, science, music, architecture, and geography. He was a poet, a composer of troubadour songs, and an artist. He wrote a lengthy medieval text on the anatomy of birds and another on the art of hawking.

Crosscurrent

Sicily, where Frederick was born and raised, was half Christian and half Arab. Frederick was exposed at an early age to the teachings of Islam. His palace guard consisted of Saracens who bowed toward Mecca at times of prayer. The call of the muezzin sounded throughout his island during the duration of his reign.

Frederick Calls for a Crusade

Frederick is crowned Holy Roman Emperor at the age of 21. He sits on the same throne as Charlemagne and his illustrious grandfather, Frederick Barbarossa, who (as you may remember) became literally pickled in Syria. At the conclusion of the coronation, he announces that he intends to lead a Crusade that will once and for all time rescue the Holy Land from the Moslems. No one expects to hear the new emperor say this. He is a bookworm who has little interest in warfare, but he sees himself as the greatest of all Christian kings and princes, destined to rule as a new Caesar. His appeal for knights to join his Crusade reflects his dream of personal glory. "Remember," he says, "how the Roman Emperor, in ancient days, with the help of his soldiery, loyal unto death, subdued the whole world."

His announcement is wonderful news. The bishops, knights, and nobles acclaim him. Frederick tells them that the new Crusade will set sail in August 1221.

Word of the Crusade is preached from pulpits throughout Christendom. A great army is recruited and preparations are made for its glorious departure from Italy. As proof of his commitment, Frederick asks Pope Honorius to excommunicate any soldier, knight, or noble who takes the vow and fails to show up for the departure. He bows before the Holy Father like a humble subject and receives the papal blessing.

Hooked on His Harem

From Rome, Frederick meanders to his kingdom in Sicily so that he can become knowledgeable in Arabian science, philosophy, art, astrology, and physical science. He becomes fluent in Arabic and commits much of the Koran to memory. This is all well and good, but Frederick starts to become a little weird. He now dresses like a sultan and surrounds himself with eunuchs. This might seem a bit eccentric, and be excusable—except for the harem. That's right. Frederick keeps a harem of sweet Saracen girls from Sicily. He has quite a collection. They range in age from 14 to 40, and vary in size, shape, and color. Even this could be taken as an eccentricity, but Frederick is supposed to be the "Holy" Roman Emperor. And there is nothing holy about having a harem. It is immoral, illicit, and downright heathen.

To make matters worse, Frederick is cultivating his harem when he should be fighting in the Fifth Crusade. While Christian soldiers are dropping dead in the desert of a mysterious plague, the emperor is reading *The Perfumed Garden* and engaging in sexual acrobatics. It's enough to unhinge even a patient pope like Honorius III.

Marriage by Proxy

Pope Honorius puts pressure upon Frederick to make his departure, only to encounter delay after delay. Something must be done. A summit is called at Ferentino to discuss the Crusade. Present at the meeting is Pope Honorius III; John Brienne, king of Jerusalem; and Pelagius, the papal legate who commanded the Fifth Crusade. These corporate heads of thirteenth-century Christendom decide that the best solution is for Frederick to marry Princess Yolanda of Jerusalem, the daughter of John of Brienne. John will hand over the throne to Yolanda, and Frederick will become king. As king of Jerusalem, Frederick must appear in the Holy Land. Otherwise, he will forfeit his crown.

A marriage is arranged between Frederick and Yolanda. Since Frederick neglects to show up, the couple is married by proxy, with Bishop James of Patti representing the absent emperor. There are feasts and celebrations for 15 days. Finally, Frederick makes his appearance in a turban and, to everyone's surprise, consents to the vows. Frederick and Yolanda actually meet and they undergo a second marriage ceremony at Brindisi. Everyone is happy. Frederick is crowned king of Jerusalem and he vows by his sacred troth to depart for Jerusalem on August 15, 1227. This gives him time to make adequate preparations.

But there's one thing you can be sure of about Frederick: He is utterly unpredictable. On his wedding night, he seduces one of Yolanda's ladies-in-waiting, and fails to show up for the honeymoon. Maybe this is understandable. Frederick, after all, is 30 and his new bride is barely 14.

Several weeks later, he finally appears in Brindisi to take his young bride to his castle in Sicily. This is an improvement. Frederick has at least come to claim his wife. Maybe the emperor has finally come to his Christian senses. Unfortunately, that's not the case. Frederick consummates his marriage and promptly places Yolanda in the harem with his Saracen concubines. The young bride cannot escape. She is guarded by eunuchs. Several years later, she gives birth to a son, Conrad, and several days after that she gives up the ghost.

Crusade Aid

By law and by tradition, the crown of Jerusalem passed, in the absence of male heirs, through the female line. This is how Guy of Lusignan and Henry of Champagne became kings of Jerusalem. But the law also said that the king must appear in his kingdom within a year of the day of his coronation. Frederick was crowned on November 10, 1226. He didn't set sail for the Holy Land until September 3, 1228.

Frederick and the Christian Army Drift

In the meantime, the August 12, 1227 date for departure has arrived. From England, Sicily, Apulia, Lombardy, and Germany, a great army of 200,000 amasses in Brindisi. But Frederick has made no effort to provide a welcome. Food supplies are low; lodgings for the knights are inadequate; feed for the horses is insufficient; only a handful of ships are in the harbor; and sanitary facilities have not been provided at the camp sites. There have been clear skies and scorching heat all summer, and the land is parched. To make matters worse, the plague makes another appearance, killing tens of thousands. The situation is insufferable.

Frederick shows up and boards a ship with his men. Hope stirs in the hearts of the Christian knights. Frederick is finally heading off to the Holy Land. The Crusade, delayed by more than 10 years, will finally get underway.

But Frederick is not heading for Acre or any port in Palestine. He is sailing for Otranto because he wants to get out of the plague-ridden city. Arriving in Otranto, he rushes off to the baths of Pozzuoli for several weeks of rest. From Pozzuoli, he sends greetings and presents to his new friend—al-Kamul, the sultan of Egypt, the very man he should be engaging in battle.

Christian Chronicles

Sultan al-Kamul of Egypt and Emperor Frederick exchanged numerous letters in which they discussed such things as the immortality of the soul, the origin of the universe, and the philosophy of Aristotle. When the sultan learned that Frederick was a student of animal behavior, he sent apes, bears, camels, and elephants to Sicily. The sultan was also greatly pleased to learn that Frederick disliked the persistent war between Moslems and Christians.

Frederick Is Excommunicated

Enough is enough! Pope Gregory IX convenes the College of Cardinals, takes out bell, book, and candle, and charges the Holy Roman Emperor with the following host of unholy crimes:

Crosscurrent

Frederick objected to his excommunication and told the pope that he had been delayed by illness, nothing more. He offered to perform whatever penance the pope prescribed in order to have the ban lifted. Gregory IX continued to curse him as the "most damnable enemy of mankind" since the creation of the world, and refused under any conditions to lift the ban.

➤ Frederick deliberately chose Brindisi as the staging ground for the Crusade, knowing full well that it was a place of pestilence.

➤ Frederick deliberately postponed the Crusade on many occasions for the mere purpose of playing a devil's game.

➤ Frederick deliberately violated his vow of Holy Matrimony by confining his wife—like a common prostitute—to his personal whorehouse.

➤ Frederick deliberately dispatched letters and presents to the leader of the Saracens in an effort to undermine the Holy War.

Having read these offenses, the pope rings the bell, closes the book, and extinguishes the candle. The Holy Roman Emperor Frederick II has been excommunicated from the Holy Mother Church. He is pronounced a "damnable hater of mankind" and "an agent of the devil." In the eyes of the Church, he is a pariah. He cannot receive the sacraments; no Christian may serve him; and he cannot be buried in consecrated ground.

After he defends his actions to Pope Gregory, Frederick seems unconcerned about the papal pronouncement. He returns to his harem, his Saracen attendants and eunuchs, and his studies of the Koran and Arabian philosophy.

The al-Kamul Deal

Frederick continues to correspond with al-Kamul, who sends an emissary to him with an intriguing proposal. Al-Kamul's brother, al-Muazzam, has started a rebellion in Damascus and is attempting to snatch the sultanate from him. If Frederick can help in the suppression of this rebellion, al-Kamul will give him the Holy Land as payment.

This offer motivates Frederick to finally launch his Crusade. He is coming—not to help the Christians—but to aid the Moslems. The Holy War has come full circle.

Frederick arrived at Acre in September 1228—late, as usual. By this time, al-Kamul had conquered Damascus and al-Muazzam was dead. The sultan no longer has need of Frederick's help. Al-Kamul says to Frederick, "It's nice of you to come, but you're too late." Frederick responds with a plea: "I am your friend, O great Sultan. It was you who urged me to make this trip. The pope and all the kings of the West now know of my mission. If I return empty-handed, I will lose much prestige. With good grace, please give Jerusalem to me so that I may lift up my head among my peers."

The exchange continues. Al-Kamul says: "I, too, must take account of opinion. If I deliver Jerusalem to you, it could lead not only to a condemnation of my actions by the Caliph, but also to a religious insurrection that would threaten my throne."

Finally, Frederick opts for a show of force. He parades his army of 6,000 knights and less than 8,000 foot soldiers before the sultan. It is pathetically small compared to the Egyptian sultan's army. But it gives al-Kamul a solution that will settle the problem and restore his friendship with Frederick.

A Christian-Moslem Alliance

The Moslems are having trouble with the Mongols, who are pouring out of the plains and deserts of northwestern Asia and invading the Middle East. They have already reached the Upper Euphrates and are threatening to swarm over Syria.

The Mongols, in the eyes of the Moslems, are even worse than the barbaric Christians. They live in tents, clothe themselves in smelly hides, eat anything edible—even lice—and slaughter everyone and everything in their path.

Crusade Aid

The Mongol expansion began when the Turkish and Turkish–Mongol tribes were united in the northwest of China by Genghis Khan. In 1206, Genghis Khan and his "golden horde" set out to conquer the world, and almost did. They took northern China, including Peking in 1211, and by 1221 they were raiding towns and villages along the Indus River. By 1240, the sons of "the great Khan" overran central Russia, the Ukraine, Korea, Poland, Hungary, Iran, and Asia Minor.

The Christians could serve as allies in the war against the golden horde of Genghis Khan. After all, the Christians are becoming civilized; Frederick wears a turban, smokes hashish, and quotes the Koran. He represents a man of considerable wisdom, understanding, and judging from his sizeable harem, refinement.

Frederick Wins—And Loses—Jerusalem

A deal is struck to the astonishment of everyone. Frederick, without a drop of Saracen or Christian blood being spilled, receives everything millions of other crusaders tried in vain to obtain—with nothing in return except a handshake and a promise of military assistance. This guy, who is a curse to the Christian world, accomplishes more than the most glorious Christian warrior—Richard the Lion Heart. He almost makes you want to scream. The emperor, with little or no effort, gets Jerusalem, Bethlehem, and Nazareth, together with Lydda, Ramleh, and Emmaus. But this isn't all. He also receives the roads from Jaffa to Jerusalem, and from Jerusalem to Bethlehem; and a large slice of Galilee as a bonus. Al-Kamil makes only one request: that Moslems be allowed to worship at the Dome of the Rock and the al-Aqsa Mosque. Naturally, Frederick agrees. What the heck? This isn't much to ask.

Christian Chronicles

The treaty was almost too good to be true. It was the work of Frederick and al-Kamul themselves, and represented their friendship and mutual trust. Frederick, on behalf of all Christians, renounced all efforts to conquer Egypt. What the pope objected to most was that an excommunicated emperor had succeeded where pious Christian kings and princes had failed. For the first time in 42 years, Christians were free to make a pilgrimage to the Church of the Holy Sepulcher in Jerusalem.

Frederick Crowns Himself

The agreement is signed on February 18, 1229. It is supposed to last for 10 years, 5 months, and 40 days. Frederick now goes to Jerusalem for his coronation at the Church of the Holy Sepulcher. The ceremony is very simple, as no priest can celebrate Mass before an excommunicate. A thousand candles burn before the altar. Frederick, wearing his richly embroidered imperial robes, marches up the aisle, grabs the crown that is laid on the altar, and places it on his head. He turns to the congregation and says: "Behold, now is the day of salvation!"

The Pope Is Not Amused!

After the ceremony, Frederick bewilders everyone by visiting the sacred places of the Moslems. To the dignitaries who accompany him, Frederick says: "My chief purpose in coming to Jerusalem is to hear the Moslems, at the hour of prayer, calling upon Allah by night."

The pope is not amused at Frederick's self-coronation. In fact, he is so outraged that he places the Holy City under an interdict. All religious services are suspended. No sacraments may be administered, not even Last Rites to the dying. No baptism performed. No penance administered. No sins forgiven. No Eucharist received. No means of sanctifying grace is available. Every Christian within Jerusalem is stigmatized by the curse that has been placed on the emperor.

Frederick doesn't linger in the Holy Land. He must return home. His father-in-law, John of Brienne, has invaded his imperial territories in Italy, including Sicily, at the head of a papal army.

On May 1, 1229, at dawn, Frederick, accompanied by his guards, leaves the palace at Acre and rides to the port and the waiting ships. On the way, he passes through the Street of the Butchers. "The butchers and other good Christians pelt him and his retinue with stones, rocks, dung, sheep entrails, and scraps of meat."

They are delighted to see him go, despite the fact that he, the most unholy of kings, will remain the only Western monarch who acquired the Holy City for the Christians.

Crusade Aid

Not only did the pope excommunicate Frederick and place an interdict on the Holy City, he also sent letters to the Templars, the Hospitallers, and the Sultan of Egypt, describing the emperor as the Whore of Babylon who must be destroyed for the simple sake of goodness.

The Least You Need to Know

➤ Frederick II is called the "stupor of the world" because of his ability to stupefy everyone he encountered.

➤ Frederick adopted Arabian customs and even cultivated a harem.

➤ The Sixth Crusade waited 10 years for Frederick so it could begin.

➤ Pope Gregory IX excommunicated Frederick because of his unholy and un-Christian conduct.

➤ Frederick signed a treaty with the sultan by which he gained the kingdom of Jerusalem without spilling a drop of blood.

➤ When Frederick crowned himself king of Jerusalem, the pope issued an interdict, suspending religious services in the Holy City.

Chapter 28

A Crusading Saint Takes Charge

In This Chapter

➤ The pope crusades against Frederick II

➤ Louis IX leads the Seventh Crusade to Egypt

➤ The pagan Khwarisimians take Jerusalem

➤ The Khwarisimians massacre crusaders at La Forbie

➤ At Mansurah, the crusader army is crushed by Saracens and disease

➤ Louis loses his army and his wealth

Pope Gregory IX refuses to ratify the pact that Frederick negotiated with the Moslems, even though it is precisely the type of agreement that he and the other popes have been striving to obtain since the start of the Second Crusade, a half-century ago. He claims that Frederick had no right to make an agreement in the name of the Holy Mother Church as he is an excommunicate and, by rights, not even the lawful king of Jerusalem.

Who is the king of Jerusalem? Three contestants stand up. The first is Frederick, who claims that he is lawful king because of his marriage to Yolanda. The second is John of Brienne, who says that the marriage is null and void and that he remains regent as Yolanda's father. The third is Conrad, the son of Yolanda and Frederick, whom the nobles in Palestine say is king by proper succession.

The Crusade Against the Crusader

It's getting crazy. The pope has now announced another Crusade—this one is not against the Turks or the Saracens, but against Frederick, the Holy Roman Emperor. In other words, we have a Crusade against a crusader. Of all the developments in the past 300 pages, this has to be one of the most mind-boggling. The Holy War has ended up with Latin Christians killing not only Greek Catholics, but one another.

The Crusade against Frederick got started in 1239, soon after Pope Gregory IX, just for spite, excommunicated Frederick a second time. To drum up support for this Holy War, the pope places on display the most famous relics in Rome, the heads of Sts. Peter and Paul. Christians from far and wide travel to Rome to behold the holy heads. The sight is so moving that many enlist to take up arms against the Moslem-loving, harem-keeping, hashish-smoking Frederick.

The taxes are being used not to save the Holy Tomb from the infidels but to seize Frederick's holdings in Sicily and southern Italy. This Crusade will persist for almost 200 years, long after the dust has settled on the Holy War against the Moslems.

Crusade Aid

When Pope Gregory IX died in 1241, his successor continued the campaign against Frederick, and in 1245 summoned a general council that stripped Frederick of all his thrones—the Holy Roman Empire, the kingdom of Sicily, and the kingdom of Jerusalem—and charged him with oppression of the clergy, attacks on the papal states, heresy, and intimacy with Moslems.

Yet Another Crusade to Free Jerusalem

Let's cut back to Gregory IX. He opts to conduct two Crusades at the same time; the Crusade against Frederick and yet another Crusade to free Jerusalem. Taxes, of course, are doubled, and everyone is sick to death of the Holy Wars and having to pay for them. To make matters worse, people who pledge to go on a Crusade but become ill or infirm have to pay the full cost for someone else to go. The Church is now confiscating the homes, properties, and possessions of its members—all for these inept and unsuccessful Crusades. One chronicler writes:

> This scandal of forcing the poor and the disabled to make payments for substitutes has affected the preaching of the Crusades to such an extent that if the clergy again preaches the indulgences of the Cross, their success is uncertain, although it is certain they shall receive numerous insults.

Christian Chronicles

Many nobles, filled with crusading fervor, sold or mortgaged their properties to churches or monasteries to raise the liquid funds necessary to equip a small army for the Holy War. In this way, many monasteries and bishoprics acquired vast estates and enormous fortunes.

Christian Chronicles

In 1241, Pope Gregory IX directed his legates to commute for a money payment the vows of people pledged to a Crusade. These payments were to be used to finance his struggle against Frederick II. Troubadours throughout Europe criticized the Church for diverting financial aid from Palestine by offering equal indulgences for the Crusade against the Holy Roman Emperor. "The faithful wondered," wrote Matthew Paris, "that the same plenary remission of sins was promised for shedding Christian, as for shedding infidel, blood."

Still, the pope can't permit the Holy City to remain in Moslem hands nor can he turn his back on the Christians who remain in Tyre, Acre, Antioch, and other Christian settlements in the Latin east. He can't forget the Templars and the Hospitallers and the promise of Byzantium. He can't allow Islam to triumph over Christianity. That would be the ultimate outrage, a denial of the intrinsic truth of the Holy Catholic Church.

No, the Seventh Crusade against the Moslems must commence, and Pope Gregory IX has the perfect monarch to lead this military operation: a saintly king named Louis.

King Louis IX

Louis IX is an intriguing fellow. He is humble, caring, and handsome, with long blond hair that falls to his shoulders and an athletic figure. But he usually wears a monk's robe with a cowl to appear ordinary.

He is incredibly devout. His mother, Queen Blanche of Castille, instilled in him a deep-seated piety. He has a Spaniard's hatred of mortal sin and a Spaniard's acceptance of religious severity. When he is a young child, his mother gives him a hair shirt to wear beneath his clothing. The hair shirt is made from the coarsest skins. It irritates the skin and causes severe sweating, chafing, and discomfort. Monks and nuns wear hair shirts under their habits so that they will be constantly reminded of the sufferings of Christ. It is a means of perpetual penance that Louis, as a lad of seven, accepts without complaint.

Instead of playing with his royal friends and relations, Louis spends most of the day with his mother in prayer. Every time he has a sinful thought, he retreats to a cell and flagellates himself until his back is a welt of bloody stripes.

The monks and clerics call the new king "Friar Louis," not only because he wanders around in a robe of coarse cloth; he is devoted to the poor, the sick, and the disabled. Every day, he visits the local hospitals and charity wards to perform the lowliest of tasks, such as the emptying of bedpans.

Louis dislikes ornamentation, fancy clothes, and expensive jewelry. But he loves relics. He is an avid collector and amasses the most impressive treasury of saintly remains in the world. From the good Christians who plundered Constantinople, he obtains splinters of the True Cross and the Crown of Thorns (that remains in pristine condition). Of course, these relics are priceless. So he is pleased to shell out millions from his treasury. In time, he also purchases such wonders as the Holy Lance (remember that one?), the Holy Sponge that was soaked in gall to wet the lips of the crucified Savior, the purple robe that Pilate draped around Christ's shoulders, the Holy Nails that were used to nail Him to the cross, and the Holy Napkin that was used by Mary Magdalene to wash His feet. Barnum and Bailey, in their heyday, never possessed such attractions.

Christian Chronicles

Louis IX founded and endowed hospitals, asylums, monasteries, a home for the blind, and another (the Filles-Dieu) for redeemed prostitutes. He ordered his governors in each province to search out the poor and the old and to provide for them at public expense. Wherever he went, the king made it a principle to feed 120 poor people every day and to wash their feet.

In addition to the preceding, Louis acquires a phial that contains the Virgin Mary's milk and another phial that contains a few drops of the Lord's Precious Blood, along with the Virgin's blue mantle and the swaddling clothes that were wrapped around the infant Jesus. He has spent tens of millions for his collection. It is so vast that the king builds a church, the famous Sainte-Chapelle, to house them. It becomes the number-one tourist attraction in the medieval world.

Louis, with his love of relics, is naturally attracted to the greatest of all relics: the empty tomb in the Church of the Holy Sepulcher. So the future saint cannot resist the notion of going on a Crusade.

The Seventh Crusade

The need for the Seventh Crusade is now urgent. The Moslem world is again divided. The Seljuk Turks in Syria are at war with the Sufi Saracens in Egypt. This rift has been going on since the days of al-Kamul. The Christian nobility of Palestine is caught in the crossfire, and has become allied with the Moslem ruler of Damascus. It is a bad move. The Egyptian sultan calls upon pagan Turks, known as Khwarisimians, with offers of booty to help him in his struggles. Before you scratch your head in bewilderment, let's sort the situation out as simply as possible:

➤ The ruler of Damascus, a Seljuk Moslem, is allied with the Christians in Palestine.

➤ The Seljuks are Turks who became Moslems, invaded the Byzantine empire, captured Jerusalem, and caused the First Crusade.

➤ The sultan of Egypt, at odds with the Seljuks, allies himself with pagan Turks from the steppes, who are called Khwarisimians.

➤ The Khwarisimians are not Mongols. The Mongols, in fact, are now invading central Persia, where many chieftains will convert to Christianity. The Khwarisimians are pagans, although a few have become Moslem.

The Khwarisimians Take Jerusalem

At the bidding of the sultan of Egypt, a vast horde of over 200,000 Khwarisimians descends upon Damascus like hungry wolves. In fact, they wear wolf skins, and survive on a regular diet of boiled herbs, water, milk, and any meat they can find. They are mercenaries without a homeland who live by ravaging one community after another. They are admirable bowmen, skilled lancers, and incredibly quick with their short hunting knives. They can not only dispatch, but disembowel the fiercest Moslem or Christian soldier before anyone can say "jackrabbit."

As they cannot capture Damascus, the Khwarisimians, whose only means of subsistence is conquest, move on to Jerusalem. The Holy City is unprepared for the attack by these wild tribesmen. It falls without much of a struggle on July 11, 1244.

The scene is horrific. The Khwarisimians race through the narrow streets of Jerusalem, murdering over 8,000 Christian men, women, and children, and pillaging everything in sight. They rush into the churches and cut the throats of the priests who are celebrating Mass; dig open the graves of the kings searching for treasure, and finding only bones, cast them into the fire. Everything is in ashes, even the Church of the Holy Sepulcher.

Christian Chronicles

After the initial massacre in Jerusalem, the Khwarisimians offered to allow 8,000 survivors to go free. They'd proceeded a few miles down the road when they saw Frankish flags flying above the Holy City. Thinking that Jerusalem had been reconquered by Christian knights, they turned back, only to fall again into the hands of the barbaric tribesmen. The Khwarisimians amused themselves with yet another slaughter. Only 300 out of the 8,000 lived to tell the tale.

The Holy City is finally and completely lost to the Christians. Two months later, it will fall again into the hands of the Moslems. Except for a six-month period in 1300, 673 years will pass before a Christian army again enters Jerusalem. That will occur on December 9, 1917, when the Turks surrender to British General Sir Edmund Allenby.

The Massacre at La Forbie

The Khwarisimian horde joins the Egyptian army at La Forbie, northeast of Gaza. The Christian army has joined with the Seljuks. The combined Khwarisimian-Egyptian force, under the command of a former slave named Baibars, engages the mighty Seljuk-Christian army and completely routs it. Over 5,000 Christian soldiers, many members of the religious orders, lay dead in the sands. The great Knights Templar and the Hospitallers will never regain their glory. The losses at La Forbie are even greater than those at the Horns of Hattin.

The disaster at La Forbie and the terrible destruction of Jerusalem has no major impact on Europe. There are no cries of lamentation, no demands for retaliation, no appearances of priests and bishops in sackcloth and ashes. Pope Gregory IX's successor, Innocent IV, unlike Innocent III, does not suffer a heart attack when he hears the news, only a slight fainting spell.

King Louis, however, is determined to undertake a Crusade even though few Christians share his enthusiasm for yet another venture to the Holy Land. He only manages to attract knights and nobles to his cause by giving them expensive presents and speaking of the great treasures of the East.

Louis, in an effort to unite all of Christendom in his Crusade, journeys to Italy in an attempt to reconcile Pope Innocent IV with Emperor Frederick II. Innocent, thinking of Frederick smoking a Turkish water pipe among the naked women in his harem, refuses. Frederick, on his part, warns his friend the sultan of Egypt that yet another Christian army is on its way to rescue the Holy Tomb.

Crusade Aid

The battle at La Forbie represented the end of the crusaders' offensive military power. The Christian nobles and knights would continue to hold castles and fortified cities for several years, but never again would they be able to amass a mighty army in the field.

In 1248, Louis assembles an expedition of 20,000 soldiers, including 4,000 armed knights, and sets sail for Cyprus, the assembly point for all the Christian armies in the eastern Mediterranean. By the time the fleet is assembled, there are 1,800 vessels off the coast of Cyprus, and the sea, according to a chronicler, "as far as the eye can see is covered with the canvas of ships' sails." From Cyprus, the army sails to Damietta in Egypt.

By the time King Louis sets out on his Crusade, it has become an article of faith that Jerusalem can only be saved when the Christians are established in Cairo, Alexandria, and Damietta. They fail to take note that the unmapped and treacherous tributaries of the Nile Delta greatly hinder access to the mainland. They also neglect to take into consideration the deadly heat of Egyptian summers, the pestilences, the Nile floods, and the desert storms. The crusaders are hell-bent on doing things the hard way.

A Bloodless Victory at Damietta

At the start, all goes well. The crusaders land at Damietta and find that the Moslems, in panic at the news of their arrival, have abandoned the city. The gates are open. The houses, shops, and palaces are intact. The granaries are filled with wheat, barley, and rice; the army quarters are filled with weapons; and the vats are full of wine and oil. It's a miracle.

The crusaders want to seize the moment and move on to Cairo, but it's June, and Louis, in planning the venture, somehow forgot that this is the time for the Nile to overflow, so it's impossible to fight in the Delta.

The armies have left home and hearth, liquidated their savings, and hurried to join Louis in Cyprus, only to be faced with months of waiting in Damietta. The Crusade already is beginning to tax the patience of a saint.

And so, we have another intermission, this one of six months, in which the crusaders sit and stare at each other day after day in the interminable heat with absolutely nothing to do. Well, almost nothing to do. Fearful that they may fall victim to lustful thoughts and "self abuse," Louis commands the soldiers to dig a huge trench around Damietta. Hour after hour, day after day, they dig the vast pit. They're obliged to remain in the trenches throughout the night to guard against Bedouin raiders, and the desert sands are filled with venomous snakes and sadistic scorpions.

The Bloody Retreat from Mansurah

Finally, the troops, whose morale has been destroyed by months in the trenches, set out for the outpost of the Moslem army at Mansurah. Louis leads his army across the river and the huge Saracen army swarms out of Mansurah to meet them. There is a tremendous battle of maces against swords, with both sides intertwined in a dance of death. John of Joinville, the illustrious chronicler of St. Louis, describes knights emerging from the fray with terrible wounds. "A blow from one of the enemy's swords landed in the middle of Erard de Siverey's face cutting through his nose so that it was left dangling over his lip." Another knight suffers a lance thrust

Christian Chronicles

Louis's brother, Count Robert of Artois, who accompanied the king on this Crusade, believed that ultimate victory over the Moslems could only be achieved by the conquest of the Nile valley. Egypt was the heart of the Moslem world, and "if you wished to kill the serpent, you must first crush its head." Louis accepted this strategy, and took the same route that led the Fifth Crusade to disaster.

between his shoulders, creating such a gaping wound that blood pours from his body as if from "a bunghole of a barrel."

Joinville manages to protect himself from the enemy's arrows by using a padded Saracen's tunic. He is pleased that he receives only five wounds, since so many knights emerge from the battle looking like porcupines.

King Louis cuts a fine figure as a Christian warrior. Joinville writes: "Never have I seen a finer or more handsome knight! He seemed to tower head and shoulders above all his people; on his head was a gilded helmet and a sword of German steel was in his hand."

The Saracens retreat, and the crusaders wait outside the walls of the city, expecting another miracle to take place. But a miracle never materializes. Instead, the Christian army is exposed to weeks of famine, and then pestilence. Scurvy, typhoid, and dysentery are rampant. The plagues of Egypt have returned with a vengeance.

So many knights die that grooms wear their armor and stand guard as sentries. There are no longer enough priests to say Mass or administer Holy Communion. There are not enough healthy foot soldiers to bury the dead. Louis is finally forced to sound a retreat.

The remains of the Christian army, riddled by disease and hunger, make their way back up the bank of the Nile toward Damietta. Joinville writes:

> The sickness that had stricken the army now began to increase to such an alarming extent, and so many suffered from mortification of the gums, that the barber surgeons had to remove the gangrenous flesh before they could chew their food or swallow it. It was pitiful to hear around the camp the cries of those whose dead flesh was being cut away; it was like hearing the cry of women in labor.

During the retreat, Louis is suffering so badly from dysentery that a hole is cut in the back of his breeches.

Louis Loses Everything

Day after day, the Saracens attack the Christians on all sides, massacring the defenseless soldiers and making prisoners of all who might fetch a hefty ransom. The trail along the riverbank is littered with thousands of dead Christian soldiers. The sultan claims that his forces have killed or captured over 50,000 men.

The king, more dead than alive, is also captured. Negotiations take place for an armistice. Damietta must be surrendered and 80,000 gold bezants (a sum equal to the entire yearly revenue of France) must be paid for the release of King Louis and the other prisoners.

Christian Chronicles

In Damietta, Queen Margaret, Louis's wife, learned of the king's capture a few days before the birth of her son. In a remarkable display of fortitude, by relinquishing much of her property and many of her possessions, she managed to stop the Venetian sailors from taking flight and leaving the city defenseless. In this way, she managed to retain Damietta so that it could be used as part of the ransom for the king.

The saintly king has lost his army and his wealth. In May 1250, Louis sails to Acre with a small retinue of knights. He is still desperately ill, but the sea air seems to revive him. On deck, he comes upon a few knights gambling at backgammon. He becomes so angry that he tosses the board overboard and delivers a scathing sermon on the sinfulness of gambling on a Holy Crusade. At times, it's difficult to endure a saint.

But Louis has a plan. He now will employ his ultimate weapon against the Moslem world. He will call upon the great Mongol horde, and let loose Armageddon. It's 1250. What better year for the end of the world?

The Least You Need to Know

➤ The Khwarisimian Turks conquered Jerusalem, destroyed many sacred shrines and churches (including the Church of the Holy Sepulcher), and massacred the Christian inhabitants.

➤ The remaining Christian army in Palestine was defeated by the Khwarisimian-Egyptian army at La Forbie.

➤ King Louis launched the Seventh Crusade and conquered the seaport city of Damietta in Egypt.

➤ Over 50,000 Christian soldiers were killed during the retreat from the Christian–Egyptian battle at Mansurah.

➤ King Louis was captured and held for a king's ransom.

➤ Louis IX was the only king of France to become a Christian saint.

The End of the Latin East

King Louis has no nuclear weapons at his disposal. If he had, he would nuke Cairo and Damascus without the slightest hesitation. He has no biological weapons, no ebola plague in a test tube. If he did have, it would be dumped on the head of every caliph, sultan, and emir, to put an end—once and for all—to the Holy War.

As a last resort, though, Louis does have one terrible weapon of mass destruction that he can deploy: He can unleash the Mongol horde on the Middle East. They'll descend from the steppes like locusts and destroy every Moslem in God's brown creation. The Mongols are not discriminate in their slaughter. Naturally, they'll kill thousands of innocent Armenian, Greek, and Latin Christians. What the heck? It's a small sacrifice. Something must be done to bring these interminable Crusades to complete closure.

King Louis Counts His Troubles

Louis is familiar with the Mongols. At Cyprus, when he was on his way to Egypt, he received two envoys from Guyuk Khan, nephew of Genghis Khan and ruler of all of Asia. They conveyed news that many of the Mongols, including the Great Khan's mother and a number of his wives, had converted to Christianity, and that a possibility existed for an alliance with the crusaders.

Quite naturally, Louis was intrigued by this proposal. He sent an embassy to meet with Guyuk Khan at the Mongol court in Karakorum. The embassy included a negotiator, a couple of Dominican friars, a few clerks, and two sergeants-at-arms. By the time they arrived in central Mongolia, Guyuk Khan was dead and the empire was ruled by Guyuk's principal widow, the ugly Ogul Hamish. She had incredibly long and sharp fingernails, along with a face that was as white as leprosy and lips that were blood red. The embassy presented the empress with gifts from King Louis, including a chest of jewels and a tent-chapel of scarlet silk, embroidered with scenes from the life of Jesus. Ogul looked at the gifts and said, "Ugh! These are unacceptable!" She then advised the ambassadors to return with chests of gold and silver "as much as may win our friendship." Ogul obviously wasn't interested in an alliance. She wanted Louis to kneel before her as a vassal.

But now things have changed. Louis has lost his army and his fortune. He is in Acre and the situation looks really grim. The Khwarisimians have destroyed Jerusalem, killing every Christian man, woman, and child. They, with the Egyptian army, have routed the Christian army at La Forbie. And they are on the move against the remaining Christian outposts on the coast of Palestine.

The situation in France is equally frightful. After the loss of his army at Mansurah, "the name of the French king became hateful and disreputable amongst both the nobles and the common people." A Franciscan chronicler says "people curse the preachers who beg alms for the Crusade."

The Crusade of the Shepherds

What's worse, yet another crazy Crusade has materialized. A weird, bearded monk called the Master of Hungary has amassed a following of 30,000 shepherds and peasants to recapture Jerusalem. The Master says that the simple people, through their honesty and humility, can achieve for God infinitely more than the nobles with their wealth and pride. "The poor," according to one chronicler, "kneel before this Master as if he is a saint and give him whatever he asks."

The Crusade of the Shepherds marches through France with standards of a lamb and the cross. "The lamb," writes a chronicler, "depicts innocence, while the cross is a sign of victory."

While Louis is in the Holy Land, the flock arrives in Paris where they receive a warm welcome by Queen Blanche, who is Louis's mother and France's regent. She showers the Master of Hungary with expensive presents and gives her blessing to the endeavor. The Master also shows her a document of authorization for the Crusade that he received from the Virgin Mary, saying that it is written in the Virgin's own hand.

In Orleans, the Master delivers a tirade against the clergy and the nobility. As he speaks, some students heckle him. A riot breaks out and the students are killed. The crusading shepherds proceed to wander through towns and villages desecrating churches and killing clergymen.

A distraught Queen Blanche is forced to order the destruction of the new crusading army. Her troops engage the irksome shepherds at Villeneuve-sur-Cher and slaughter them like lambs with their battle-axes and broadswords. The body of the Master of Hungary is found in the mud. He is scarcely recognizable except for his magnificent long beard.

Louis is in a funk. He spends his time repairing and strengthening the fortresses at Acre, Jaffa, Caesarea, and Sidon. Every day, he can be seen mingling with the masons, carrying stones and baskets full of quicklime. He is attempting to do penance for the tens of thousands he can lead to their deaths and the thousands who remain in captivity in Egypt. "If I depart," he tells his advisers, "this land is lost."

The Assassins

But he must make alliances to protect the people and to reclaim Jerusalem. The saint seeks friendship with the Assassins. He knows that they are at odds with the sultan of Egypt and that their friendship might become very valuable. They can execute political hits that will send the entire Arab world into a tizzy, if not a tailspin. He sends gifts—chests of jewels, rolls of scarlet cloth, cups of gold—to the Old Man on the Mountain. The Chief Assassin sends Louis the shirt off his back and a gold ring of the finest workmanship with this inscription: "With this ring I espouse you and we shall be one."

Crosscurrent

By opening discussions with the Assassins, Louis IX and members of his court became aware that Islam, far from being a monolithic structure, was riddled with different sects. The Assassins, they finally realized, were an offshoot of the Shiite sect that had its origins in Persia. The Shiites venerated Ali, the son-in-law of Mohammed, more than they venerated Mohammed. Those who obeyed the laws of Ali regarded those who obeyed the laws of Mohammed as heretics who must be put to death.

Meetings are held between Christian nobles and the master Assassins to initiate a reign of terror from Cairo to Damascus. Don't shake your head at this. Strange circumstances produce strange bedfellows. What's more, this is still the Middle Ages when the end always justifies the means.

The Mongol-Christian Alliance

But more alliances must be made. And so, Louis, once again, reaches out to the Mongol horde. In 1253, he sends a new group of ambassadors, including William of Rubruck, to meet with the Mongol Emperor Mongka at Karakorum. Louis thinks that Mongka must be a marked improvement over the awful Empress Ogul; anyone would be. A group of Armenian Christians under King Hethoum also arrives in Mongolia to pay homage to the Great Khan and to urge him to invade Syria to put an end—once and for all—to the Moslem menace. The Mongols agree. Why not? They were planning to invade Syria anyhow.

A deal is hatched. The Christians will assist the Mongols in their conquest of the Middle East. In return, the Mongols will restore Jerusalem to the Christians—but under the Khan's auspices. It's not much of a deal for the Christians, but they have no place else to turn.

The Mongols, under Mongka's brother Hulagu, move west, leaving utter destruction in their tracks. They are without mercy and totally savage. They live on nothing but rancid horsemeat and fermented mare's milk, and their diet reflects their disposition. On long marches when they run out of food, they'll eat anything—often slicing up members of the army.

No one is safe from the Mongols, not even the Assassins. The Assassins, after all, killed one of Genghis Khan's sons for a few bucks, and the Mongols want to take their revenge. Before the Assassins can do King Louis's bidding, the Mongols wipe out their outposts in Persia and put an end to their operations.

The Mongols move on to Baghdad, the seat of the Abbasid Caliphs for five centuries, and put to death over 80,000, including Caliph Al Mustasim himself, who is smothered in a carpet. The slaughter takes five days. The Christians in Baghdad are spared, along with the Christian churches.

The cities of upper Mesopotamia are next to fall. The Mongol army crosses the Euphrates and is at the gates of Aleppo. It falls in a few days. The same scenario takes place. The Moslems are slaughtered and the

Christian Chronicles

The Emperor Mongka's mother had been a devout Christian, and many of his wives professed Armenian Christianity. Mongka, however, attended Buddhist, Moslem, and Christian services, saying that there is only one God, who can be worshipped anywhere.

Christians are spared. It's all going along as planned. The Mongols are the vivid realization of the Horsemen of the Apocalypse.

Next on the list is Antioch, but the city is spared because it is controlled by Armenian Christians who pay homage to Hulagu and the "golden horde." The two Christian rulers, King Hethoum and his son-in-law Bohemond VI, join the Mongol army as it marches on Damascus. The pagan horde with Christians holding its banners is carrying out the Crusade dream of ridding the world of the scourge of Islam. Moslem Syria no longer exists, and the Christian kingdom in Palestine is safe—but only as long as the good Christians genuflect before the Great Khan. This is certainly not what Urban II had in mind that day in Clermont so many pages ago.

Then, several things occur that change the torturous course of the Crusades.

First, Louis returns home. Queen Blanche, his mother, has died, and France has no ruler. He sets sail from Acre with his wife and children on April 24, 1254, but vows to return.

Then, as the Mongols are preparing their invasion of Egypt, Mongka, the Great Khan, dies in China. Various members of the Great Khan's family are fighting for the throne. This forces Hulagu to return to Mongolia with most of his army. Before leaving, Hulagu sends an embassy to Egypt demanding that the sultan become his vassal, and an amazing thing happens to the Mongolian ambassadors.

As soon as they arrive in Egypt, they're led into a courtyard and decapitated. A new sultan, a chap named Qutuz, has come to the throne, and he's no pussycat like his predecessor. In fact, he's the most fearsome creature on the face of the earth. Qutuz is a *Mameluke.*

Warrior Words

Mameluke, in Egyptian, means *owned.* The Mamelukes were white slaves who came from the Russian steppes. They were strong and muscular, with Oriental features. Mamelukes could reproduce but they could not replicate themselves. Their children were Moslem, and therefore not enslaveable. What's more, they were completely unsuitable to serve as Mamelukes, as they had not been raised in the wild steppes and then removed from everything they knew. The Mameluke system demanded a constant supply of children. For this reason, the Mameluke population in Egypt kept growing.

The Mamelukes

In Egypt, the Mamelukes are converted to Islam, placed in barracks, and subjected to years of fierce military training and brainwashing under a drill instructor they call "father." They are groomed to serve as the personal bodyguards of the sultan. They are trained for nothing except to kill all enemies of Islam, especially Mongols and Christians. Every Mameluke is called ibn Abdullah, "son of Abdullah" (Mohammed's father) so they'll have no sense of self-worth or individuality. They are Arabian automatons—without mercy, without compassion, without a drop of decency.

Mamelukes originally were also disposable. They were trained to be loyal to one sultan. When a new sultan was elected, the old Mamelukes had to be replaced. This process, as you can imagine, was not always pleasant. After all, what could you do with a used Mameluke? But that changed when Sultan Fakhr ad-Din died during the battle with King Louis's army at Mansurah. The new sultan, a guy named Turanshah, orders the disposal of the existing Mamelukes in accordance with the custom. But the Mamelukes, who have grown in number and intelligence, decide to get rid of Sultan Turanshah instead.

Christian Chronicles

Baibars, the Mameluke head of the Egyptian army, killed Sultan Turanshah by stabbing him, setting him on fire, and drowning him in a river. This permitted him to claim that the sultan died three deaths: by sword, by fire, and by water.

Crusade Aid

Before the massacre at the Pools of Goliath, the Mongols had never been defeated in battle. As the Mamelukes went on to conquer Damascus and Aleppo, they became a power that the Mongols would never be able to challenge. Gradually, the Mongols turned their backs on the West, returned to Mongolia, and became Buddhist pacifists.

Sultan Baibars

Now on the throne of Egypt sits a former slave named Qutuz ibn Abdullah. He leads thousands of other Mamelukes, all named ibn Abdullah, against the remains of the Mongol horde.

Hearing that the golden horde has crossed the Jordan, the Mamelukes set out to meet them at the Pools of Goliath in northern Galilee on September 3, 1260. The Mamelukes greatly outnumber the Mongols, and most of them remain concealed while Baibars, the Mameluke head of the Egyptian Army, mounts a frontal attack with a small force. When Baibars and his warriors retreat over a hill, the Mongols pursue them, only to run headlong into the vast Mameluke army. So much for the Mongols! They are massacred to the last man. King Louis's ultimate weapon has been defused in the desert.

The Mameluke military machine proceeds to conquer the strategic cities of Damascus and Aleppo. At Aleppo, Baibars politely asks if he can be appointed Governor of Aleppo. Sultan Qutuz smiles and says no. Baibars responds as every good Mameluke should. He takes out his dagger and stabs Qutuz in the back.

Baibars is now the sultan. He is a tall, heavy-set Circassian (someone from the Caucasus region of Russia) with red cheeks, blue eyes, and brown hair. He is good-looking and extremely muscular. When he was sold as a slave, he fetched an incredibly high price of 800 copper coins. He has a curious white spot in one of his eyes and a penetrating gaze that terrifies everyone who meets him. He is also a rabid Islamic fundamentalist, kind of like a medieval Ayatollah Khomeini, who lays down the law of the Prophet with a vengeance. Anyone in his realm who drinks an alcoholic beverage (even a beer at a beheading) is put to death. Anyone who consorts with a prostitute or a loose woman is emasculated. Anyone with a loose tongue loses it.

The Christian cities on the coast of Palestine are subjected to the domino effect. Baibars and his highly disciplined army drag huge siege engines across the sands. These are not the puny weapons of the First Crusade that hurled stones and human heads. These weapons represent heavy artillery. They can hurl quarter-ton missiles that can punch holes through the thickest of walls in a matter of seconds.

It all begins in 1265. Caesarea is first to fall. Next is Haffa. Then, in a series of lightning raids, the Mamelukes destroy the Christian kingdom of Armenia, capturing Adana, Tarsus, and Sis, the capital city. The palace is plundered; the cathedral burned to the ground; and the inhabitants put to the sword.

Christian Chronicles

Baibars was the greatest and the least scrupulous of the Mameluke rulers. Moslem tradition honors him next to Harun and Saladin. Baibars organized the government of Egypt so well that no incompetence among his successors availed to unseat the Mamelukes from power until their overthrow by the Ottoman Turks in 1517. He gave Egypt a strong army and navy; cleared its canals, roads, and harbors; and built the mosque that bears his name.

The next year, the Mamelukes attack Safed, the great castle of the Knights Templar that stands over upper Galilee. The Templars surrender upon receiving assurance from Baibars that their lives will be spared. The Templars should have known better. The

Mamelukes are not only cold-blooded killers, they're psychopathic liars. As soon as they gain control of the castle, the Mamelukes behead all of the startled knights. So much for chivalry! Baibars makes Safed his headquarters in Palestine and surrounds it with the severed heads of thousands of Templars.

Crusade Aid

For 267 years (1250–1517), the Mamelukes ruled Egypt and sometimes Syria (1271–1516). Their reign was marked by a continuous series of pogroms and political assassinations. Historians credited them with saving the Middle East and Europe from the Mongols, rescuing Palestine from the crusaders, and driving the last Christian warrior from Asia.

Baibars then marches to Toron, on the coast; it falls without a fight. Then he heads south to Aleppo, giving orders to his army to kill any Christian man, woman, or child they come upon. He is always on the move. His secretary complains: "Today he is in Egypt, tomorrow in Arabia, the day after in Syria, and in four days in Aleppo."

The dominos continue to fall. Next is Acre. Baibars and his Mameluke army employ a ruse. They now possess tens of thousands of uniforms, lances, and banners of killed or captured crusaders. Baibars outfits his vast army so that it will appear as a great crusader army coming to the rescue. The outlying towns and villages throw open their gates to the masquerading Mamelukes, only to suffer complete and utter destruction.

In February 1268, Baibars attacks Jaffa, which resists his assault for 12 days. For some strange reason, he permits the garrison to go free, but massacres everyone else. This merciful gesture is made because the fortress is well defended and a siege would take many months. Baibars is too antsy to wait. He wants to comb through the crusader states with a red-hot rake.

Antioch Is Annihilated

After destroying the castle of Beaufort, the second great stronghold of the Templars, Baibars turns toward Antioch. Antioch has been in Christian hands for more than 170 years. When the garrison surrenders, the Mamelukes enter the city and close the gates so that none can escape. The few who survive the carnage are sold as slaves.

Baibars, however, is deeply distressed. The prince of Antioch, Bohemond VI, is nowhere to be found. It appears that he has gone off for a holiday with the count of Tripoli. What a disappointment! Baibars writes the vacationing prince a letter to inform him of the demise of his principality:

> Our purpose here is to give you news of what we have just done, to inform you of the utter catastrophe that has befallen you. You should have seen your knights prostrate beneath the hooves of our horses; your houses stormed by pillagers and ransacked by looters. You should have seen the crosses in your

churches smashed, the pages of the false Testament scattered, the tombs of the Patriarchs overturned. You should have seen your Moslem enemy trampling on the place where you celebrate the Mass; cutting the throats of monks, priests and deacons upon the altars. Since no survivor has come forward to tell you what happened, we have informed you of it, and since no one is in a position to give you the good news that you have saved your life at the loss of everything else, we bring you the tidings in this personal letter.

Christian Antioch—the first great crusader state, the city where the Holy Lance was recovered, and where the Christians experienced one of their most glorious victories— is now a mound of rubble. It is so devastated by fire and plunder that it will never recover.

Louis the Saint

While the Final Beast rises over the Middle East, Louis longs to meet him in a great battle foretold in the Book of Revelation that will bring an end to the sad spectacle of human history and bring forth the Parousia—the return of Jesus Christ and the Last Judgment.

The only remaining Christian outpost in the East is Acre, and the Mamelukes are at the gates. The last of the crusaders cry out to Louis in total despair. Hugh of Revel, the Master of the Hospitallers, writes:

> We know not to whom we should complain, and show the wounds of our heart, so pierced and so anguished, if not to those who to our knowledge are moved by deep compassion for our sufferings. Nor do we need to describe the hardships we have endured in the Holy Land for such a long period of time nor the magnitude of our losses in property and lives. We believe that almost all of this must be known to you. These sufferings, these losses, do not appear to be coming to an end; instead, they increase and multiply daily.

The heart of King Louis is breaking. For the love of Christ, he must set off on another Crusade. He must take some action to save the last vestige of hope in the Holy Land. He cannot allow two centuries of incredible suffering, sacrifice, and slaughter to end in the triumph of Islam.

He gathers all his resources for one last attempt to destroy the Anti-Christ and to save Christianity from the clutches of Islam. But there is little interest in this venture. The dream of the Crusade has faded. Less than 10,000 set sail from Aigues-Mortes in the summer of 1270.

This time, the king lands his inadequate force in Tunisia, hoping to convert its ruler to Christianity, and to attack Egypt from the west. This would be the first step toward the restoration of all of North Africa to Christianity, as in the days of St. Augustine,

Bishop of Hippo. He hardly touches African soil when he falls "sick of a flux in the stomach," and dies with the word "Jerusalem" on his lips.

His retinue realizes that Louis is a saint and that his remains must be preserved. His body is boiled in water and wine until the flesh falls from the bones. His bones are placed in a casket and transported to the Abbey Church of St. Denis. His heart, entrails, and other organs are placed in gold vessels and conveyed to the great cathedral of Montreale in Palermo. By the turn of the fourteenth century, he will be canonized.

Baibars continues his conquests. He takes the Templar fortress called Safita and moves on to conquer Krak des Chevalier, an outpost that even Saladin found impregnable. He invades Anatolia and retires for a brief rest in Aleppo. He decides to poison a few of his generals who show signs of ambition. There is a mix-up and Baibars mistakenly drinks from one of the poison cups. He suffers severe spasms, falls to the palace floor, and dies in a fit of rage. It is now the task of the new sultan, al-Ashraf Khalul, to lay siege to Acre and put an end to the grand follies of the Crudsades.

Acre

It is 1291, exactly 195 years after the launching of the First Crusade amidst great cheers and high hopes, when Sultan al-Ashraf Khalul leads a massive Mameluke army of 40,000 cavalry and 160,000 foot soldiers to Acre. The soldiers drag over 200 huge siege engines through the mud and sleet to the walls of the city. Two of these catapults ("the Victorious" and "the Furious") are so massive that it takes 100 pairs of oxen to transport them from Cairo. There are now more weapons of destruction at Acre than have ever before been gathered at one place.

The siege begins on April 5 at the crack of dawn and will persist for 40 days and nights, without let-up. One chronicler writes: "The Saracens assailed the city with fire, stones and arrows so that the air seemed to be stiff with arrows. I have heard a very honorable knight say that a lance that he was about to hurl from a tower among the Saracens was all notched with arrows before it left his hand."

The end is inevitable. The remaining Christians attempt to make a mass exodus by sea from the city. Thousands get away, but there is a severe shortage of ships. Large numbers are left on the quayside. One chronicler tells of 500 ladies of noble birth crowding the harbor and offering sailors whatever they ask for a place in a boat.

Christian Chronicles

The noise inside Acre was deafening. The walls trembled as they were struck by the massive boulders and the booming of the sultan's kettledrums could be heard throughout the city at all times of the day and night. Against the Moslem mines, the Christians built countermines. At several points, the mines met and there was fierce hand-to-hand fighting deep beneath the seaport city.

Acre is smashed to pieces by the siege engines so that it can never again serve as a base for the Franks. In celebration of this final victory, Khalul permits his soldiers to massacre or enslave 60,000 prisoners.

All that remains is a mopping-up campaign that al-Ashraf Khalul performs with great pleasure. All the remaining Christian fortresses along the seacoast surrender without a struggle. Tyre, the great city where Richard clashed with the forces of Saladin, is abandoned. Many Christians escape to Cyprus; many more are killed or sold in the marketplaces of Cairo and Damascus.

It is the middle of August. There is not a single structure in Palestine that is held by the Latin Christians. The region has been stripped of all vegetation, all strongholds, all Christian shrines. There is no indication, save for scattered ruins, that the great adventure ever took place. It has all come to nothing at all—like dust in a desert storm or a forgotten dream of a tomb in a holy city.

Crusade Aid

Peter of Flor, who served with the Templars, took charge of a Templar galley and invited the richest women of Acre to accompany him to Cyprus. The payment for this passage was all the jewels and gold the women possessed. In this way, he garnered a great fortune.

The Least You Need to Know

➤ Knowing the precariousness of the Christian position in the Middle East, King Louis sought alliances with the Assassins and the Mongols.

➤ The Mongols conquered Baghdad, Aleppo, and Damascus, and were then defeated by the Mamelukes.

➤ The Mamelukes were slaves who became the masters of Egypt.

➤ In rapid succession, the Mamelukes captured every Christian castle, fortress, and city in the Middle East, except the port city of Acre.

➤ Louis attempted to mount a final Crusade but died in Tunisia, and later became Saint Louis.

➤ In 1291, the Mamelukes conquered Acre, massacred or enslaved all remaining crusaders, and destroyed every vestige of the Latin Christian presence in the East.

Glossary

Acre   A seaport city in Palestine that was occupied by the crusaders.

Adhemar of Le Puy   The Roman Catholic bishop who became the official ruler of the First Crusade.

Alexis Comnena   Emperor of Byzantium. At 46, he was adamantly determined to oust all the Turks from his empire. His call to the West for help triggered the First Crusade.

anathema   A curse in the eyes of the Roman Catholic Church.

Anatolia   The medieval term for the vast plateau between the Black Sea and the Mediterranean Sea. It was later called Turkey, as it was the land of the Turks.

Anna Comnena   The emperor Alexis Comnena's bright and beautiful teenage daughter. Her account of her father's reign became a masterpiece of world literature.

Antioch   A city in Syria that became a principality of the Crusader states.

Ascalon   An Egyptian seaport that was the site of a great battle between the Saracens and the crusaders.

Assassins   A Moslem sect of assassins who specialized in suicide missions. The youths who went out on these missions were called *hashshasheen* or "drinkers of hashish," hence, the term assassins.

Baibars   A ruthless Mameluke who became the sultan of Egypt and put an end to the Great Crusades.

Baldwin   The most intelligent and complex of the crusaders. He was 32 when he headed off with his brother Godfrey of Bouillon for the Holy Land.

benefice   Every church, diocese, monastery, convent, and cathedral was considered to be a benefice.

Bohemond   The fiercest Frank and the most unpredictable of the leaders of the First Crusade. He was 40 years old when he set out for Jerusalem, but he retained a young man's fierce ambition and fiery temper.

Boniface   The Marquis of Montferrat who became the ruler of the Fourth Crusade.

Byzantine Catholic   The Greek Catholic Church that arose from Constantinople rather than Rome. The leader of the Byzantine Catholic Church was the eastern emperor, rather than the pope.

Byzantium   Another name for the Byzantine Empire that stretched from Constantinople into Asia Minor.

caliph   The fountain of all religious truth, the ultimate judge, and the owner of an Arab state.

chivalry   A knight in the kingdom of the Franks was called a *chevalier*. The word comes from *cheval*, an Old French word meaning horse, because knights were mounted warriors. The code of conduct for a chevalier was aptly called chivalry.

Clermont   A town in France where Pope Urban II proclaimed the First Crusade.

Constantinople   The capital city of the Kingdom of Byzantium.

crusader states   The five areas that were carved out of Palestine and Syria as states: the Kingdom of Cilicia, the Principality of Antioch, the County of Edessa, the County of Tripoli, and the Kingdom of Jerusalem. All states were united under the king of Jerusalem.

Damietta   A seaport city in Egypt that was viewed as the key to the Nile and the subsequent conquest of Cairo.

dignitary   Everyone in a church office, from the simple parish priest to the lofty cardinal.

doge   The chief magistrate of Venice. The word comes from the Latin *dux*, meaning ruler.

Dorylaeum   The site in Syria of Bohemond's great victory over the Turks.

Edessa   A city in Cilicia that became the first crusader colony.

emir   An Arab chieftain who is a descendant of the prophet Mohammed.

Eucharist   Holy Communion, the wafer that contains the actual elements of the body and blood of Jesus Christ.

excommunication   Being cast out of the Catholic community because of some horrendous sin.

Fatimid   The Saracens, Egyptian Moslems who trace their lineage from Fatima, the daughter of the prophet Mohammed.

Frank   French.

Frederick II   The Holy Roman emperor who led (if you call it that) the Fifth Crusade and prided himself on his harem and his love of Arabian culture.

Godfrey of Bouillon   The most forthright and reliable of the crusaders of the First Crusade. He was 35 when he headed out to Jerusalem, and he was grave, handsome, strong, pious, and almost humorless.

Greek fire   A medieval form of napalm made from sulfur and resins.

Guy of Lusignan   A French noble who became king of Jerusalem by marrying Sibylla, the widowed sister of King Baldwin IV.

Hattin   The site of a key battle where the crusaders, under King Guy, were routed by Saladin.

Hauberk   A long coat of rings of armor that extends from the neck and shoulders to below the knees. It's slipped over the head and is incredibly heavy.

holy fire   A medieval disease caused by moldy rye in the bread. It made the peasants break out in sores, vomit blood and bile, and foam at the mouth like rabid dogs.

Holy Sepulcher   The tomb that contained the crucified body of Christ.

Hospitallers   A military order of monks who originally cared for patients at the Hospital of St. John in Jerusalem.

indulgence   A pardon from the penalty of sin that can be full (plenary) or partial.

interdict   An official decree of separation from the Roman Catholic Church and its sacraments.

jihad   Holy War for Islam. The first *jihad* was in the seventh century, when Arabs conquered the Byzantine Christians' lands in Syria, Persia, and Palestine. Zengi led a Holy War against the Franks that destroyed the Christian army and ended the First Crusade.

Kerbogha   The emir of Mosul who attacked the crusaders after they conquered Antioch. He was the mightiest of Turkish rulers of his time.

Khwarisimian   Pagan Turks from the steppes who were recruited by the Moslem Turks to battle the Mongol hordes.

King Arslan   Known as the "Red Dragon," this Sultan of Nicea was responsible for the wholesale slaughter of the Crusade of the Poor.

King Louis IX   The French king who led the Sixth and Seventh Crusades and became a great Christian saint.

King Richard I   The Lion Heart, a military genius with no talent for government who lived to wage war.

knight   The word *knight* comes from the Old English *cniht,* meaning *boy,* because knights were originally servants. When servants were granted land and property by the lord they became part of the nobility.

La Forbie   The site of an important battle in which the Franks found themselves sandwiched between the Khwarisimians and the Egyptians.

Lateran Council   The ecumenical council of the Roman Catholic Church that affirmed the pope supreme over all temporal rulers and instituted a crusade tax on all Christians.

Latin Church   The Roman Catholic Church.

Little Peter   See Peter the Hermit.

livery   Distinctive clothing of the knights, from *livree,* the Frankish word for *deliver,* because they were delivered to the knight's entourage twice a year.

Mameluke   Means "owned" in Egyptian. The Mamelukes were white slaves who came from the Russian steppes. They were strong and muscular, with Oriental features. They later took power in Egypt, and their leader, Sultan Baibars, led the force that overran all the Christian states and enclaves of the Middle East.

Mahdi   The leader who is expected to unite the Moslem world in a war against all infidels.

Mansurah   The site outside Cairo of the headquarters of the Egyptian (Saracen) army.

Mongol   A member of the golden hordes from Mongolia that invaded Asia and central Europe during the thirteenth century.

Nicea   The city that stood as a gateway to Asia Minor.

noblesse oblige   A pledge of martial valor and feudal fidelity, of unquestioning service to all knights, all women, all the weak, and the poor.

Nur ed-Din   The great Moslem general who united Turks and Saracens.

Pax Dei   The "peace of God," days in which no spilling of blood was allowed.

penance   Punishment for sin.

Peter the Hermit   Also known as Little Peter and Cucu Peter, this fascinating figure was a pop hero of the eleventh century. He freely gave of all his possessions to the poor and lived in abject poverty. Some thought he might be the Second Coming. He was a forceful preacher who summoned hundreds of thousands to join him in the Crusade of the Poor or the Peasants' Crusade.

plenary indulgence   Full pardon of the punishment for sin.

purgatory   A place in the afterlife where souls are sent to fulfill their penance before entering the Kingdom of Heaven.

Raymond of Toulouse   The oldest, most sophisticated, and richest of the leaders of the First Crusade. He was 56 when he embarked on the great adventure.

Reynald of Chatillon   A Christian count who was a real kook and almost single-handedly gave rise to the Third Crusade.

Richard the Lion Heart   See King Richard I.

Romania   The name Christians gave Byzantium.

Saladin   His name was Yusuf ibn Ayyub (Joseph, son of Job). He called himself Salah al-Din, which means Rectifier of the Faith. He was born in 1138 at Tekrit on the upper Tigris of Kurdish—not Semitic—stock. He destroyed the Christian army of the Second Crusade. His battle against Richard the Lion Heart in the Third Crusade ended in a truce.

Saracens   The Greeks carelessly referred to all inhabitants of the Arabian peninsula as *Sarakenoi* or Saracens, from the Arabic *sharqiyun,* meaning Easterners. The Saracens were nomads from the Syrian-Arabian desert.

scimitar   A long, curved, and incredibly sharp sword.

see   The place from which a bishop governs all the churches in his jurisdiction. It comes from the Latin *sedes,* meaning seat, and is the town or village in which the bishop maintains his throne, or *seat.*

Seljuk   The Turks who became Moslems by invading Asia Minor.

serf   A peasant reduced to the status of a slave.

Shiite   Means "the party of Ali," and is the Moslem group accounting for about 15 percent of the followers of Islam. They believe in a leader, an *imam,* who will one day return as a messiah to restore the Caliphate to its true nature. The Shiites split from the Sunni Moslems after the prophet Mohammed's death.

St. Bernard   The great Christian preacher who summoned the nobility to the Second Crusade.

St. Louis   See King Louis IX.

Sufis   Moslem mystics, called Sufis because of the simple robe of wool *(suf)* that they wore, they believed that a mystical revelation of God could only be received through exercises of devotion, meditation, obedience to a Sufi master (a *mullah*), and a complete abandonment of personal desire.

sultan   A Moslem ruler who remains answerable only to a caliph.

Sunnis   The great majority of Moslems, estimated at 85 percent. For the Sunnis, an *imam* (leader) is simply the man who leads others in prayer on Friday.

Tancred The 17-year-old nephew of Bohemond, who was bold, brash, ambitious, and, odd as it may sound, deeply pious. He originally came from Normandy in northern France. He conquered many territories in the Holy Land and became hailed as the "Prince of Galilee."

Templars A military order of monks who were originally stationed in the Temple of Jerusalem.

tournament The word comes from the Latin word *tornus,* meaning *lathe.* It refers to the circular nature of the contests held between knights, with one group of combatants succeeding another.

Urban II He was born a French noble, abandoned Rome to become a simple monk, and later was selected as Pope. He was 60 when he summoned the French nobles to Clermont and urged them to wrest the Church of the Holy Sepulcher from the Seljuk Turks. Shortly thereafter, five nobles merged their armies and headed to the Holy Land on the First Crusade.

vassal A noble lad who has served as a page and aspires to become a knight.

villain During the Middle Ages a serf or a peasant was called a villain, from the Latin *villanus,* meaning a farm servant.

Zengi The son of a slave and a Turk, he became the leader of the *jihad,* against the Christians, and many Moslems looked upon him as the *Mahdi,* the Redeemer of Islam.

Further Reading

This is just the briefest overview of the thousands of works that have been written about the Crusades, from chronicles of the time to contemporary character studies of the major players. To find more books about specific Crusades or areas of interest, consult the bibliography of any of the books listed under "General Overviews."

Chronicles

Anyone interested in the Crusades should read the chronicles (brief excerpts from which are sprinkled throughout this book). These are eyewitness accounts, both Moslem and Christian, of the Holy Wars, and they're anything but dull. They're filled with mind-boggling stories of sex, drugs, and violence, raw and raucous R-rated scenes of medieval history. Many passages, in fact, were much too graphic to include in this book for general readers. Seek out:

Chronicles of the Crusades by M. R. Shaw. New York: Viking Penguin Books, 1972.

The Chronicles of the Holy Crusades by Elizabeth Hallam. New York: Welcome Rain Publishers, 2000.

Contemporary Sources for the Fourth Crusade by Alfred Andrea. New York: Ayer Company Publishers, 2000.

For Moslem chronicles, turn to:

The Crusades Through Arab Eyes by Armin Maalouf and Jon Rothschild. New York: Schocken Books, 1989.

For lovers of the First Crusade:

The First Crusade: The Chronicle of Fulcher of Chartres and Other Material by Edward M. Peters. Philadelphia: The University of Pennsylvania Press, 1998.

General Overviews

For a general overview of the Crusades, by all means, read ...

The Dream and the Tomb by the great historical writer, Robert Payne. Originally published in 1983, it recently has been re-issued in paperback by Cooper Square Press (New York: 1999). Every chapter is a finely crafted jewel.

Of equal readability are two works by the great English scholar Malcolm Billings.

My favorite is ...

The Cross and the Crescent by Malcolm Billings. This is a beautifully illustrated book that was published by Sterling Publishing (New York) in 1990 and, sad to say, is now out of print.

Billings's most recent work is ...

The Crusades: Five Centuries of Holy Wars by Malcolm Billings. New York: Sterling Publishing, 1996. It's also a beauty for the mind and eye and this glorious book remains in bookstores. Billings worked for many years for the British Broadcasting Company; he writes to be read. Seek him out. He's great company.

Scholarly Works

If you want a detailed and scholarly account of the history of the Crusades, look for:

A History of the Crusades by Sir Stephen Runciman. New York: Cambridge University Press, 1987. It has become a definitive work for all medieval scholars.

For those who seek a more compact overview, there are several terrific books, including:

A Concise History of the Crusades by Thomas Madden. New York: Rowman and Littlefield, 1999.

God Wills It: An Illustrated History of the Crusades by Wayne B. Bartlett. New York: Sutton Publishing, 2000.

The Crusades: Cultures in Conflict by Pamela Kernaghan and Tony McAleavy. New York: Cambridge University Press, 1993.

The Oxford Illustrated History of the Crusades edited by Jonathan Riley-Smith. New York: Oxford University Press, 1997. The work contains a series of articles on all phases of the Holy Wars.

Related Reading

For those of you who want to discover more about medieval warfare, including the correct way to swing a battle-axe, there is no better source than ...

Western Warfare in the Age of the Crusades, 1000–1300 by John France. New York: Cornell University Press, 1999.

If your interest remains more with piety than pikes, pick up ...

Preaching of the First Crusade: The Mendicant Friars and the Cross in the Thirteenth Century by Christoph T. Maier. New York: Cambridge University Press, 1997.

For a Moslem view of the Crusades, turn to ...

Arab Historians of the Crusades by Francesco Gabrieli. New York: Barnes and Noble, 1989.

Should you seek simply to go off on the First Crusade and to skip the rest, seek out a copy of ...

People of the First Crusade by Michael Foss. New York: Arcade Publishing, 1998. Surely, no characters in any modern novel are more compelling.

If you're an art lover, go out and buy ...

Art and the Crusade in the Age of St. Louis by Daniel H. Weiss. New York: Cambridge University Press, 1998. It will grace your coffee table.

For sheer fun, no book on the crusades is better than ...

The Crusades by Terry Jones (of Monty Python fame) and Alan Ereira. New York: Facts on File, 1995. The book was developed to accompany the authors' television series which was presented for the Arts and Entertainment Channel. It is not only hilarious but also incredibly insightful.

Author's Favorites

My favorite character remains Richard the Lion Heart. Everything about him was bigger than life. My favorite scene in the history of the Crusades is Richard marching before the army of Saladin, defying anyone to engage him in battle. For this reason, I savor every book about him. I especially like ...

Warriors of God: Richard the Lionheart and Saladin in the Third Crusade by James Reston. New York: Doubleday, 2001.

Lionhearts: Saladin and Richard I and the Era of the Third Crusade by Geoffrey Regan. New York: Walker and Company, 1999.

And for a more scholarly portrayal ...

Richard I by John Gillingham. New Haven: Yale University Press, 1999.

Let's face it. Richard should be the subject of an epic movie made by someone of David Lean's stature. In the 1950s, a movie was made about him with Laurence Harvey in the lead. It remains for me the most grievous case of miscasting!

The most outrageous incident of the Crusades remains the fall of Constantinople. The crusaders were called to save Constantinople and they ended up sacking it and leaving the great Byzantine city in ruins. The best and most mind-boggling studies of this incredible atrocity are …

The Fourth Crusade: The Conquest of Constantinople by Donald E. Queller and Thomas F. Madden. Philadelphia: The University of Pennsylvania Press, 1999.

An Ungodly War: The Sack of Constantinople and the Fourth Crusade by Wayne B. Bartlett. New York: Sutton Publishing, 2000.

Index

F

295